RHETORIC AND THE DEAD SEA SCROLLS

RHETORIC AND THE DEAD SEA SCROLLS

Purity, Covenant, and Strategy at Qumran

Bruce McComiskey

THE PENNSYLVANIA STATE UNIVERSITY PRESS
UNIVERSITY PARK, PENNSYLVANIA

Library of Congress Cataloging-in-Publication Data

Names: McComiskey, Bruce, 1963– author.
Title: Rhetoric and the Dead Sea scrolls : purity, covenant, and strategy at Qumran / Bruce McComiskey.
Description: University Park, Pennsylvania : The Pennsylvania State University Press, [2021] | Includes bibliographical references and index.
Summary: "Investigates the rhetorical strategies used by the Essenes in the Dead Sea Scrolls. Illustrates strategies based on identification, dissociation, entitlement, and interpretation in response to evolving historical contexts"— Provided by publisher.
Identifiers: LCCN 2021013543 | ISBN 9780271090153 (hardback) | ISBN 9780271090160 (paper)
Subjects: LCSH: Dead Sea scrolls. | Rhetoric—Religious aspects—Judaism. | Essenes. | Qumran community.
Classification: LCC BM487 .M343 2021 | DDC 296.1/55—dc23
LC record available at https://lccn.loc.gov/2021013543

Copyright © 2021 Bruce McComiskey
All rights reserved
Printed in the United States of America
Published by The Pennsylvania State University Press,
University Park, PA 16802–1003

The Pennsylvania State University Press is a member of the Association of University Presses.

It is the policy of The Pennsylvania State University Press to use acid-free paper. Publications on uncoated stock satisfy the minimum requirements of American National Standard for Information Sciences—Permanence of Paper for Printed Library Material, ANSI Z39.48–1992.

For my father
Thomas Edward McComiskey

May he lift upon you the countenance of his favor for eternal peace.
—*Rule of the Community* (1QS, column II, line 4)

CONTENTS

Acknowledgments | ix

Introduction | 1

1 Rhetorics of Identification, Distinction, and Persuasion in *Miqṣat Ma'aśeh ha-Torah* (4QMMT) | 24

2 Performative Rhetorical Strategies in the *Rule of the Community* (1QS) | 48

3 Dissociation as a Rhetorical Strategy in the *Damascus Document* (CD) | 73

4 Impurity and Purification as Material Rhetoric in the *Purification Rules* (4QTohorot A and B) and the *Temple Scroll* (11QT) | 100

5 Hermeneutics/Rhetoric in the Book of Habakkuk and the *Habakkuk Pesher* (1QpHab) | 131

Conclusion | 173

Notes | 185
Bibliography | 203
Resources for the Study of the Dead Sea Scrolls | 219
Index | 221

ACKNOWLEDGMENTS

This book is dedicated to my father, Thomas Edward McComiskey, who is responsible for its existence in more ways than even I know.

I want to thank the participants of the Jewish Rhetorics Seminar at the Conference on Rhetoric and Religion in the 21st Century in Knoxville, Tennessee (October 4–7, 2018). The group was led by Janice Fernheimer and included Eliza Gellis, Davida Charney, Jamie Downing, Jeff Ringer, Kyle Piscioniere, Samuel Stinson, and Ben Crosby. I learned a lot about the long view of Jewish rhetorics from these fine scholars.

Portions of this book have been previously published. Chapter 1 is a longer and revised version of "Laws, Works, and the End of Days: Rhetorics of Identification, Distinction, and Persuasion in *Miqṣat Maʿaśeh ha-Torah* (Dead Sea Scroll 4QMMT)," *Rhetoric Review* 29, no. 3 (2010): 221–38, reprinted by permission of the publisher (Francis & Taylor Ltd.). Chapter 2 is a longer and revised version of "Performative Rhetorical Strategies in the *Rule of the Community* (Dead Sea Scroll 1QS)," *Journal of Communication and Religion* 38, no. 3 (2016): 89–106. A short portion of Chapter 4 appeared previously in "Material Rhetoric and the Ritual Transfiguration of Impure Flesh in the *Purification Rules* (Dead Sea Scrolls 4QTohorot A and 4QTohorot B)," in *Rhetoric Across Borders*, edited by Anne Teresa Demo (Anderson, SC: Parlor Press, 2015), 13–22. I am grateful to these editors and presses for permission to revise and reprint.

INTRODUCTION

I first heard about the Dead Sea Scrolls in the early 1970s. I was nine or ten years old, sitting in an adult Sunday school class, which my father was teaching. Dr. Thomas Edward McComiskey was a well-known Old Testament theologian, and Moody Bible Institute had contracted him to teach an early Sunday school class on the Dead Sea Scrolls and then preach later that morning. My task in this class was to advance slides of the scrolls as my father talked about them. My father had acquired these slides himself on a trip to Israel several years before, and they were among his most prized possessions.

I'm sure I wasn't very good at my job, since all I probably heard was, "Blah, blah, blah, blah, blah, *slide, Bruce*. Blah, blah, blah, blah, blah, *slide, Bruce*."

When the Dead Sea Scrolls were first discovered in 1947, my father was an undergraduate student at Philadelphia Bible College (now Cairn University), and as the earliest scrolls were very slowly being published throughout the 1950s and 1960s, he was working to complete three master's degrees in theology at three different schools and a PhD in Near Eastern and Judaic Studies at Brandeis University. I remember my father explaining what it was like to be an Old Testament theologian during that time. He said that he and many of his colleagues felt a strange combination of excitement and dread each time a new biblical scroll was published: excitement that these ancient manuscripts may be closer to God's words than any other manuscripts previously known, and dread that they might be different, not just linguistically, but theologically. As it has turned out, most of the biblical scrolls are very close to previously known manuscripts, including the standard Masoretic Text, with only a few minor differences, and none theologically salient.

For theologians like my father, the biblical texts among the Dead Sea Scrolls play a vital role in confirming existing beliefs. However, for rhetoricians like me, these biblical texts hold little interest. There is a long tradition of rhetorical criticism in studies of the Old Testament and the Hebrew Bible, and if the biblical scrolls found in the Judean desert are similar to the traditional Masoretic Text, then there is little new rhetorical work to be done on those scrolls. Thus, while there may be much work remaining in the rhetorical criticism of biblical texts, the biblical manuscripts among the Dead Sea Scrolls contribute little new material to that work.

But the biblical texts represent only some of the scrolls that were discovered in the caves above the western shores of the Dead Sea. The so-called nonbiblical or sectarian texts discovered in these caves include mostly unknown hymns, biblical commentaries, parabiblical works, rule texts, wisdom poetry, prayers, calendars, and horoscopes. These nonbiblical texts are called "sectarian" because most of them were written by a community of Israelites led by deposed Zadokite priests, whose ideas about purity and ritual were not accepted at the time as Temple orthodoxy.[1] During the late Second Temple period, the Bible as we know it was in the process of being canonized, and different sects emerged as a result of different communal interpretations of the emerging canon.[2] The deposed Zadokite priests were likely a faction of (or at least allies with) the Sadducees until their own interpretations of the emerging biblical canon became so conservative and apocalyptic that they exiled themselves from Jerusalem, reidentified themselves as Essenes, and began to compose scrolls that would reflect the evolution of their beliefs in relation to the shifting rhetorical ecologies in which they lived. The leadership of the Essene community wrote numerous scrolls that are (or, I will argue, *should be*) of great interest to rhetoricians because they represent strategic, sometimes suasive uses of language that are often unique to the time and place in which they were composed or are different inflections of existing genres.

Throughout this book, I interpret the intersections between the rhetoric of certain texts among the Dead Sea Scrolls and the rhetorical ecologies in which they circulated.[3] Rhetorical ecologies may include material (environmental, economic), discursive (ideological, institutional), and historical (temporal, dynamic) elements, all of which condition how texts generate meaning and acquire significance.[4] Although the elements that comprise rhetorical situations (author, purpose, audience, exigency, constraint, etc.) are critical to any understanding of historical texts, Barbara A. Biesecker (1989) explains that these categories describe only a static view of a rhetorical moment, not its socially dynamic and historically evolving character as a response to ongoing material pressures and discursive forces. But attention to rhetorical ecologies is not intended to replace the critical understanding of rhetorical situations. It is intended to emplace texts and their situations within larger structures of meaning and matter. As Marilyn M. Cooper points out, "Language and texts are not simply the means by which individuals discover and communicate information, but are essentially social activities, dependent on social structures and processes not only in their interpretive but also in their constructive phases" (1986, 366). Thus, rhetoric does not simply occur in static contexts; rather, it occurs in dynamic processes of circulation (production, distribution, exchange, and consumption) within material, discursive, and historical systems, all of which effect influence to varying degrees in a web of interaction.

Extensions of rhetorical situations into rhetorical ecologies occur most productively in discussions of public discourse. For example, Jenny Edbauer (2005) argues that public rhetorics push outside the boundaries of rhetorical situations into fluid networks of distributed social connections not visible through the elemental terministic screens of author, audience, and text. Drawing more overtly from the metaphor of ecology, Michael Weiler and W. Barnett Pearce describe public discourse as

> a system [that] can be imagined most usefully as a kind of ecosystem in which various individual discursive subsystems interact in relations of conflict and mutual dependence. Rhetors are forced to act within the confines of the ecosystem, and their discourses must reflect the web of relationships among its species and their surroundings. But as the rhetorical ecosystem evolves, as any living thing must, so too do its discursive possibilities, and within the

system there is ample room for authorial creativity and cleverness. The rhetorical options available are thus constrained but not determined by the intertextuality of or "spaces" in the array of discourses that confront rhetors. Context both fits rhetorical action and is reconstructed by it.... To theorize the public sphere and its discourse is to suggest a kind of *rhetorical ecology* in which the intentional, strategic activities of many rhetors are in inescapable tension with, yet accommodative to, multiple patterns of intertextuality. (2006, 14–15)

And Nathaniel A. Rivers and Ryan P. Weber argue that "public discourse gets enacted through a complex system of multiple, concatenated documents and rhetorical actions produced through the combined agency of rhetors, audiences, texts, objects, history, and institutions" (2011, 195). This complex system, Rivers and Weber argue (and Cooper, Edbauer, and Weiler and Pearce would agree), is best understood as rhetorical ecology.

The Dead Sea Scrolls comprise a collection of texts produced and circulated both in response to specific rhetorical situations and within the larger networked systems of historically evolving rhetorical ecologies. The institution of the Temple and the emerging canonization of the Hebrew Bible are the earliest and most fundamental aspects of the rhetorical ecology that gave rise to the community of Essenes and the texts they copied and composed. During the First Temple period (1200–586 BCE), David's son Solomon finished building the First Temple in the Israelite capital city of Jerusalem (circa 1000 BCE), a newly permanent site for ritual and worship, and there Solomon declared Zadok and his descendants as the only legitimate line of high priests. These Zadokite high priests and other priestly attendants administered the rites and rituals that were becoming settled orthodoxy, and they gathered together their sacred texts and compiled them into more unified works. The Jerusalem Temple as the center of Israelite worship, the high priesthood of the Zadokite line, and the process of canonizing sacred texts would continue through the destruction of the First Temple and well into the Second Temple period (516 BCE to 70 CE).

By the middle of the Second Temple period, several shifts had occurred in the rhetorical ecology of Israel, and these shifts motivated certain rhetorical responses within the emerging community of Essenes. In 332 BCE, Alexander the Great conquered Israel, initiating a long and tumultuous time of Greek occupation in the region. Despite Greek occupation, Zadokite high priests continued to perform rites and rituals in the Jerusalem Temple, at least until Antiochus IV Epiphanes, king of the Greek Seleucid empire, installed Menelaus (a non-Zadokite Israelite) into the high priesthood in 171 BCE. In addition to economic and political oppression, Greek leaders would now have the religious influence they needed to Hellenize worship in the Temple itself. This Hellenization would defile the Temple, thus violating the covenants between God and the Israelites, a kind of "final straw" that resulted in the Hasmonean revolt against Greek rule in 167 BCE. Judah, one of the Hasmonean brothers, secured an alliance with Rome, which resulted in Greek withdrawal from the region. By midcentury, there was a period of relative independence for the Israelites, and in 152 BCE the Hasmoneans installed Jonathan as high priest. Jonathan purified the Temple of Greek (pagan) defilement and returned it to its historical status as the center of Israelite worship. With the increasing drive to record and standardize sacred knowledge in written documents, sectarian communities emerged based on ideological interpretations of these increasingly settled texts. Jonathan, who "subscribed to a Pharisaic outlook" (Eshel 2008, 51), interpreted these sacred texts liberally, increasing the times and locations of Temple rites and rituals in order to accommodate growing numbers of Israelites during this time of relative peace. However, the Essenes interpreted these same sacred texts conservatively, viewing many of Jonathan's ritual practices as impure, thus defiling the Temple. So the Essenes exiled themselves to the desert, awaiting their return to a pure Temple and strict adherence to the regulations of Torah law.

This is the rhetorical ecology in which *Miqṣat Ma'aśeh ha-Torah* (4QMMT) was composed. 4QMMT was originally an epistle written to the reigning Hasmonean high priest and his administration around 150 BCE, so its initial audience is most likely Jonathan (152–142 BCE). While 4QMMT is considered a founding document of the exiled Essene community (who probably did not yet occupy the settlement at Qumran), it also represents a clear desire to return to the Temple in some capacity. Thus, although one rhetorical purpose of 4QMMT is to describe sectarian *distinctions* in the interpretation of Torah law between the Essenes and the Pharisaic Hasmonean priests, the other rhetorical purpose is to create *identification* between the two factions, invoking scripture as a common bond. The end of days was quickly approaching, the Essenes wrote, so the Temple must be pure and its rituals must be executed according to the strictest interpretation of scriptural law. There is evidence that 4QMMT succeeded in its purpose of distinction but failed in its purpose of identification, since, according to the *Habakkuk Pesher*, the Hasmonean high priest tried to murder the Essene leader, the Teacher of Righteousness, on the Day of Atonement. This violent response from 4QMMT's audience would lead the Essenes to establish and define their community as the only true Israel.

Following Jonathan's death in 142 BCE, Simon (another Hasmonean and non-Zadokite) was declared high priest (142–134 BCE), and a decree was formalized that all subsequent high priests would be Hasmonean, permanently ending any hope that the Zadokites might return to power in the Temple. Three more Hasmoneans were appointed high priest during the next six decades: John Hyrcanus (134–104 BCE), Aristobulus I (104–103 BCE), and Alexander Jannaeus (103–76 BCE). During the reigns of these three Hasmonean high priests, the Essenes established a unique system of ideas that would define their community (the Sons of Light) against all other communities (the Sons of Darkness), including non-Essene Israelites. Two characteristics of this evolving rhetorical ecology became especially relevant for the development of Essene separatist ideology under Hasmonean rule: the rapid expansion of Israelite territories and the irreversible (unpurifiable) defilement of the Jerusalem Temple.

John Hyrcanus, who is referred to in scroll 4QTestimonia as the "man of Belial" (Eshel 2008, 87), began a process of expanding Israelite territories into the surrounding Hellenized communities, thus exposing Israelites to a defiled pagan population. Hanan Eshel explains that when John Hyrcanus became high priest in 134 BCE, "he inherited a rather small kingdom." However, "by the time he died in 104 BCE he had gained control of the Hebron Hills, Samaria, Galilee, and some areas in Transjordan" (2008, 63), including Idoumea, the region that would produce Antipater and Herod. According to Antony Kamm, both John Hyrcanus's military expansionism and his lust for political and religious power "caused members of the party of the Pharisees, who had openly supported the Maccabees [Hasmoneans], to suggest that he should give up the office of High Priest and concentrate on matters of practical government" (1999, 154), since he "may not have scrupulously observed Torah commands" (Greenspoon 1998, 337). Unfortunately for the Pharisees, John Hyrcanus "took offense and transferred his patronage to the Sadducees, whose members were largely of the rich priestly nobility and were less likely to look askance at worldly aspirations" (Kamm 1999, 154).

Two events represent John Hyrcanus's desire to centralize control over both religion and politics: the destruction of the Samaritan temple on Mount Gerizim and the construction of a Hasmonean state palace in Jericho. Early in the final decade of the second century BCE, the region of Samaria was already inhabited by Israelites, though they were deeply Hellenized, when John Hyrcanus advanced his armies to claim the land (Bourgel 2016, 506). The Samaritans living near the Israelite temple on Mount Gerizim viewed themselves as independent of the Jerusalem Temple, conducting the full range of cultic obligations with legitimate Zadokite priests and collecting temple taxes from nearby residents. The Hasmoneans, now high priests and political rulers, were not descendants of Zadok as required by Torah law. They were, according to 1 Maccabees 2:1, "members of the lower priestly family of the Jehoiarib" (Bourgel 2016, 520). In order to centralize cultic worship in Jerusalem and preserve his authority over Israelite religious practice, John Hyrcanus destroyed the Samaritan temple and did not allow the structure to be rebuilt. Jonathan Bourgel explains, "In this context, the existence of another priesthood (even if based not in Jerusalem but on Mount Gerizim), which regarded itself and was regarded by many as the legitimate Aaronide priesthood, was certainly seen by John Hyrcanus as a potential threat to his authority and legitimacy as high priest, which had to be removed" (2016, 520). So remove it he did. The Essene leadership, descendants of Zadok (the high priestly line of Aaronide priests), must have taken this event as an indication of their own fate in Jerusalem.

During the middle of the final decade of the second century BCE, seeking to represent his new political Hasmonean state materially, John Hyrcanus built a fortified palace in Jericho, about twenty-two miles northeast of Jerusalem, territory that had been won during the Hasmonean revolt several decades earlier. Unfortunately, this act of rebuilding Jericho directly violated Joshua's curse on the city, and the Essenes believed that John Hyrcanus not only brought the wrath of the curse upon himself and his sons, Aristobulus and Antigonus, who both suffered untimely deaths, but also upon the land of Israel and the Temple sanctuary. According to Eshel, "The people of Qumran interpreted Joshua's curse on the builder of Jericho to refer to John Hyrcanus I, who built the agricultural estate and Hasmonean palace in Jericho" (2008, 11). But neither the destruction of an Israelite temple nor the construction of a cursed palace stopped John Hyrcanus or his Hasmonean successors from their expansionist activities.

Another one of John Hyrcanus's sons, Alexander Jannaeus (103–76 BCE), continued this process of territorial expansion until, by the turn of the century, he had extended John Hyrcanus's territory "along the coastal plain (all except for the city of Ashkelon) and across the river Jordan until it matched in extent the kingdom of David and Solomon" (Kamm 1999, 154). At this same time, more locally, Alexander Jannaeus had seen the city of Jerusalem itself grow "fivefold, from a relatively small area in the City of David with some five thousand inhabitants to a population of twenty-five to thirty thousand inhabitants" (Levine 2002, 92). Shortly before 103 BCE, Alexander Jannaeus married his brother Aristobulus's widow, Salome Alexandra, who secured for him the office of high priest. Unfortunately, it is a direct violation of Israelite law for a high priest to be married to a widow, causing a rebellion that Alexander Jannaeus crushed by executing six thousand of his own citizens (Kamm 1999, 154). Alexander Jannaeus would continue his expansionist military pursuits throughout his term as high priest, during which he lived in violation of Torah law, defiling the Temple beyond any means of purification, and he would inflict "immense cruelty" (Greenspoon 1998, 337) upon all who dared oppose him.

During the years leading up to the first century BCE, the Essenes had given up the hope of rejoining an authentic nation of Israel or returning to a pure Temple in Jerusalem. Thus, they exiled themselves to the desert, occupying the settlement of Qumran around 100 BCE (Magness 2002, 65). There they worked to develop and solidify their separatist beliefs, writing scrolls with two central rhetorical functions in the context of this Hasmonean rhetorical ecology: to establish the Essenes as the true Israel (the *Rule of the Community* and the *Damascus Document*) and to establish Qumran as the legitimate Temple (the *Purification Rules* and the *Temple Scroll*).

The *Rule of the Community*, one of the first and most central scrolls composed during the early years of the Essene occupation of Qumran, establishes specific procedures for initiation into, and annual renewal of, the Essenes' new covenant with God. The audience of the *Rule of the Community* is neither Hasmonean priests nor non-Essene Israelites, who were counted among the Sons of Darkness, along with Egyptians, Romans, and Greeks. Instead, this scroll is strictly intended for an audience of Essene priests and leaders who lived in the settlement of Qumran and called themselves the Yahad.⁵ The Yahad's covenant described in the *Rule of the Community* is a new formulation of the old Mosaic covenant (the promise of material blessings in exchange for obedience to the law), which was continually violated by wayward Israelites and the Hasmonean priests who misled them. This new covenant recommitted members of the Yahad to strict obedience to the law, and it reformulated inclusion in the covenant from national inheritance (old covenant) to voluntary commitment (new covenant) and recast the blessings and curses of the covenant from material (old) to metaphysical (new). Since the Yahad's disputes with Hasmonean Temple priests were based on technical matters related to legal observance, the Mosaic law (which, more than any other biblical covenant, requires strict adherence to legal regulation) became the ideological emphasis in the community's formation and its covenant. The *Rule of the Community* describes this new covenant in detail and lays out specific procedures (material rhetoric in the form of performative speech acts) for initiation into, and annual renewal within, the community of the new metaphysical covenant, the new and true Israel. Material rhetoric (more than just distinction and identification) establishes a real community with defined boundaries and ranked membership, ready for the end of days. The initiation and renewal ceremonies described in the *Rule of the Community* created a material foundation for this separatist community, and they likely took place at Qumran and were administered by powerful Essene priests and leaders.

Since membership in the Essene community extended well beyond the reconstructed walls of the Qumran settlement, more rhetorical work was required than just the material establishment of the community. Common Essenes did not live at Qumran; they lived in villages and towns throughout Israel—among the very people who had become the Sons of Darkness, marked for destruction in the end of days. The audience of the *Damascus Document* (CD and its Cave 4 copies) are these Essenes, and the scroll's purpose is to mandate rhetorical dissociation in order to maintain a unified and coherent concept of *Essene* among community members who lived their daily lives surrounded by iniquity. Thus, once the Essene community was established through material rhetoric in the *Rule of the Community*, the community was then pruned and maintained through dissociative rhetoric, removing incoherent ideas that might give rise to contradiction or impurity. Throughout the *Damascus Document*, for example, *apparent Israelites* are dissociated from *real Israelites*, leaving the remaining concept *Israelites* coherent in the context of Essene ideology. And since not all Israelites were sincere in their commitment to Essene regulations, the *Damascus Document* also dissociates *apparent Essenes* from *real Essenes*, leaving the remaining concept *Essene* unified and pure, offering punishments for insincerity or disrespect.

The rites of initiation and renewal described in the *Rule of the Community*, and the practice of rhetorical dissociation described in the *Damascus Document*, ensured an authentic Israel uninfected by pagan Hellenistic impurities. However, if the Jerusalem Temple was no longer a legitimate institution for Israelite worship, then the Essenes (now the authentic Israel) would require a different legitimate Temple in which to perform the rites and rituals required by their new covenant. Since the Jerusalem Temple was illegitimate because it was impure, the new Temple would require a new level of purity, both among authentic Israelites who worshipped there and within the new Temple itself.

In an authentic Israel, each individual Israelite is pure. The *Purification Rules* explains how ritual impurities are embodied through discourse in the flesh of Israelites and how these embodied impurities are erased through ritual practices, such as isolation, bathing, and sprinkling with a purifying liquid called *me niddah*. Through a material rhetoric of entitlement, sacred discourses, like the Hebrew Bible and the Essene scrolls, especially the *Purification Rules*, inscribe qualities of purity and impurity in the physical bodies of Israelites. These same discourses describe material practices for the ritual purification of individual impurities, leading to the status of purity required by the Essenes' new covenant. Through a material rhetoric of ritual speech acts, Israelite impurities vanish from their bodies, leaving only pure flesh.

In a legitimate Temple, both the collective nation of Israel and the physical structure of the sanctuary are pure. The *Temple Scroll* explains how moral impurities are materialized through discourse in the nation of Israel and the sanctuary itself and how these material impurities are erased through ritual practices, such as required festivals and communal sacrifices. Sacred discourses entitle the nation of Israel and the physical structure of the sanctuary with purity and impurity, and these material impurities require ritual purification in order for the new covenant to remain valid and its metaphysical blessings to remain available. If individual Israelites, the nation of Israel, and the Temple sanctuary are pure when God returns to wage the final war against the Sons of Darkness, then God will join forces with the Essenes (the true Israel, the Sons of Light), and they will live forever in divine glory, as the new covenant promises. In the case of both the *Purification Rules* and the *Temple Scroll*, the acquisition of impurity and its purification are material processes, so they are best explained through material rhetoric.

From 100 until 63 BCE, Hasmonean high priests continued to acquire territory and wealth, and they continued to interpret Torah law liberally, leaving the Temple defiled, at least according to the Essenes. During this time, although there were some internal Israelite uprisings against perceived violations of the law by high priests (especially Alexander Jannaeus), most Israelite communities were not under direct threat of conquest, so they were able to live and worship as they wished. However, in 63 BCE, Roman armies under Pompey conquered Jerusalem, ending Israelite independence and subjecting Israelite territories to the perils of Roman political intrigue. Upon final victory, Pompey entered the Temple's holy of holies where only the high priest was allowed, thus defiling the inner sanctuary. Kamm writes, "In the meantime Hyrcanus II was confirmed as high priest (63–40 BCE) and appointed ethnarch of Judea, a term for a ruler which implies that he is subservient to another authority, in this case the governor of Syria" (1999, 157), who was Marcus Scaurus at the time, though that office changed hands frequently. During the Roman occupation, high priests were stripped of political influence, reduced to impotent administrators.

Although Rome occupied Israel, Israelite culture and religion were allowed to continue with few restrictions (Kamm 1999, 167), as long as the Israelites paid Roman tribute, accepted Roman imperial rule, and did not revolt (which they occasionally did anyway, though unsuccessfully). However, in 40 BCE, Antigonus, grandchild of the Hasmonean high priest Alexander Jannaeus, declared himself both high priest and king of Judea (174), directly challenging the hegemony of Roman governance in the region. In 37 BCE, Herod the Great, an Idoumean and an Israelite with loyalties more to Hellenistic Rome than to Jerusalem, acquired Roman armies and defeated Hasmonean Israel, installing himself as king of the region. Once in power, Herod exiled Antigonus to Rome where Antony ordered his execution, and Herod named a non-Hasmonean, Ananelus, as the next high priest from 37 to 36 BCE, effectively ending the Hasmonean dynasty of high priests and turning the position into a political appointment.

With Rome in power, Herod as king, and political appointees serving as high priests, the Essenes viewed themselves as living in the last days before the apocalypse that was foretold by the biblical prophets. By this turbulent time, the Essenes had fully separated themselves from all other Israelites and pagans, both physically at Qumran and ideologically in the territories, awaiting the final battle between the Sons of Light (Essenes) and the Sons of Darkness (everyone else) in the coming days. This is the rhetorical ecology in which the Essenes composed their unique genre of commentaries called *peshers*, most of which date to the second half of the first century BCE, including the *Habakkuk Pesher*.[6] For the Essenes, living under Roman occupation must have reminded them of their ancestors' fall to Babylonian forces and subsequent exile from Judah, and hermeneutics/rhetoric enabled them to codify these comparisons analogically.

The biblical prophets revealed abstract oracles from God and interpreted these oracles based on their own concrete historical circumstances. In the case of the prophet Habakkuk, those circumstances were the turbulent events in the late seventh century BCE that were leading to the Babylonian exile. In the narrative of his prophecy, Habakkuk explains that he offered up a complaint to God about internal and external strife in Judah (the Southern Kingdom) and received an oracle that predicted conquest and exile as the consequence for discord and disobedience. In prophecy, the oracle itself is universal and ahistorical, a divine message communicated directly to the prophet. Since the power of genuine oracular prophecy (or the reception of divine oracles) had been lost during the Second Temple period, the Essenes relied on what they called "mysteries" to reinterpret original oracles for a new historical circumstance.

In the *Habakkuk Pesher*, the Essenes revealed mysteries from God regarding an already-delivered oracle (the one in the book of Habakkuk) and reinterpreted the oracle analogically for their own concrete historical circumstances. In the case of the Essenes, those circumstances were the turbulent events in the late first century BCE that were leading to the Roman destruction of the Second Temple. Following are just a few of the analogies drawn by the Essenes (or provided through God's mysteries) in the *Habakkuk Pesher*: Habakkuk's evildoer equals the Essenes' Wicked Priest, Habakkuk's upright man equals the Essenes' Teacher of Righteousness, and Habakkuk's Chaldeans equal the Essenes' Kittim, or Romans. Also, the destruction of Jerusalem and the exile of its people are prophesied in the book of Habakkuk and are recognized in the *Habakkuk Pesher* as present realities (or at least inevitabilities) for the Essenes. As Eshel points out, identifying the Romans (using the thinly veiled sobriquet Kittim) in written texts about the apocalypse may have caused the need to transition from written to oral interpretation (2008, 179) and hide sacred texts that might be destroyed as heretical or confrontational.

By 66 CE, the entire region in and around the Roman province of Judea had descended into utter chaos. The Israelites revolted, but the Romans crushed every effort the Israelites made to acquire independence from Roman occupation and exploitation. In 66 CE, Roman general Vespasian marched troops into Judea and began to quell the rebellion and subdue the region, killing any who might oppose the Romans. By 68 CE, most of the province of Judea had been laid to waste, except for Jerusalem, which Vespasian was saving for last. But Vespasian returned to Rome to assume his role as emperor, leaving another Roman general, Titus, to finish the siege of the city, which he did in a most brutal fashion in 70 CE (Kamm 1999, 192–95). It is in this context of conquest and brutality that the Dead Sea Scrolls were deposited and hidden in the caves above the western shores of the Dead Sea. It is likely that some of the caves near Qumran had already functioned as a kind of library containing the Essenes' sacred scrolls for over a century. Cave 4, for example, was painstakingly carved out of the limestone cliff in a location that was near Qumran and thus more accessible than many of the natural caves; it contained around 550 different texts, over half of the total number that we now know as the Dead Sea Scrolls. Caves 1 and 2, on the other hand, were likely used as makeshift hiding places for scrolls deposited only after the revolts of 66 CE and before the destruction of Qumran in 68 CE (Schiffman 1995b, 53–54). Whatever the original functions of the caves, the fact is that the scrolls were concealed there for nearly two thousand years, until their (re)discovery.

Early in 1947, a young Ta'amireh Bedouin named Muhammad edh-Dhib was tending goats around the cliffs and hills just west of the Dead Sea.[7] Realizing that one of his precious charges had gone missing, he scaled the craggy rock face, searching the caves and listening for bleating. Edh-Dhib stopped at one cave in particular, listened, and threw a rock into it, hoping to scare the goat into revealing its hiding place. But instead of bleating, edh-Dhib heard the sound of shattering pottery. Nomadic Bedouin tribes often supplement their meager subsistence with money exchanged for ancient artifacts they find in the desert. So edh-Dhib entered the cave, opened the clay jars he found there, and removed some ancient scrolls, taking them back to his family for safekeeping until they could be sold. A few months later, these Bedouins traveled to Bethlehem and sold seven scrolls edh-Dhib had found to two different antiquities dealers: Faidi Salahi bought three scrolls and Khalil Iskander Shahin (known as Kando) bought four. On November 29, 1947, Professor Eleazar L. Sukenik of the Hebrew University in Jerusalem traveled to Bethlehem and purchased two of Salahi's scrolls (the *Psalms Scroll* and the *War Scroll*), acquiring the third scroll, a fragmentary copy of portions of Isaiah, a week later. These three scrolls would remain at the Hebrew University in Jerusalem for nearly twenty years.

On the very day that Sukenik returned to Jerusalem, November 29, 1947, the United Nations approved Resolution 181, the UN Partition Plan for Palestine, sparking a war between Palestinian Arabs and Jewish Zionists, who had immigrated to the region after the Holocaust of World War II. After six months of war, on May 15, 1948, Israel was declared a state. Sukenik's son, Yigael Yadin, recalled in his 1957 book, *The Message of the Scrolls*, "I cannot avoid the feeling that there is something symbolic in the discovery of the scrolls and their acquisition at the moment of the creation of the State of Israel. It is as if these manuscripts had been waiting in caves for two thousand years, ever since the destruction of Israel's independence [by the Romans in 70 A.D.], until the people of Israel had returned to their home and regained their freedom" (quoted in Shanks 1998, 15; brackets in the original). The discovery of the Dead Sea Scrolls would lend ideological validity to Jewish claims of rightful ownership in the land of Israel.

Intense conflicts throughout the region, from the winter of 1947 to the late spring of 1948, caused some delays in the purchase and transmission of Kando's four texts, the *Great Isaiah Scroll*, the *Habakkuk Pesher*, the *Rule of the Community*, and the *Genesis Apocryphon*. In April 1947, Kando sold his scrolls to Mar Samuel, the metropolitan of Jerusalem in the Syriac Orthodox Church, and they remained in Samuel's possession until he moved to the United States in 1949. Although Samuel's scrolls were displayed in museums throughout the United States and had generated much excitement among academics, no one came forward to purchase the scrolls. Needing funds for his church, Samuel placed a classified advertisement in the *Wall Street Journal* on June 1, 1954, announcing the sale of "The Four Dead Sea Scrolls" (Shanks 1998, 19, 21). Working through intermediaries, Yadin purchased the four scrolls for the new nation of Israel, adding them in 1955 to his father's collection at the Hebrew University in Jerusalem. All seven scrolls sold by edh-Dhib and his family were published and made generally available to scholars during the 1960s, and in 1965 the Israeli government established the Shrine of the Book to house these seven priceless documents, making the original scrolls available for study.

Since their initial discovery in 1947, both Bedouins and archaeologists have searched the caves above Qumran for more scrolls. In particular, Roland de Vaux, a French Dominican priest and director of the Catholic École Biblique in East Jerusalem (then part of Jordan), and Gerald Lankester Harding, director of the British Department of Antiquities in Jordan, excavated the area around the site of the first discoveries, finding ten new caves and thousands of fragments. They supplemented their own discoveries with thousands more fragments purchased from Bedouins (mostly with Kando as intermediary) who had beaten de Vaux and Harding to their locations, including the treasure trove of texts hiding in what is now Cave 4. In 1953, de Vaux gathered together a small group of scholars at the Palestine Archaeological Museum in East Jerusalem, including Josef Milik, John Allegro (who was later replaced by John Strugnell), Frank Moore Cross, Jean Starcky, Patrick Skehan, and Claus-Hunno Hunzinger (who was later replaced by Maurice Baillet). These scholars were mostly Catholic, and not one was Jewish or Israeli (because of the location of the museum in Jordan, and also because of overt anti-Semitism).

De Vaux, the leader of the team, assigned scrolls to scholars according to specialization, and these scholars inappropriately assumed rights of ownership over their scrolls. By 1958, almost all of the texts we know as the Dead Sea Scrolls had been discovered by archaeologists or purchased from Bedouins, and by 1961 most of the fragments, especially the huge cache from Cave 4, had been reconstructed into relatively coherent texts. However, after just a few years of enthusiastic reconstruction, de Vaux's scroll team seemed to lose some of its energy, slowing publication of the fragments to a snail's pace. Academics outside this small cadre of scholars were denied access to the fragments and their reconstructions, even as the reconstructed scrolls sat in the Palestine Archaeological Museum deteriorating from neglect.

During the Six-Day War in 1967, Israel captured East Jerusalem from Jordan, thus also taking control of the Dead Sea Scrolls housed in the Palestine Archaeological Museum, which the Israelis renamed the Rockefeller Museum. Israeli archaeologists entered the Palestine Archaeological Museum and seized control of the scrolls that were stored there. Unfortunately, these

Israeli archaeologists agreed to let de Vaux's original team publish the scrolls themselves, not realizing at the time that the pace of publication would continue to be painfully slow (Shanks 1998, 48–50). Hershel Shanks explains that "in 1985, well over half the texts from Cave 4 remained unpublished and inaccessible to scholars who were not on the team" (1998, 47). Twenty-five years had passed, and scholars from around the world, who knew very well that the scrolls existed, wondered why these texts were not being published for general examination, leading to some conspiracy theories that have proven to be unwarranted in hindsight. The refusal, or indolent neglect, to publish the Dead Sea Scrolls from the 1960s through the 1980s was not a Vatican conspiracy to conceal information damaging to Catholicism. The scrolls do not challenge any fundamental beliefs of Christianity (except, perhaps, its utter uniqueness at the time). They do, however, represent the only primary texts known to us from the late Second Temple period, which is enough, surely, to make the discovery of the Dead Sea Scrolls one of the greatest archaeological finds of the twentieth century.

From 1955 to 1989 (thirty-four years!), the editors in chief of the Oxford Clarendon series Discoveries in the Judean Desert (DJD)—first Roland de Vaux, then Pierre Benoit, and finally John Strugnell—had overseen the publication of only seven volumes of Dead Sea Scrolls manuscripts. In 1990, Strugnell made anti-Semitic comments in an interview for an Israeli newspaper. He was removed from his position as editor in chief of the DJD series by the Israel Antiquities Authority and replaced by Emanuel Tov (Vermes 1999, 6–7). Tov immediately redistributed the scroll manuscripts to around sixty new scholars and demanded faster results. Over the next nineteen years, from 1990 to 2009, Tov oversaw the publication of thirty-two more volumes in the DJD series, finally completing the task of publishing the Dead Sea Scrolls that had been discovered by 1958. Since 2009, debates have continued to rage about the accuracy of the DJD reconstructions, and new technologies have enabled scholars to see letters that were invisible to the naked eye just a few decades ago. The scrolls have also been translated into dozens of languages, making them available to scholars across the world. While theologians have created a cottage industry of criticism about the Dead Sea Scrolls, rhetoricians have taken little notice of these unique and important texts.

The rhetorical strategies described or exemplified in ancient Israelite and Jewish texts have long been of interest to communication scholars and rhetorically minded theologians. However, despite general interest, one period of this ancient textual tradition has been ignored by rhetoricians. In "Ancient Traditions, Modern Needs: An Introduction to Jewish Rhetoric," Samuel M. Edelman (2003) divides ancient Jewish rhetorics into three periods: the classical biblical period, the Hellenistic period, and the talmudic period.[8] Texts from both the classical biblical period and the talmudic period have received ample attention from rhetorical critics because the texts from those periods, the Torah and the Talmud, have been well preserved and available to scholars for centuries. However, only scant research has been conducted on the Hellenistic period of Israelite and Jewish rhetorics because only scant texts have survived from that time—until fairly recently, that is.

Until the mid-twentieth century, most of what scholars knew about this tumultuous time in Israelite history, the late Second Temple period, came from the Septuagint and from later histories of Judaism written by Philo, Pliny, and especially Josephus. The Septuagint shows no clear signs of sectarianism. Philo and Pliny never favored any particular sect of Judaism. Josephus did align himself most closely with the Pharisees, though he says that he spent quite a bit of time living among Sadducees and Essenes as well. The Pharisees had taken control of the Temple through bribes to their Roman oppressors during the first century BCE, and it was their ideological interpretation of Israelite scriptures that would endure into the talmudic period. Until the Dead Sea Scrolls were discovered, almost all we knew about late Second Temple Judaism came through nonsectarian scriptures and histories, or through Pharisaic histories and later rabbinic (also mostly Pharisaic) interpretations. There was, in other words, a nearly four-hundred-year gap in our understanding of the evolution of Israelite and Jewish rhetorics from the end of the classical biblical period to the beginning of the talmudic period, and what we had assumed to be true was generally not, though we had no way of knowing this yet.

The dearth of primary documentary evidence from the Hellenistic period of Israelite history would be filled in just a short time during the middle and late decades of the twentieth century with the discovery and publication of the Dead Sea Scrolls. And it was the fact that the scrolls filled this gap in our understanding of Judaism's historical trajectory that attracted some of the best-known biblical scholars to their study. Lawrence H. Schiffman writes, "What captured my attention was the opportunity to uncover the unknown missing links between the Judaism of the Bible and that of the

Talmud and to trace the links between prophet and priest on the one hand and Talmudic rabbis on the other.... Up until the discovery of the Dead Sea Scrolls, no contemporary documentary evidence existed for the intermediate [or late Second Temple] period" (1995b, xix).

This treasure of texts from a period of Israelite history with little other primary documentary representation should have triggered a firestorm of interest among scholars dedicated to studying ancient Israelite and Jewish rhetorics, but it has not. In 1990, Carol A. Newsom pointed out that "the rhetoric of a sectarian community is of particular interest, since such a community must be rather self-conscious about the creation of the discourse that gives it identity" (122). Thus, Newsom remarked, "It is curious that so little attention has been paid to the rhetorical dimensions of Qumran literature" (121). Twenty years later, in 2010, Newsom would conclude, again, that "the literature of a sectarian community has particular affinities for this type of analysis"—that is, rhetorical criticism—because "the Qumran community was deeply involved in using language to effect persuasion" (200). However, Newsom continued, "rhetorical criticism is as yet a little used method in Qumran studies. This near absence of rhetorical criticism is both surprising and unfortunate" (200). I do not know of any source on rhetoric in the Dead Sea Scrolls prior to the publication of Newsom's 1990 article on rhetorical strategies in the *Hodayot* (*Hymns*) and *Serek Ha-Yahad* (the *Rule of the Community*). To my knowledge, since 1990, fewer than a dozen articles have been published on the subject.[9]

Surely this lack of rhetorical criticism applied to the Dead Sea Scrolls in general is a missed opportunity. While it is true that the sectarian Dead Sea Scrolls present a difficult hermeneutic task for rhetoricians, it is a task worth engaging, since without a better understanding of the Dead Sea Scrolls, our knowledge of ancient Israelite and Jewish rhetorics in general remains incomplete. Reflecting on the status of scholarship about Israelite and Jewish rhetorics in 2003, Edelman explains, "We are in need of careful scholarly studies of the diachronic movement of Jewish rhetoric and case studies illuminating particular moments and theories in this tradition" (2003, 114).

The chapters of this book comprise a "case study" of rhetoric in certain texts among the Dead Sea Scrolls, thus illuminating a particular moment in Israelite rhetoric during the Second Temple period. The conclusion examines how the Dead Sea Scrolls illuminate the "diachronic movement" of rhetoric in its transition from the classical biblical period to the talmudic period.

In chapter 1, I discuss the Dead Sea Scroll called *Miqṣat Ma'aśeh ha-Torah* (or 4QMMT). This scroll was originally an epistle composed by leaders of the Essene community and addressed to the priests who administered the Temple in Jerusalem around 150 BCE (though it was also copied later for circulation and study). It is distinctly persuasive in purpose, since the Essenes, who had been deposed from Temple administration, believed that the ruling Jerusalem priests were not correctly executing Torah law, thus leading the entire nation of Israel into a state of impurity. Since purity was a requirement of the historical covenants, especially the Mosaic covenant, the Essenes believed that the imprecise rituals practiced by the Temple priests would lead the Israelites toward a fate of utter destruction in the end of days. In order to identify with their audience, thus creating an amicable relationship through their language, the Essene community emphasized their points of agreement with the Jerusalem priests by citing commonly revered scriptures introduced with the phrase "it is written." This phrase and the citations that follow it create a common substance of beliefs between the Essenes and their audience, preparing the rhetorical ground for their statement of differences. Although the Essenes and the Temple priests could agree on aspects of Torah law, it was in their practical application (locations of sacrifices, durations of rituals) that differences emerged, and the Essenes introduced their different interpretations of Torah law with the phrases "we say" and "we think." The exigency for articulating these differences of interpretation is the eschatological "end of days," in which God returns to judge the Israelites and condemn them if they are impure. The rhetorical purpose of 4QMMT, at least for the Essenes, was to encourage the ruling priests to purify their practice so that the Essene community could end its self-imposed exile and rejoin the Temple cult. Unfortunately for the Essenes, despite the conciliatory and respectful tone of their epistle, it was ultimately not well received.

Chapter 2 explores the *Rule of the Community* (1QS) as a description of performative procedures for initiating and renewing membership in the community of the new covenant, the Yahad. According to the Qumran community, the old Mosaic covenant had been utterly violated, and the curses of the old covenant were upon them. Only a new covenant, emphasizing selective membership, metaphysical blessings, and personal commitment could reverse their path toward destruction. Since the crisis of covenant is primarily based on the infelicitous performance of rituals at the Jerusalem Temple, speech act theory offers a useful rhetorical means to explain the performative response from the Essenes. The *Rule of the Community* describes two ceremonies. The first, an initiation ceremony, emphasizes commissive speech acts, including blessings, acknowledgments, confessions, curses, and oaths. The second, an annual renewal ceremony, emphasizes verdictive speech acts, including isolation, obedience, and sincerity. Through the speech acts performed in each of these ceremonies described in the *Rule of the Community*, the Yahad established a new Mosaic covenant based on personal choice and metaphysical blessings, discarding the old Mosaic covenant (with its assumption of national inheritance and material blessings) as eternally void.

In chapter 3, I explore dissociation as a rhetorical strategy in the *Damascus Document* (CD). The *Damascus Document* was a guidebook composed for members of the Essene community who lived in the camps among other Israelites and Gentiles, and were thus constantly exposed to sources of impurity and temptations to sin. The authors of the *Damascus Document* use dissociation in order to maintain ideological coherence in the Essene community by removing through argumentation sources of incoherence. Dissociation resolves ideological incoherence in communities by rhetorically carving away problematic notions that are incompatible with the concepts that represent communal ideals. These incompatible notions may arise in the natural process of linguistic change, and they may arise from shifts in historical circumstances. Once an ideal concept has become incoherent, dissociation divides the concept into a real aspect and an apparent aspect, with the real aspect maintaining the desired coherence, and the apparent aspect taking away with it the incoherence that threatens the community.

In the case of the *Damascus Document*, the authors persuade their audience to accept five key dissociations, hoping to maintain the coherence of the community in the face of rampant iniquity. First, the *Damascus Document* resolves the incoherence in the concept *humanity* by dissociating *apparent humanity* (Gentiles) from *real humanity* (Israelites), separating God's chosen people from those marked for destruction in the end of days. Second, the authors resolve the incoherence of the concept *Israelites* by dissociating *apparent Israelites* (nonremnants) from *real Israelites* (remnant), separating those who truly observe God's covenantal regulations from those who assume their salvation as a birthright. Third, the *Damascus Document* resolves the incoherence of the concept *remnants* by dissociating *apparent remnants* (non-Essenes) from the *real final remnants* (Essenes, the Yahad), arguing that only the Essenes will remain when God returns to earth in both glory and judgment. Fourth, the authors resolve the incoherence of the concept *Essene* by dissociating *apparent Essenes* (fraudulent members) from *real Essenes* (sincere members, who considered themselves the *true* Israel), emphasizing punishments for transgression. Fifth, the *Damascus Document* resolves the incoherence of the concept *Israel* through a double dissociation, removing *apparent Israel* (Ephraim) from *real Israel* (Judah), and then removing *old Israel* (Judah) from *new Israel* (Damascus), thus returning *Israel* to its original status as a coherent ideal concept. Each year, the inspector of the Essenes judges all community members regarding their execution of each of these dissociations, elevating or demoting them in the community hierarchy accordingly.

Chapter 4 analyzes the relationships among a few different scrolls, particularly the *Purification Rules* (4QTohorot A and 4QTohorot B) and the *Temple Scroll* (11QT), in the context of ritual and moral impurity and their erasure. In the *Purification Rules*, ritual impurities are embodied through discourse in the flesh of Israelites, and these embodied impurities are then erased through specific ritual practices. In the *Temple Scroll*, moral impurities are materialized through discourse in the nation of Israel and the sanctuary itself, and these impurities are erased through required festivals and sacrifices. Since ritual and moral impurities have a material existence, material rhetoric explains how impurities are both acquired and erased. This chapter uses two theories of material rhetoric to examine the *Purification Rules* and the *Temple Scroll*, entitlement and speech act theory. First, Kenneth Burke explains entitlement as a process in which salient discourses like the Torah and the Essene scrolls inspirit things, infusing them with meaning, so that these things become the signs of words (rather than the other way around). Second, J. L. Austin ([1962] 1975) explains speech acts as intentional actions that materialize effects in people and the world around them. Whereas ritual and moral impurities are acquired through entitlement, they are erased through speech acts, ensuring the holiness of God's people in the end of days.

In chapter 5, I examine the *Habakkuk Pesher* (1QpHab) as an example of hermeneutics/rhetoric, or rhetoric in which interpretation forms the substance and structure of the work. Hermeneutics/rhetoric is most fully grounded in the work of Hans-Georg Gadamer, especially *Truth and Method*. For Gadamer, interpretation and the communication that is based on it emerge from the cyclical interaction of individual prejudices, historical traditions, and the fusion of horizons. The result of this fusion of horizons is the manifestation of hermeneutics/rhetoric. The *Habakkuk Pesher* is an interpretation of the book of Habakkuk in which sequential *lemmas* (quotations and paraphrases) are immediately followed by peshers (interpretations). I begin my critical journey in this chapter with an analysis of the book of Habakkuk, exploring the ways in which Habakkuk's prejudices interact with historical traditions in a prophetic fusion of horizons. Habakkuk's prejudices derive from internal and external Judean strife, his traditions are based on divine oracles and the Mosaic covenant, and these horizons (prejudices and traditions) are fused in the practice of prophecy and later redactions of prophetic texts. The result of this cyclical process is prophetic hermeneutics/rhetoric.

Since the book of Habakkuk is an interpretation of divine oracles, not an objective recording of them (because divine oracles would be incomprehensible to situated human understanding), the *Habakkuk Pesher* is a *double* interpretation, or an interpretation of an interpretation. Pesher methodology, then, requires interpreters to believe that true prophetic oracles remain hidden behind situated interpretations of them in the prophetic books (like Habakkuk), that these oracles are relevant for all time (not just the time of their delivery), and that the only remaining access to these original oracles is pesher interpretation. Thus, the Essenes interpret Habakkuk's First Temple prejudices (Chaldean oppression) as being different from their own Second Temple prejudices (Roman oppression) only in a situational, experiential, human sense, but not in a divine or universal sense. While Habakkuk's traditions relate to oracular revelation and covenant theology, the traditions of the Essenes relate to the loss of oracular revelation and broken covenants that must be established differently rather than simply renewed. The fusion of horizons that occurs in pesher methodology is thus a double cyclical process of interpretation, and this double process is the substance and structure of hermeneutics/rhetoric in the *Habakkuk Pesher*.

The conclusion broadens the scope of my analysis from "case studies" of specific texts among the Dead Sea Scrolls to the ways in which the Dead

Sea Scrolls inform a more general understanding of the "diachronic movement of Jewish rhetorics" (Edelman 2003, 114). When the Roman destruction of the Jerusalem Temple in 70 CE is considered the single most salient rupture in Israelite and Jewish histories, then the late Second Temple period does not receive the attention it deserves. With 70 CE as the rupture, we understand the destruction of Jerusalem as the impetus for establishing synagogues as new institutions designed to replace the religious functions of the Temple. Yet then we overlook the fact that the Essenes established Qumran as an alternative Temple nearly two centuries before. With 70 CE as the rupture, we understand the dissolution of the Jerusalem priesthood as the impetus for the rise of rabbis. Yet then we overlook the fact that the Essenes were led by a community council of three priests and twelve men, who were not priests. Nearly two centuries before the destruction of the Temple, the Essenes chose primarily lay leadership, eschewing the requirement of a traditional priestly hierarchy. Finally, with 70 CE as the rupture, we understand the destruction of the Temple institution and the dissolution of its priestly administration as the cause of the loss also of the sacrificial cult, which rabbis replace with prayer, good works, and knowledge of the Torah. Yet then we overlook the fact that the Essenes had abandoned the sacrificial cult nearly two hundred years before, offering instead their prayers for purification and atonement, not animals.

The Dead Sea Scrolls complicate the history of Israelite and Jewish rhetorics because they are concrete documentary evidence that the rupture we once believed 70 CE represented is, in fact, no rupture at all. The Dead Sea Scrolls teach us that the shift from biblical to rabbinic Judaism was a slow process, a gradual transition over the course of centuries in which many rabbinic innovations now seem to have clear precedents, though they are not identical. Surely these transitional texts from Qumran should be of interest to scholars of Israelite and Jewish rhetorics, since they fill a gap in our historical understanding in some surprising ways. For this reason, I share Newsom's concern that only a few scholars have applied rhetorical methodologies to the Dead Sea Scrolls. Nevertheless, I believe it is an intellectual journey worth taking, and I hope this book encourages others to explore rhetoric and the Dead Sea Scrolls.

CHAPTER 1

RHETORICS OF IDENTIFICATION, DISTINCTION, AND PERSUASION IN *MIQṢAT MAʿAŚEH HA-TORAH* (4QMMT)

Miqṣat Maʿaśeh ha-Torah (hereafter 4QMMT) is one of the many texts found in the Judean desert caves near Qumran. It represents the Essene community's effort, through rhetorical identification and distinction, to correct impure priestly orthopraxy in the Jerusalem Temple following the successful Hasmonean revolt against Greek rule and the installation of Hasmonean high priests in the Temple cult.[1] Six copies of 4QMMT were found in Cave 4 near Qumran (the 4Q in the manuscript designation means Cave 4 at Qumran), but only fragments of each copy survived the ravages of time and mishandling. Copy 4Q394 (or 4QMMTª) is the most complete of the fragmented manuscripts. Other copies either repeat lines or reveal text beyond the final line of 4Q394, for a total of about 130 extant lines of Hebrew text.[2] Paleographic analysis dates the six copies of 4QMMT to between 75 BCE and 50 CE (Kampen and Bernstein 1996, 2). However, linguistic analysis, which shows traces of earlier Second Temple period language and usage, suggests that the provenance of the six copies was an older original, perhaps as early as 150 BCE.[3] In other words, we do not have an original text of 4QMMT; we have copies that were circulated and studied at Qumran. The original document, however, was probably one of the founding documents of the Essene sect.

4QMMT is unusual among the Dead Sea Scrolls. Many of the scrolls are biblical—that is, copies of texts that would become the Hebrew Bible. Most of these texts were composed prior to the Second Temple period and were either copied at Qumran for distribution and study or were brought to the caves from the Temple in Jerusalem. The remaining scrolls are nonbiblical, of sectarian origin.[4] Most of these nonbiblical texts were composed, not just copied, by members of the Qumran community for *internal* use— that is, the members of the sect who composed or copied the texts used them for the sect's own social and religious purposes. These sectarian texts include, for example, rules of the community, *pesharim* (commentaries), liturgies, and calendars. But 4QMMT is one of only a few genuine epistles among the sectarian Dead Sea Scrolls. It was composed by members of the Essene community (or, more likely, their head priest) for an explicitly *external* audience, the priests (or high priest) who controlled the Temple in Jerusalem.[5] The purpose of the text is clearly rhetorical. As Carolyn J. Sharp explains, 4QMMT "was likely composed with great care toward the goal of persuading its reader(s) to undertake some significant action or change of ideological position related to cultic practice" (1997, 208).

There are three distinct sections in the composite text of 4QMMT. Each section was assigned a letter by the first editors of the text, Elisha Qimron and John Strugnell (1994). First, in section A, we find the last few phrases describing a 364-day solar calendar that would replace the lunar calendar used by Temple priests. Although only small fragments of the solar calendar remain in 4QMMT, we know it well from other Qumran scrolls, including Enoch, Jubilees, and the *Temple Scroll* (Schiffman 1996, 83). The lunar calendar followed by the priests in the Jerusalem Temple caused certain festivals requiring harvests and sacrifices to fall on the Sabbath. However, the commandment to keep the Sabbath holy demands complete rest. The Essene community considered harvesting and sacrificing to be forbidden work on the Sabbath, thus a form of sin, and so relied on a solar calendar according to which no festivals fell on this holy day.[6] Second, in section B, we find a list of laws and works of the law that the leader of the Essene sect hopes will be adopted in Jerusalem priestly orthopraxy.[7] Although all Second Temple Israelites agreed that the Torah states universal laws, the works and deeds of (or practices associated with) the laws were the subject of heated debate:

incorrect interpretation of the law leads to impure priestly orthopraxy, which leads to sin, which leads to eternal torment. These are not, in other words, merely academic debates; they are debates about matters that result in salvation or damnation. Third, in section C, we find a final exhortation directed to a singular "you," the Jerusalem high priest, who is probably Jonathan, a Hasmonean (and non-Zadokite) installed in this highest office following the successful revolt led by the Hasmonean family against Hellenistic religious oppression.[8]

The rhetorical purpose of 4QMMT is distinctly persuasive, to recommend pure priestly orthopraxy so that the Jerusalem Temple will not be in a state of defilement at the end of days (*aḥarit ha-yamim*). In *The Philosophy of Literary Form*, Kenneth Burke explains that "every document bequeathed us by history must be treated as a strategy for encompassing a situation, . . . as the *answer* or *rejoinder* to assertions in the situation in which it arose" ([1941] 1973, 109). 4QMMT is, of course, a response to a specific situation, the defilement of the Jerusalem Temple, and the stakes are high. The members of the Essene community believed that God left the Temple for heaven, abandoning the Israelites, when his Temple was impure. And if God descended from heaven in final judgment only to find his Temple defiled, the end of days may see the total destruction of humanity, not a glorious time of redemption and victory for pious Israelites. All of the rhetorical elements of persuasion are present: concerned writers (Essene priests), a specific audience (Jerusalem priests), a pressing subject (laws and works governing priestly practice), a definite purpose (to reestablish the purity of the Jerusalem Temple), and an exigent context (the end of days, which the Essene community believed was fast approaching). 4QMMT, then, represents an intentional act of persuasion, a deliberate attempt to change the minds of powerful Israelite priests regarding impure priestly orthopraxy so that the Essene community might return to worship in a pure Temple (Regev 2003, 253).

In this chapter, I explore both the rhetorical situation (exigencies, rhetors, audiences, and constraints) of 4QMMT and also the rhetorical ecology surrounding the text, including the constantly evolving social politics and sacred intertextuality characteristic of that place and time. In particular, the Essenes used direct references to the Torah as a way to create identification with their audience in a rhetorical ecology marked by religious and political power struggles. The Essenes used the introductory formulae "we say" and "we think" to buffer the presentation of their differing interpretations of Torah law so that the audience might be more inclined to accept the veracity of these differences. And the Essenes used an eschatological framework to lend a sense of urgency to the implementation of Essene legal procedures in the Jerusalem Temple, employing, in the process, a conciliatory style, reasoned argument, personal sincerity, and appeals to common memory as rhetorical strategies for persuasion. Before I address the Essene community's use of specific rhetorical strategies in 4QMMT, I will first explore certain salient aspects of the rhetorical ecology from which 4QMMT emerged and into which it was intended to return.

POLITICS AND PRIESTS

During the 900s BCE, Solomon succeeded David as king of the Israelites in a ceremony performed by Zadok, one of David's chief priests.[9] The succession was not without difficulties, however, since David did not officially determine his heir until very late in his life. Solomon was David's sentimental choice, but David's eldest living son, Adonijah, had a more legitimate claim to succession. In a hasty ceremony, Zadok crowned Solomon king of the Israelites. Wishing to put these succession woes behind him and consolidate Israelite sentiments in his favor, Solomon constructed the First Temple in Jerusalem as a permanent home for the ark of the covenant, which contained the Ten Commandments. The Jerusalem Temple would replace the temporary camps and portable tabernacle that was tended by the Levites during the Israelites' time in the desert. Solomon was hoping that a centralized location for social and religious practices would unite the Israelites. Further, Solomon installed Zadok, who supported Solomon's succession to the throne, as sole high priest and decreed that all high priests from that time forward would come from the line of Zadok (Werman 2000, 624–25). The Zadokite high priests held power in Jerusalem for centuries (both before and after the destruction of Solomon's Temple) until their line of succession was usurped in the mid-second century BCE by Greek forces who had economic and political interests in the region.

Onias III, son of Simon II and member of the Zadok family, was high priest from 190 to 174 BCE (Kamm 1999, 147). As Kamm explains, Onias III was loyal to the Greek leader Seleucus IV. However, in 175 BCE, when

Onias III was in Antioch seeking a more secure peace and reporting his activities to Seleucus IV, the Greek leader was assassinated and replaced by Antiochus IV. Onias III, fearing that his association with Seleucus would cost him his own life, did not return to Jerusalem (where he could easily be located), though he would later be killed by Menalaus. Joshua, Onias III's brother, bribed Antiochus IV into installing him as high priest in Onias III's absence, and, as a part of the deal, Joshua built a Greek-style gymnasium near Jerusalem. While Joshua (a Zadokite) was not the first high priest to allow Hellenistic practices, including pagan sacrifices, in the Jerusalem Temple, he was perhaps the first who actively sought to Hellenize priestly orthopraxy, though his time as high priest was short-lived. When Joshua sent his envoy Menelaus to pay tribute to Antiochus IV in 171, Menelaus outbid Joshua, and Antiochus IV installed Menelaus in the office of high priest. While Onias III and Joshua may not have been the best high priests, allowing certain impure (Hellenistic) practices to take place in the Jerusalem Temple, they were at least born of the priestly Zadokite line, as Solomon had decreed (Kamm 1999, 147). Leonard J. Greenspoon points out that "the Oniads traced their lineage back to Zadok, whom Solomon had secured in this position, and Jews worldwide generally agreed that Zadok's descendants had been chosen by God for the priestly leadership" (1998, 327). Menelaus, though probably of a priestly family, was not of the high priestly line of Zadok, and under Menelaus Hellenization continued apace until Judaism, viewed by Antiochus IV as an ever-increasing annoyance, was effectively outlawed.

Menelaus, whose term as high priest lasted from 171 to 162 BCE, was, according to Josephus, "a wicked and an impious man; and, in order to get the government to himself, had compelled his nation to transgress their own laws" (1987, 332). Under Menelaus's watch, Antiochus IV sent decrees and implemented laws "that struck at the very heart of Jerusalem" (Greenspoon 1998, 328). Greenspoon continues:

> All distinctive Jewish customs and ceremonies were forbidden, including Sabbath and festival observance and circumcision. All Torah scrolls were to be seized and burned. All sacrifices and offerings to God at the Jerusalem Temple were abolished. Anyone who persisted in carrying out these or other Jewish rites was subject to

the death penalty. To demonstrate that the provisions of these decrees were not empty threats, those in charge of Seleucid forces, together with their allies among the Jews, began a concerted and public effort to implement them. Nowhere were their actions more provocative than at the Temple itself, which they turned into a place of worship for the Greek god Zeus Olympius. The altar on which daily sacrifices had been offered to the God of Israel was desecrated, and in its place an altar to Zeus was erected. On 25 Kislev 167 BCE (during the first part of the winter) a pig was sacrificed on this altar, a direct insult to the traditions of Judaism. Statues of Greek gods appeared in the Temple and elsewhere in Jerusalem. Throughout Judea, into Samaria, and to a lesser degree elsewhere in his empire Antiochus IV seemed determined that the monotheistic faith of Israel be utterly destroyed and that those brave or foolish enough to resist be killed. (328–29)

While it is unclear whether Menelaus encouraged, tolerated, or was angered by Antiochus IV's efforts to crush the Israelite faith, what is nevertheless perfectly clear is that Menelaus allowed the prohibition of Jewish practices and the desecration of the Temple to happen without attempting to intercede.

Some of the Israelites living in Jerusalem abided by the new decrees enforced by Antiochus IV, perhaps fearing for their lives, or perhaps enticed by the luxuries that came with a Hellenistic lifestyle. Of those who left Jerusalem, some fled into the countryside or desert where they could engage in unofficial ritual observances. Others, however, led by the powerful Hasmonean family beginning in 167 BCE, revolted in the style of guerilla warfare, surprising and defeating Antiochus IV's forces wherever and whenever they could. Annoyed by these Hasmonean victories, and more interested in engaging his armies in Egypt, Antiochus IV came to the belief that the Jewish revolt was a response to Menelaus, who made a convenient scapegoat. So, according to Josephus, Antiochus IV had Menelaus killed and replaced him with Alcimus (another non-Zadokite), who was high priest from 162 to 159 BCE (1987, 332). What Antiochus IV did not realize is that the Jewish revolt was a response to Hellenization and defilement of the Temple, not a response to Menelaus, and Alcimus did nothing to slow the process of Hellenization. So the Jewish revolt under the Hasmoneans continued, much to Antiochus IV's chagrin. Several of the Hasmonean brothers were killed in battle during the revolution, but before his own death at the hands of Antiochus IV's armies, Judah secured an important alliance with Rome, which was accepting alliances with any forces who would oppose Greece (Greenspoon 1998, 333). Following Alcimus's death in 159, no succeeding high priest was appointed, and the position was left vacant until 152, when, following the ultimately successful Hasmonean revolt, Jonathan (a Hasmonean and non-Zadokite) was installed as high priest and began the process of returning the Temple to its former status as the center of Jewish worship in Judea.

In his new role as high priest, Jonathan began to purify the Jerusalem Temple of Hellenistic defilement and return the Temple to its central role as the governing institution of Judaism. When Jonathan was killed in 142, his younger brother Simon was appointed high priest, continuing the Hasmonean policy of anti-Hellenism, and thus Jewish purity. Two years later, an assembly of priests and Israelites declared that all subsequent high priests must be born of the Hasmonean dynasty, ending any Zadokite claims to the high priesthood (Hodge 2003, 45–46). Although most Second Temple Israelites believed that the Zadokite line was predestined by God to administer the Jerusalem Temple, surely even the remaining Zadokite priests, who had been ousted from their rightful office some years before, did not oppose the victorious Hasmoneans, at least not yet.[10] Without the brave leadership of the Hasmonean brothers, the Temple would still be defiled. Most scholars date 4QMMT to the early years of the Hasmonean dynasty, perhaps shortly after Jonathan had purified the Temple of Hellenistic defilement and the Hasmoneans had established some priestly practices that were inconsistent with Zadokite practices. Although the rhetorical purpose of 4QMMT is to change the high priest's mind regarding certain works of the law, the tone is more respectful and less polemical than later sectarian texts. Thus, despite the dissolution of the Zadokite line of high priests, the Zadok family must have identified with the Hasmoneans as fellow pious Israelites in the fight against Hellenization, while simultaneously distinguishing themselves from the impious practices that resulted in the defilement of the Jerusalem Temple. It is in this context, during the late 150s or early 140s BCE, that 4QMMT was first composed.

"IT IS WRITTEN": COMMON LAWS AND THE RHETORIC OF IDENTIFICATION

In *A Rhetoric of Motives*, Burke describes identification as a process whereby two or more individuals or groups perceive a union of interests despite their unique qualities. Burke writes, "A is not identical with his colleague, B. But insofar as their interests are joined, A is *identified* with B. . . . In being identified with B, A is 'substantially one' with a person other than himself. . . . A doctrine of *consubstantiality*, either explicit or implicit, may be necessary to any way of life. For substance, in the old philosophies, was an *act*; and a way of life is an *acting-together*; and in acting together, men have common sensations, concepts, images, ideas, attitudes that make them *consubstantial*" (1969, 20–21). And, later, Burke continues, "Any specialized activity participates in a larger unit of action. 'Identification' is a word for the autonomous activity's place in this wider context" (27). Burke's notion of identification is useful here because it transcends the rhetor-audience relationship characteristic of traditional articulations of the rhetorical situation and allows us to examine the larger rhetorical ecology that brings rhetor and audience together in the context of social and historical discourse. Solomon's effort to unify the Israelite community with a central Temple and a permanent priestly administration had succeeded for centuries, but this relative unity was beginning to break down in the late Second Temple period, when sectarian disputes over scriptural interpretation and ritual practice resulted in bitter rivalries. Impure priestly orthopraxy may have been the immediate exigency for 4QMMT, but the rhetorical ecology of disintegrating unity among competing Israelite factions also led the Essene community to work toward identification. Finding commonalities is not just a good way to open a persuasive argument; it is also, through intertextual reference to the sacred Torah, a way to connect the immediate text and situation of 4QMMT with more positive aspects of its rhetorical ecology, such as unity of purpose and devotion to one God.

While the rhetorical purpose of 4QMMT was in part to state differences between the Essene community's own ritual practices and the practices of the Jerusalem priests, the fact is, as E. P. Sanders points out, "the Qumran community [also] had much in common with other Jews of the same place and time" (2000, 32). Sanders explains, "The vast majority of Jews in the ancient world had these characteristics: (a) they believed in and worshipped the God of Israel; (b) they accepted the Hebrew Bible (often in translation) as revealing his will; (c) consequently they observed most aspects of Mosaic law; (d) they identified themselves with the history and fate of the Jewish people" (8). Moreover, Sanders continues, "virtually all Jews believed that God required sacrifices, that he had specified that they must be offered in the Temple in Jerusalem, that he appointed hereditary priests, and that he designated certain days during certain seasons as times of festivals. The Qumran sectarians entirely agreed" (16). Regarding 4QMMT, Hannah K. Harrington states that "both sides agreed that priests were the main officiants at the sanctuary, that Jews should contribute certain gifts to them, and that all Israel should maintain a certain purity code which increased when visiting the sanctuary. The point at issue here was one of degree" (1997, 128). And Jesper Høgenhaven argues that "a relationship of fundamental agreement exists between the 'we' [authors] and the 'you' [audiences of 4QMMT] regarding the authoritative tradition and its implications" (2003, 200). Sanders, Harrington, and Høgenhaven do not deny the critical importance of the differences between the Essene community and other Israelites of the time, of course; they do recognize, however, the importance of understanding those differences in the context of *common* beliefs among Second Temple Israelites.[11]

Israelites of the Second Temple period were monotheists who believed in one God, the God of Israel. The Israelites were God's chosen people, and they had a covenant and a book of laws (the Torah) to prove it. Jonathan G. Campbell points out that "the scriptures making up the canonical Torah were fixed in early post-exilic times" (2000, 184), so all Israelites of the latter half of Second Temple period would have studied and interpreted the same Torah, encountering, thus, the same laws therein. The Ten Commandments are the most recognizable of these laws; however, there are also many more laws and commandments throughout the entire Torah. The laws stated explicitly in the Torah were common to all Jewish sects of the Second Temple period (and, of course, before and after). One cannot, in other words, identify an Essenic or Pharisaic or Sadducean copy of Leviticus or Deuteronomy. These common laws formed, and continue to form, the foundation of the Jewish faith (Harrington 2001, 124).

Direct reference to the laws of the Torah, using the citation formula "it is written" (*katub*), is a deliberate rhetorical attempt to construct consubstantiality and promote identification between the author(s) and the audience(s) of 4QMMT. Moshe J. Bernstein points out the relative frequency with which "it is written" appears in the fragments of 4QMMT: "'It is written' (*katub*) is a quotation formula that appears no fewer than eleven times in 4QMMT (the editors reconstruct two additional instances)" (1996, 39). And, according to George J. Brooke, "nearly all the phrases which follow *katub* [it is written] can be identified as citations of scripture" (1997, 71).[12] Brooke identifies at least a dozen "clear explicit quotations of scripture" (79), several of which are provenanced in the biblical scrolls. Table 1 highlights a few of the most complete direct citations of scripture in 4QMMT, each introduced with the formula "it is written," placed next to their corresponding biblical passages, quoted from Martin G. Abegg, Peter Flint, and Eugene Ulrich's translation in the *Dead Sea Scrolls Bible* (1999).[13]

Despite the fact that the author(s) of 4QMMT invoke scripture as a means to identify with their priestly audience, it is evident that even their citations of scripture also serve a distinctly persuasive purpose. Høgenhaven writes, "The way in which biblical quotations and allusions are used and interpreted is likely to constitute a major rhetorical device in a text such as 4QMMT" (2003, 190). Brooke explains that "the explicit citations of scripture, including those citations which are mild adjustments of scriptural word

TABLE 1 Common laws among Israelites: "It is written," or the irrefutable word of God

4QMMT	Dead Sea Scrolls Bible
[... it is written that ...] ... he will not sow his field [or his vineyard with two species] because they are holy. (lines 80–81)	[You shall not sow your vineyard with two kinds of seed, or the wh]ol[e yield will have to be forfeited, both the seed which you have sown and the yield of the vineyard]. (Deuteronomy 22:9)
And [further] it is writ[ten in the book of Moses that] an abomination [is not] to be brought [into a house, for] an abomination is odious. (lines 91–92)	And [you shall] not [bring an abomination into your house, or you will be set apart for destruction like it]. You shall [utterl]y detest it, and you shall utterly abhor it, [for it is set apart for destruction]. (Deuteronomy 7:26)
And further it is written that [you shall stray] from the path and you will undergo evil. (line 97)	For I know that after [my] de[ath] you will [utterly] corrupt yourselves, [and turn aside from] t[he w]ay which I have commanded [yo]u; and [disaster] will b[efall you in the da]ys [to come]; because you will do [e]vil in [the sig]ht of the Lord. (Deuteronomy 31:29)

order or grammatical forms, show that the compilers of MMT had a lively attitude to scripture which was not bound by its precise letter but which was very careful to fit it suitably, in its own phraseology, to the context of the debate" (1997, 85). Thus, "in MMT several citations use nothing but the phraseology of the scriptural source, but they are adjusted, abbreviated, or reordered slightly so that they fit the new context suitably and are appropriate to the author's interpretive need" (88). The authors of 4QMMT cite scripture as a means to identify with their audience, using the Torah as a common substance, so that the distinctions they make between themselves and their audience might be taken in a positive way, in a context of common values.

The rhetorical ecology of Second Temple Judaism was dominated by a complete devotion to the truth of the Torah. However, the Essenes believed that the Jerusalem priests were basing their religious, ceremonial, political, and legal judgments not on the Torah but rather on their own greed and on political demands from Greek patrons. To point this out to the Jerusalem establishment, however, would mean certain death. Instead, members of the Essene community presented their arguments in the context of a common belief in Torah law, citing examples of passages about which both communities could agree. This initial attempt to create, through intertextual reference, a sense of identification between authors and audiences in the larger context of social disintegration led to another inevitable purpose of 4QMMT: a statement of differences.

"WE SAY" AND "WE THINK": WORKS OF THE LAW AND THE RHETORIC OF DISTINCTION

Torah law is constant, unchanging. If we open the Torah tomorrow, we will find no new commandments, none will be missing, and the wording will be unaltered. Yet when we turn away from explicitly cited scriptural laws in 4QMMT and examine the works that are *based on* the law (that is, the procedures to be followed, for example, in sacrificing sin offerings), we begin to see more and more sectarian interpretations. These interpretations shift readers' attention away from the relative security of common Torah laws, which form the basis of identification among all Israelites, and turn readers' attention instead toward the sectarian commitments that caused ideological rifts to form among the various Second Temple sects.

Florentino García Martínez points out that, in addition to the citation of scripture, there is also in 4QMMT a discussion of "works and deeds" associated with Torah law, implementations, interpretations, and so on (1996b, 25); 4QMMT is "a collection of some of the practices, [some] of the works, which according to the prescriptions of the law should be done in order to be rewarded" (26). It is in this process of interpretation, generating sectarian works and deeds from common laws, that one group of Israelites may begin to differentiate itself from other groups. Brooke notes that "it is remarkable in MMT that there is a very clear differentiation between the use of *katub* [it is written] and verbs of saying (*amar*) or thinking (*haśab*). 'It is written' (*katub*) is nearly always associated with scripture explicitly or in summary form, whereas the opinions of the group behind MMT are expressed in terms of thinking or considering or saying" (1997, 71).[14] Such wording acknowledges the human origin of the ideas expressed, as opposed to the implied origin, God, in the passive formula, "it is written."

When the letter of the law can be understood and followed, then it should be followed. However, where the letter of the law is obscure or the circumstances of its origin are obsolete, then the law must be elaborated and clarified with additional regulations or works. The "we say" and "we think" formulae that begin statements of interpretation, statements that counter the interpretations of Jerusalem priests, also counter the rhetorical purpose of identification that we see in 4QMMT's direct citations of scripture. Yet these differing interpretations are the very exigency for 4QMMT. Without the differences, there would be no need for identification. Burke explains, "To begin with 'identification' is, by the same token, though roundabout, to confront the implications of *division*. . . . Identification is affirmed with earnestness precisely because there is division. Identification is compensatory to division. If [humans] were not apart from one another, there would be no need for the rhetorician to proclaim their unity" (1969, 23). It is in the process of interpretation, of generating division in the differences among interpretations, that one group of Israelites may begin to differentiate itself from other groups.

There are at least twenty-four different regulations or works of the law described throughout the six extant copies of 4QMMT (Abegg 1999, 139), some corresponding to biblical passages and others having no correspondence at all. Since my purpose is to discuss the rhetorical function of these works, and not to debate their technical or theological implications, I represent here only the most complete of the works in 4QMMT, and only those that begin with the explicit formula "we say" or "we think." I present these works in table 2, with the proposed Essene works of the law in the left-hand column and the presumed practice at the Jerusalem Temple in the right-hand column. In addition, I review one more work, not represented in the table, as a more elaborate case study.

Although the authors of 4QMMT explicitly cite scripture throughout the epistle as a way of creating identification with their audience, the regulations and works of the law (quoted above) are only *based on* scripture; they are interpretations and applications ("works") of the laws in the Torah. For example, some works and regulations address ambiguous notions of timing in the law. When the law says that a sacrifice should be eaten before the next day, does that mean that it must be eaten by sunset or dawn? When the law says that leprosy is cleansed on the seventh day, does that mean that the leper can eat sacred food on the seventh day or should the leper wait until dawn on the eighth day? Other works and regulations address ambiguous procedures in the law. Can a priest purify a vessel and its contents by pouring pure liquid into the vessel, or does the pure vessel and its liquid become impure by contact? Still other works and regulations are based on definitions. Is a male fetus in the womb of a sacrificed animal considered a "son," and thus subject to the laws regarding ritual slaughter, or is it merely a natural part of the mother's body? Many of these works and regulations are *based on* scripture, but a few, in fact, appear not to be. The works outlined in 4QMMT illustrate how ambiguous laws, or ambiguous situations not addressed in the laws, may require interpretation, and the peril of incorrect interpretation is impurity, and, thus, sin.

Now that I have developed a general sense of the works and regulations that make up section B of 4QMMT, I want to examine more closely one such work that I did not include in table 2. This work has to do with the place of slaughter:

> And concerning what is written: (Leviticus 17:3) ["When a man slaughters within the camp"—they] [slaughter] outside the camp—"a bull, or a [she]ep or a she-goat": the pl[ace of slaughter

TABLE 2   Pure and impure works of the law: "We say" and "we think," or contested practices based on interpretations of the Torah

Pure Works of the Law Described in 4QMMT	Impure Works of the Law Practiced in the Jerusalem Temple
[And concerning the thank-offerings] which they postpone from one day to another, w[e think] that the ce[real]-offering [should be eaten] with the fats and the meat on the day of their sa[crifice]. (lines 12–16)	Thank-offerings must be consumed entirely by sunset on the day of the sacrifice. Temple priests may have allowed Israelites to delay consuming thank-offerings until the day (or several days) after consuming the meat sacrifice, thus leading Israelites into sinful sacrificial practices. (Harrington 1997, 124; Schiffman 1996, 86)
[And concerning pregnant animals, we think that] the mother and son [should not be sacrificed] on the same day. [. . . And concerning who eats, w]e think that one can eat the son [who was in the womb of his mother after she has been slaughtered]. (lines 39–41)	The Torah forbids the sacrifice of mother and son on the same day, but does not mention the unborn fetus inside a pregnant sacrificial animal. Live male fetuses are sons, which require sacrificial slaughter at least one day after the slaughter of the mother. Temple priests may have considered fetuses to be an inseparable part of the mother's own body (not a "son") and thus not subject to laws governing ritual slaughter. (Harrington 1997, 125)
And also concerning flowing liquids: we say that in these there is no purity. Even flowing liquids cannot separate unclean from clean because the moisture of flowing liquids and their containers is the same moisture. (lines 58–61)	Pouring pure liquid from a purified vessel into an impure vessel with impure liquid makes all impure, since impurity travels through unbroken streams of water. Temple priests may have attempted to purify vessels and liquids by pouring pure liquids from pure vessels into impure liquids in impure vessels, thus leading Israelites to use impure implements in sacred rituals. (Elman 1996, 106–28; Grabbe 1997, 93–95)
And also concerning lepers: we s[ay that] they should [not] enter the holy purity, but instead [reside outside the camp], alone. [And] also it is written that from the moment he shaves and washes he should reside outside [his tent for seven] days. And it happens that when they are unclean, [lepers approach] the holy purity, the house. (lines 67–71)	Lepers were permitted to conduct sacrifices and consume sacred food in the Temple only after they were ritually cleansed. Cleansing rituals for lepers take effect at the end of the seventh day following purification (shaving and washing). Temple priests may have allowed lepers into the Temple to sacrifice and consume sacred food before the end of the seventh day following purification, making all they touched impure. (Grabbe 1997, 93; Harrington 1997, 125)

is the north of the camp.] And we think that the temple [is the place of the tent of meeting, and Je]rusalem is the camp; and outside the camp is [outside of Jerusalem;] it is the camp of their cities. Outside the ca[mp . . .] . . . [. . .] You shall remove the ashes from the altar and bur[n there the sin offering, for Jerusalem] is the place which [he chose from among all the tribes of Israel . . .] [. . .] [. . . they] do not slaughter in the temple. (lines 30–38)

Here 4QMMT cites two brief passages from Leviticus 17 (establishing identification) and then follows these passages with a discussion of where sacrifices should take place (clarifying distinction). These two cited passages would serve as a kind of shorthand to indicate a much longer passage that would immediately come to mind for the audience. The author of 4QMMT, in fact, praises the audience for his deep knowledge of the Torah. I will here cite the longer passage from *The Dead Sea Scrolls Bible*:

And the Lord spoke to [Moses, saying, "Speak to] *Aaron* and to all the children of Israel, and sa[y] to them: 'This is what [the LO]R[D] has commanded, [sayi]ng, "Any man from the house of Israel [*and the stranger who*] *resides in Israel* who slaughters an ox, or [lamb, or goat, in the cam]p, or who slaughters it outside the camp, and [has not brought it] to the door of the tent of meeti[ng *so as to sacrifice it as a burnt offering*] *or an offering of well-being to the LORD to be acceptable as* [*a pleasing odor, and has slaughtered it without and*] *does not bring it* [*to the door of the tent of me*]*eting to offer it* as an offering to LORD before the taber[nacle] of the LORD, [t]hat m[an] shall be guilty of bloodshed; he has shed blood and shall be cut off am[ong] his people. This is so [the children of] Israel will bring their sacrifices which they sacrifice i[n the] open field, that they may bring them to the L[ORD, t]o the door of the tent of meeting, to the priest, and sacrifice them for sac[rifices of well-being to the LORD. And the priest shall sprinkle] the blood on the altar [of the LORD at the door of the tent of meeting, and burn the fat for a pleasing odor] to the [L]ORD. And they shall no [longer] sacrifice [their sacrifices to the goat idols with which they play the harlot. This shall be a statute forever to them throughout their generations."'" (Leviticus 17:1–7)

On the surface of it, this law seems clear; however, members of the Essene community believed that the Jerusalem priests either were not implementing the law properly or were not aware of a more accurate interpretation (to which, of course, the Essene community was privy).

The "camp" and the "tent of the meeting place" were meaningful structures in the time of Moses, when the Israelites had only a portable tabernacle. However, from the time of Solomon through the Second Temple period (excepting only the Babylonian exile), with a centralized Temple complex, the accurate execution of this law required priests to understand what, in the context of this new construction, is equivalent to the structures that were present when the law was written. What, then, is the "camp" when there is no camp? What is the "tent of the meeting place" when there is no tent? If "camp" and "tent" are not just obsolete terms, but the immutable words of God, then it is not acceptable to say, "Well, that doesn't really apply anymore. We don't have to worry about that." The absence of camps and tents (temporary structures) from the permanent Temple did not make God's words obsolete. There must always and forever be camps and tents, but the Temple authorities must interpret which of the new permanent structures *represent* those older temporary structures.

If these terms are interpreted inaccurately (that is, the priests misunderstand what permanent structures represent the original camp and tent of meeting), then the Jerusalem priests may well be defiling the Temple with impure priestly orthopraxy, or innocent Israelites may be consuming impure meat, slaughtered in a profane way, thus incurring sin without awareness of their impure deeds. In the days of Moses, when Israelites wandered in exile throughout the wilderness, the tabernacle was located inside the "tent of meeting," which was immediately surrounded by the "camp" of the Levites, which was, in turn, surrounded by the dwellings of the tribes of Israel (Harrington 1997, 111). According to Leviticus, the only sacred location for the performance of meat sacrifices is inside the camp, so that the sacrificial animals may be brought to the priests and Levites for dispatch. There priests and Levites would drain the blood of the animal and burn its fat as a thank-offering to God, returning the meat to the pious Israelite for ritually pure consumption. All remaining lands were considered "outside the camp," and thus not sacred locations for the conduct of pure sacrifices. Any Israelites who sacrificed animals outside the camp, and so did not bring the sacrifice to the priests or Levites inside the camp, were guilty of bloodshed, and, thus, sin. The punishment for bloodshed is exile, which, in the Judean wilderness, was often a sentence of death. Again, this regulation is not mere quibbling over this or that place; it is an argument about the exclusivity of monotheistic Judaism in the context of a mostly pagan world. If Israelites were required to sacrifice all animals inside the camp, then, by default, they were also forbidden to sacrifice "outside the camp" any animals to any other gods or idols, especially, as Leviticus suggests, the goat-idols.

The authors of 4QMMT believed that the Temple structure was the permanent equivalent of the temporary and portable tent of meeting, and that Jerusalem was the permanent equivalent of the temporary and portable camp (Sharp 1997, 214). Thus, the rituals associated with meat sacrifices offered by pious Israelites during the time of the Second Temple would have to be performed inside Jerusalem (the "camp") and the animal would have to be presented to the priests and Levites in Jerusalem for proper dispatch. Yet the borders that defined Jerusalem city were at times under dispute. Harrington explains that before the Hasmonean family took control of the Temple, Jerusalem was extremely small, "encompassing less than the present Temple Mount and the ancient City of David. Nehemiah had actually reduced the area of Jerusalem to the Temple Mount and the Ophel hill south of it" (1997, 120). The Hasmoneans sought to enlarge the area of Jerusalem, incorporating what the authors of 4QMMT must have considered profane land. Harrington writes, "In the time of the Hasmonean kings the city was expanded to include much of the Upper City, the more modern Hellenistic city which had developed outside of the ancient city walls" (120; see also 127). Thus, the authors of 4QMMT explain that when Israelites sacrifice to "the north of the camp" (line 31), they also "[slaughter] outside the camp" (line 31). North of the old Jerusalem city is Gentile territory, which is profane, unsuitable for the holy act of sacrifice.

In addition to their liberal interpretation of Jerusalem's geographical boundaries, Temple authorities at the beginning of the Hasmonean dynasty may also have understood the "camp" and the "tent of meeting" in liberal and/or metaphorical (not necessarily literal) ways, thus allowing Israelites living in outlying regions to sacrifice and consume meat (that is, without requiring their presence at the Temple). Aharon Shemesh and Cana Werman suggest that the Temple establishment may also have considered the law to be altogether obsolete and no longer applicable to sacral rites performed since the construction of the Jerusalem Temple (2003, 121). Yet, as Dirk Büchner points out, the authors of 4QMMT considered all sacrifices performed outside of Jerusalem to be profane: "The one who slaughters outside [the camp, that is, Jerusalem] is more likely to perform profane slaughter as a sacrifice to goat-deities than the one who slaughters inside [the camp]"; thus, "those slaughtering outside the camp are not engaging in culturally acceptable behavior" (1997, 157, 158). Harrington agrees, suggesting that "outside of this camp [that is, Jerusalem] of ordinary pure Jews was the Gentile world with which contact was to be avoided due to its idolatrous influence as well as its effect on ritual purity" (1997, 126). Such impure and profane behavior, whether on the part of common Israelites, priests, or Levites, would not simply be considered a mistake; it would be a sin, a detriment to holiness, and the penalty is exile. And, Harrington points out, "these different concepts of holiness stem, at least in part, from ambiguities present in Scripture" (127). If there are no longer sacred camps and tents of meeting, as there were in the time of Moses, then these sacred places needed to have exactly corresponding locations in the (Second Temple) present, otherwise sacrifices are made in vain and sacred places are defiled. It is clear from 4QMMT that members of the Essene community believed that sacrifices were being performed at the wrong locations and that the priests and Levites in the Jerusalem Temple were not overseeing these sacrifices properly.

Although the Essene community believed that its own interpretations were True (with a capital *T*), they presented their differing interpretations with words that imply human origin, "we say" and "we think." Such wording acknowledges the greater degree of social, political, and religious power held by the Jerusalem priests over the Essene community. 4QMMT is a persuasive document, in other words, but its claims are attenuated in deference to priests with more power. Yet to the priestly audience of 4QMMT, these differing interpretations of Torah law must have resonated much more with the rhetorical ecology surrounding late Second Temple Israel, which was marked by divisive factions quibbling over this and that and questioning the ultimate authority of the Jerusalem Temple priests. Only the most persuasive arguments would succeed in such a rhetorical climate, and the Essene community believed there could be no more persuasive motive for changing priestly orthopraxy than the imminent end of days.

"THIS IS THE END OF DAYS": ESCHATOLOGY AND THE RHETORIC OF PERSUASION

As the Essene community's beliefs evolved over time, the sectarian Dead Sea Scrolls became increasingly shot through with eschatological theology, making "the end of days" one of the most influential concepts in Essene ideology. Yet with 4QMMT, we are dealing with a text that was composed early in the Qumran sect's formation, probably predating the community's settlement at Qumran.[15] Although the phrase "the end of days" appears several times in 4QMMT (the same phrase that holds deeply eschatological meaning in later scrolls), Martínez claims that the meaning of "the end of days" in 4QMMT is transitional (1996b, 23–26). In its earliest biblical usage, such as in the Torah, "the end of days" has a temporal meaning, indicating "days to come" or "the future." In its later Qumran usage, such as in the *War Scroll*, for example, "the end of days" has a deeply eschatological meaning, indicating the time when God will judge humanity and put an end to wickedness in the world with a bloody sword. In its transitional usage in 4QMMT, "the end of days" has both a temporal and an emerging eschatological sense in which God's judgment is not immediately imminent but is certainly approaching fast enough that reforms will be effective only if they are instituted with some urgency. According to Stanislaw Medala, "the end of days" in 4QMMT is "the time to take concrete steps to deal with rebellion, destruction of cities, and prostitution" (1999, 10). It is the time for priests to "adopt an exemplary life style so as to influence the conduct of the people in a positive way" (10). And it is "some indefinite future when the individual will experience personal joy and will be made justified . . . for performing deeds prescribed in the Book of Moses in the way described by the authors of the letter" (10–11).

The Essene community's emerging eschatological theology, which would later become downright apocalyptic, forms another layer for the exigency of 4QMMT's original composition and conditions its tone and style of address. Whereas section B focuses on identification with the audience through the common *law* and distinction from the audience through sectarian *works* of the law, section C (where most occurrences of the phrase "the end of days" appear) focuses on persuading the audience to *act*, and act righteously, according to both law and works, with the hope that the Essene community might "rejoin the Temple cult" (Regev 2003, 244, 253).

In section C of 4QMMT, the sectarian authors tell their audience, the Temple establishment, that some of the blessings and curses foretold in the Torah and the Prophets have already come true, making "the end of days" inevitable and not far from the present. Whereas later Qumran texts prophesy an "end of days" filled with violent war and bloody redemption, 4QMMT's notion of redemption in "the end of days" appears to require only a change of heart on the part of wayward Israelites: "And it is written that [all] these [things] shall happen to you at the end of days, the blessing and the curse [. . . and you shall ass]ent in your heart and turn to me with all your heart [and with a]ll your soul [. . . at the e]nd [of time]" (lines 99–102). The end of days in 4QMMT is a return to God and, we see a few lines on, a return to a more strict observance of God's law: "And this is the end of days, when they will return in Israel to the L[aw . . .] and not return [. . .] and the wicked will act wickedly and [. . .] " (lines 107–8). Some, however, will not (re)turn their hearts and souls to God and renew their commitment to correct observance of the law; they will continue to act wickedly. The authors of 4QMMT do not want the Temple priests to be among those who continue in their wicked ways, thus leading other Israelites into wickedness. The Essene authors write, "Reflect on all these matters and seek from him so that he may support your counsel and keep far from you the evil scheming and the counsel of Belial, so that at the end of time, you may rejoice in finding that some of our words are true" (lines 114–16). Not taking a chance on their own souls, however, the Essene sect makes it clear that they have already separated themselves from impure Temple practices and the people who conduct them. The time to return to the strict observance of the law is now, and the Essene community hopes that all of Israel will heed their warning and yield to the will of God.

The authors of 4QMMT have in mind the best interest of the Temple establishment and, indeed, all Israelites, and so the tone of the text is largely "conciliatory" (Grossman 2008, 4) and "respectful" (Høgenhaven 2003, 201), a "reasoned argument" (Sharp 1997, 213) reflecting "no political tension between the authors and the addressee" (Regev 2003, 254), even as it states some differences of opinion.[16] Although later sectarian texts are polemical in tone and are committed to self-preservation, not general conversion, these "later" qualities are simply not present in the early document, 4QMMT. The tone of 4QMMT is respectful, conciliatory, and accommodating, and the language is directed at describing what the authors believe are legitimate differences regarding critical matters of priestly orthopraxy, especially regarding ritual purity. Høgenhaven correctly points out that "explicitly polemical utterances are avoided," and "a relationship of fundamental agreement exists between 'we' and 'you' regarding the authoritative tradition and its implications" (2003, 199, 200). And Eyal Regev argues that the audience "is not accused of any sin or misdeed in the past or present, nor do the [Essene] authors doubt his authority" (2003, 252). Sharp explains that this conciliatory tone was employed in 4QMMT "to encourage reception of the document's message" (1997, 208). The ultimate purpose of 4QMMT is persuasive, not divisive, despite the articulation of ritual differences, and the conciliatory tone supports that purpose.

The authors of 4QMMT believe that their personal sincerity and seriousness about following the letter of the law would soften the hearts of their audience. They write, for example, "And you k[now that there is not] to be found in our actions deceit or betrayal or evil" (lines 93–94). There is not, thus, a veiled motive to usurp power in the Temple, only an attempt to purify the priestly orthopraxy of the present administration. And the Essene community is so serious about observing the law that they have refused to commune with Israelites who have been led astray by inattentive priests: "[And you know that] we have segregated ourselves from the rest of the peop[le and (that) we avoid] mingling in these affairs and associating with them in these things" (lines 92–93). Here, as Daniel R. Schwartz points out, "the author of MMT is telling his addressees, with whom he has various legal arguments, that—as opposed to 'the multitude of the people'—they and he are all serious in their religion. The point of the statement that the writer and his community have 'separated themselves' from the multitude of the people is to prove their religious sincerity" (1996, 77). Further, one way to usurp power in the Temple would be to warn Israelites who visit Jerusalem that their sacrifices are impure and that the Temple administration is to blame. The authors of 4QMMT are careful to say that this is not their approach to the problem. The Essene community is not challenging the Temple establishment's authority over Israelites in general; the community is instead attempting to correct impure Temple practices by writing straight to the priests themselves. Toward the end of 4QMMT, instead of writing in a combative or polemical tone, which would not achieve their purpose, the authors of 4QMMT gently remind the Temple priests of the content of their letter and compliment the priests for their depth of knowledge and intellect: "And also we have written to you some of the works of the Torah which we think are good for you and for your people, for in you [we saw] intellect and knowledge of the Torah" (lines 112–14). Such a compliment must have been unexpected, given the divisiveness among Israelite sects that had developed late in the Second Temple period; however, it may also have been viewed as disingenuous given the previous corrections of the Jerusalem priests' misunderstandings of Torah law.

One final appeal used for persuasive effect in 4QMMT is to call upon the writers' and audience's common history as recorded in the Torah, a communal memory that would (so the hope goes) effect an emotional connection in the audience to the arguments throughout the text. The authors of 4QMMT write, "And [. . .] remember the kings of Israel and reflect on their deeds, how whoever of them who respected [the Torah] was freed from his afflictions; those who sought the Torah [were forgiven] their sins. Remember David, one of the 'pious' and he, too, was freed from his many afflictions and was forgiven. Reflect on all these matters" (lines 109–14). Invoking collective memory is a powerful means to create identification, and invoking the memory of David in particular recalls eschatological themes, since the Davidic writings refer often to the end of days. In 4QMMT, the invocation of the most illustrious Israelites (kings, especially David) and their deep connection to the laws of the Torah is a strategy for creating identification between the Jerusalem establishment and the very reason that this establishment exists—the law.[17]

While it is useful to understand 4QMMT as the material manifestation of a rhetorical situation, it is also useful to understand this text as part of a larger rhetorical ecology, in which social relations shift with the political climate and discursive resources shift with each new text. In terms related to the rhetorical situation of 4QMMT, we see that the exigency is the perceived impurity of Jerusalem priestly orthopraxy and the coming of the end of days; the rhetors are deposed Zadokite priests who wish to purify the Jerusalem Temple of its defilement; the audience is the Jerusalem high priest (and his administration), who has developed interpretations of Torah law that are in conflict with the Essene community's interpretations; the constraints are the relations of power enacted in Temple worship. These concepts (exigencies, rhetors, audiences, constraints) form a powerful heuristic for understanding the immediate context of 4QMMT. Yet there is more going on in and around this text than can be explained by reference to exigencies, rhetors, audiences, and constraints. Without a complete understanding of the shifting social relations among the sects of Second Temple Judaism, or the evolving power structures in the Jerusalem Temple, or the emergence of an eschatological sense of the end of days among the Essene community—without a clear sense of these shifting and evolving aspects of Second Temple Jewish discourse, we cannot ever know 4QMMT to its fullest extent.

Identification and distinction are not *just* rhetorical strategies composed in fulfillment of a particular exigency; they are also strategies for dealing with the evolving rhetorical ecology that serves as the social and historical context of 4QMMT. The emerging sense of eschatology in 4QMMT is not just a good way to lend urgency to the arguments about works of the law; eschatological urgency is the product of shifting power structures in the Jerusalem Temple and anxieties about ritual impurity and priestly corruption. A conciliatory tone and reasoned argument in 4QMMT are not just stylistic devices designed to seduce the audience into a mood of acceptance; they are also part of a larger communicative climate in which religious authority is divine and, thus, beyond question. Appeals to sincerity and honesty are not just rhetorical strategies for engendering trust in the audience; they are responses to the usurpation of the historical succession of Zadokite priests and the installation as high priest of the highest bidder. And the appeal to communal memory is a direct attempt to place the audience's mind outside the context of the immediate rhetorical situation of two opposed factions and inside the common rhetorical ecology of Israelite ancestry and divine covenant.

Understanding ancient texts such as 4QMMT as material responses to rhetorical situations is obviously important; however, the study of situational categories (exigencies, rhetors, audiences, and constraints) should not constitute our stopping point. Such concepts tell us much about the immediate rhetorical situation of a manuscript, but they tell us little about the rhetorical ecology that gave rise to the situation. This ecology is as much a part of rhetorical study as the situation itself, and only the understanding of texts as situational *and* ecological will further our understanding of ancient texts such as 4QMMT. In the next chapter, I examine one of the first documents composed by the Essenes after moving to Qumran, the *Rule of the Community* (or 1QS). The rhetorical ecology had shifted between 4QMMT's composition around 150 BCE and the composition of the 1QS around 100 BCE, and the rhetorical strategies employed in this later text consequently became decidedly more material in structure and purpose. A different text at a different time yields a different analysis.

CHAPTER 2

PERFORMATIVE RHETORICAL STRATEGIES IN THE *RULE OF THE COMMUNITY* (1QS)

In 150 BCE, with the hope still alive of returning to the Jerusalem Temple cult, whether as priests or as common Israelites, the Essenes used rhetorical strategies of distinction *and* identification (citation of scripture, conciliatory tone, etc.) in 4QMMT. The rhetorical purpose of 4QMMT centered around purifying the Temple of Hellenistic defilement, and how best to do it, and the audience was probably the first Hasmonean high priest, Jonathan (152–142 BCE). However, by 100 BCE, when both the *Rule of the Community* and the *Damascus Document* were being composed in multiple drafts over time, the hope of the Essenes returning to a pure Temple had vanished. In these and other subsequent scrolls, gone, too, are all rhetorical strategies based on identification with external groups. Although Jonathan's central concern was purification, later Hasmonean high priests focused less on purity and more on securing religious and political power, expanding Israelite territories, and interpreting Torah law liberally in order to accommodate the burgeoning population of Hellenized Israelites. After Jonathan's death, powerful Israelites gathered in the Temple and declared his brother Simon (142–134 BCE) *both* ruler of the Israelites *and* high priest, and they declared that all subsequent high priests should descend from the Hasmonean family. These two watershed declarations formally usurped both the Zadokite line of high priests and the Davidic dynasty of Israelite rulers, ending historical traditions in Israel's two most salient institutions, the Temple and the monarchy. Simon's son, John Hyrcanus (134–104 BCE), continued the Hasmonean drive to incorporate more land into Israelite territory, while also centralizing control over Israelite religion (by destroying the Samaritan temple) and politics (by constructing a fortified palace in Jericho).

When the Essenes were composing the *Rule of the Community*, another Hasmonean, Alexander Jannaeus (103–76 BCE), was both high priest and king of Israel, and territorial expansion was his central concern. The *Nahum Pesher* refers to Alexander Jannaeus as the "Angry Lion" or the "Lion of Wrath" (fragments 3–4, column I, lines 5–8) because he murdered all who opposed him, whether foreign or Israelite (Eshel 2008, 122–24). Under Alexander Jannaeus's theocratic tyranny (as the Essenes saw it), Israel expanded to its original size under David and Solomon (Kamm 1999, 154), and Jerusalem's urban population grew fivefold (Levine 2002, 92). Since Alexander Jannaeus forced subjugated nations to convert from their Hellenized pagan religions to Israelite monotheism, many integrated citizens made pilgrimages to Jerusalem in order to fulfill their new religious obligations in the Temple cult. However, rather than a full theological substitution, these converts most often incorporated Israelite monotheism into their existing pagan religions. Thus, the Essenes believed that the Temple, Jerusalem, and the nation of Israel were all in shambles with no hope of recovery, since they were constantly exposed to Hellenized people and ideas.

Under the rule of Alexander Jannaeus, in a rhetorical ecology marked by the utter failure of Israelite institutions, the Essenes exiled themselves to Qumran in order to establish their community as the Sons of Light and condemn all others as the Sons of Darkness. With priests and Israelites violating God's law and forsaking their hereditary covenants, the Essenes conceived a new voluntary and metaphysical covenant devoted to the strictest interpretation of Torah law.[1] The community that emerged from this new commitment called itself the Yahad (*yaḥad*).[2] The highest-ranking member of the Yahad was its founder, the Teacher of Righteousness (*moreh ha-ṣedeq*), who was followed after his death by a succession of individuals called the Instructor (*maśkil*), probably all from the Zadokite line of priests. The Instructor headed a group of Essene leaders called the Community Council (*'atṣat ha-yaḥad*), which consisted of three priests (probably Zadokites) and twelve men (not priests) (1QS, column VIII, line 1).

The *Rule of the Community* describes two annual ceremonies performed by the Instructor at Qumran, one initiating new members into the community of the new covenant and the other renewing each existing member's commitment to strict legal obedience, turning now toward material, performative rhetorics (such as speech acts) in order to create a tangibly pious community, clearly distinct from all other wicked communities in the end of days. During these ceremonies, each individual was expected to engage in specific acts of performative rhetoric, reciting *new* blessings, curses, acknowledgments, confessions, and oaths (illocutions) and taking personal responsibility for their rhetorical effects (perlocutions).

The Yahad believed that the rhetoric of the priests who administered the Jerusalem Temple was, unfortunately, successful from a *persuasive* standpoint, since Israelites believed that their worship was proper and their sacrifices were effectual, resulting in purification and atonement. However, the Yahad also believed that the rhetoric of the Jerusalem priests was unsuccessful (or infelicitous) from a *performative* standpoint, since the Temple was administered by the wrong bloodline of priests, their procedural execution of sacrificial rites was incorrect, and their interpretation of Torah law was too liberal. Since all non-Essene Israelites were victims of infelicitous performative rhetoric, they were marked for eternal destruction in the impending apocalypse. The remnant of Essenes would be saved through their personal and *performative* commitment to the metaphysical speech acts of the new Qumran covenant.

Among the Dead Sea Scrolls, the *Rule of the Community* is one of the most salient texts for rhetorical criticism, since it details the metaphysical exigency for a new covenant, the rhetorical procedures for enacting covenant initiation and renewal, and the material punishments for inappropriate communication within the community. Although there is a strong tradition of research on the *Rule of the Community* that stretches over several decades (emphasizing themes like its relationship to the Hebrew Bible and the New Testament, its requirement of purity and punishments for impurity, the identity of the community it describes, and its use of ancient Hebrew), the unfortunate fact is that very little of this research addresses the rhetorical strategies used in the text.[3] Newsom's two articles (1990, 2010), mentioned in the introduction, are the only exceptions of which I am aware.

Both of Newsom's articles on rhetoric in the Dead Sea Scrolls treat multiple texts, but in each case, one of those texts is the *Rule of the Community*. In "Kenneth Burke Meets the Teacher of Righteousness," Newsom uses Burke's theories of intracommunal identification and symbolic co-optation to show that both the *Hodayot* and the *Rule of the Community* deal rhetorically "with a common issue, the problem of disaffection" (1990, 122). Here Newsom analyzes a short section of the *Rule of the Community* (column VII, lines 15–25), focusing on the rhetorical effects of the punishments listed for various violations of community law, especially challenges to the authority of its leaders. Later, in "Rhetorical Criticism and the Dead Sea Scrolls," Newsom (2010) begins with a general description of themes and constraints in rhetorical criticism, including genre, value, author, audience, argumentation, and style, and applies these themes to the *Damascus Document*, the *Hodayot*, and the *Rule of the Community*. When she analyzes the *Rule of the Community* specifically, Newsom focuses on what she calls the "motivational rhetoric" that emerges from the textual reshaping of the scroll throughout its various versions, ending with 1QS. This motivational rhetoric in the *Rule of the Community* is effected primarily through style (especially the use of infinitives) and frames of value (especially the new covenant). Newsom's discussions of rhetoric in the *Rule of the Community* are important but very brief.

In the pages to come, I examine the Yahad's shift from the failed (or infelicitous) persuasive rhetoric of the Jerusalem priests to a performative rhetoric directed at each individual Israelite who makes a personal commitment to follow God's law as it is interpreted, in its most strict sense, by the Essene leaders at Qumran. First, I use speech act theory as a method for analyzing the failed rhetorical strategies of the Jerusalem priests, thus justifying the Yahad's perception that the Mosaic covenant is void and needs to be reformulated. Next, I use performative rhetoric to analyze the speech acts that dominate the covenant initiation and renewal ceremonies. These strategies (or ceremonial speech acts) were employed in this rhetorical context as a way of ritually and materially transfiguring flesh and spirit from a state of condemnation to a state of redemption. Finally, I examine the Yahad's punishments for infelicitous communication committed within the context of community life itself. Through these applications of performative rhetoric to the ceremonial communication described in the *Rule of the Community*, I hope to illuminate a characteristically Second Temple Israelite use of rhetoric.

DUALISM, COVENANT, AND ESCHATOLOGY

Three related assumptions ground the *Rule of the Community* and its ceremonial procedures: (1) the human psyche is divided into good and evil spirits (*ruaḥ*), with the majority of Israelites, and certainly the rest of humanity, living according to the rule of their evil spirit; (2) the Mosaic covenant (*berit*), that God will be Lord to the Israelites if they obey his commandments, had been violated by wayward priests and their followers, so that the broken covenant must be formally replaced by a new covenant and renewed annually; and (3) the end of days is near, when God will judge the Israelites and all the rest of humanity according to their obedience or disobedience to the law, and either redeem them or punish them eternally.

Various forms of dualisms were common among religions in the ancient Near East; however, most were represented by competing divinities in the context of polytheistic ideologies. The dualism in the *Rule of the Community* is unusual for this time and place, since it is a dualism of the spirit in the context of a monotheistic ideology.[4] The *Rule of the Community* explains that each person was created by God with two spirits, one founded in truth and the other in deceit.[5] Until God's return in the end of days, however, the lot of all humans is to manage their dual spirits, traveling only along paths of light, seeking assistance from the Prince of Lights and the angel of God's truth (and, thus, since we are in a dualistic ideology, not traveling along paths of darkness, rejecting the deceit of the Angel of Darkness) (column III, lines 17–25). The Sons of Light, those obedient Israelites who follow God's commandments always and exactly, are marked by their straightness of path, their spiritual enlightenment, their knowledge of justice and truth, their respect for the law, and their enthusiasm, compassion, and prudence (column IV, lines 2–6).[6] The Sons of Darkness, conversely, have strayed from the straight path of strict obedience to God's law and have been seduced by the worldly desires for power and wealth. They are marked by unholy qualities, including their deceitful spirit, their irreverence toward the law, and their hardness of heart (column IV, lines 9–11).[7]

Unfortunately, the Yahad believed that the Hasmonean priestly establishment that was in charge of the Jerusalem Temple had strayed from the straight path, the paths of light, and had succumbed to the enticements (greed, lust, power) of the paths of darkness. According to the Qumran community, the Jerusalem high priest and his administration were repeatedly violating God's law, and, as the leaders of the central institution for Israelite cultic worship, these same priests were therefore implicating all other Israelites in the same sinful practices. Thus, the Mosaic covenant in particular was broken and void. The covenant given to Moses on Mount Sinai was a promise from God made to the entire Israelite nation. The covenantal rewards and blessings promised to the Israelite nation, in return for obedience to the law, included safety in the promised land, prosperity in farming and herding, and the fruitful multiplication of the Israelite generations, among many other things. As they are described in Deuteronomy 26–28, these blessings and curses are *all* material in nature, and their fulfillment will take effect sometime in the temporal future. However, according to the Yahad, the entire Israelite nation (with the *exception* of the Essene community itself) had violated, and was constantly violating, the condition on which the promise was based, thus forfeiting the blessings associated with the covenant, and incurring the wrath of the material curses associated with its violation. It was only the members of the Qumran community who believed the Mosaic covenant to be void, since the rest of the Israelites worshipped exactly as the Jerusalem priests instructed them to, in strict accordance with what they believed was required by the covenant.

According to the Yahad, since national identity was no longer sufficient to claim access to the blessings of the covenant, and the material blessings associated with the covenant were void anyway, then a new and different covenant would need to be established in order to disassociate the Qumran community from its wicked and wayward counterparts. While obedience to the law remained the central obligation for the Israelites in the new Qumran covenant, the Yahad made three salient changes that reflected their evolving ideological beliefs: first, the participants reflected in the new covenant would shift from God-Israelites to God-Yahad; second, access to the new covenant would shift from passive historical inheritance to active individual commitment; and third, the blessings and curses promised in the new covenant would shift from material to metaphysical.

In order to regain access to future blessings associated with the Mosaic covenant, the Qumran community shifted the binding relationship of the covenant from God-Israelites to God-Yahad (Christiansen 1998, 69). As Ellen Juhl Christiansen points out, "While *berit* (covenant) in the biblical background stands for a divinely-established covenant relationship with Israel as a nation, the interpretation [in the *Rule of the Community*] limits covenant relationship to a voluntarist group within Israel" (1998, 69). Thus, the *Rule of the Community* reflects "a change from an ethnic [national] to a particularistic [Essene only] definition of what covenant-belonging means" (69). John J. Collins agrees, explaining that the Yahad "rejected the notion that all Israel has a share in the world to come" (2014, 192). Collins continues, "The covenantal community [at Qumran] was no longer equated with ethnic Israel. The continued use of covenantal language then gives an impression of continuity but in fact masks a sharp rupture with biblical tradition" (192). According to the Essenes, it was no longer sufficient to simply *be* an Israelite; the requirement of the new covenant was to *choose* salvation and join the Yahad.

Commensurate with the shift in covenantal relationship (from God-Israelites to God-Yahad) is another shift from the *historical inheritance* of the covenant (Israelites as God's chosen people) to the *individual choice* to enter into the new covenant and to renew dedication to its strict legal obligations on an annual basis (Christiansen 1998, 86–88). Craig Evans explains that "the idea [of the new covenant described in the *Rule of the Community*] is not simply to escape damnation, but (positively) to take possession of what God has promised" (2003, 63). The blessings associated with the new Qumran covenant would be granted by God on an individual basis, according to each person's active dedication to correct legal observance, and not on the basis of passive historical or genealogical belonging to the Israelite nation.

The new Essene covenant was *reformulated* in Qumran *not* to emphasize the material blessings and curses of an inherited covenant *but* to emphasize the *metaphysical* blessings and curses of an eschatological covenant. Jeff S. Anderson explains that, although blessings and curses are a common biblical means to signify transitions, "the community [at Qumran] adapted both content and form of blessings and curses to its own needs" (2014, 186). Since the realization of these blessings and curses would occur not just in a temporal future but in the eschatological "end of days," the Essenes reformulated them to match the metaphysical nature of the new covenant. The members of the Yahad were convinced that the metaphysical blessings of this new covenant would be theirs in the end of days if they dedicated (and annually rededicated) themselves to the strict legal obligations that the Jerusalem establishment and the nation of Israel had neglected.

In the end of days, the straightness, understanding, and purity of the Sons of Light will earn for them eternal blessings and atonement (1QS, column IV, lines 6–8), and it is precisely the promise of eternal rewards received in the end of days that more than justifies the rejection of fleeting pleasures during the dominion of the Angel of Darkness. Conversely, in the end of days, the deceit, greed, and lust of the Sons of Darkness will earn for them horrible divine punishments, eternal damnation, destruction, weeping, and the absence of a savior (1QS, column IV, lines 11–14). Since membership in the Essene community, and thus participation in the new eschatological covenant, were determined by individual and conscious choice (not by birthright), the Yahad established specific ceremonial processes to mark initiation into and renewal of dedication to the new covenant. These ceremonial processes were dominated by the verbal repetition of specific blessings, curses, acknowledgments, confessions, and warnings, all of which function as performative rhetorical strategies in the *Rule of the Community*.

SPEECH ACTS AS RHETORICAL STRATEGIES

During the 1960s, J. L. Austin developed speech act theory as a pragmatic branch of the philosophy of language, and a number of scholars subsequently explored the relationship between speech act theory and rhetoric.[8] In *How to Do Things with Words*, Austin begins with a general distinction between constative and performative utterances: constative utterances report or describe information and are either true or false; performative utterances (as the name implies) perform actions and are either felicitous or infelicitous (happy or unhappy, satisfied or unsatisfied, fulfilled or unfulfilled), but never true or false ([1962] 1975, 6). Austin suggests that performative utterances have three forces: locution, illocution, and perlocution. Locution is the act of uttering. Illocution is the act performed by means of uttering (promise, threat, blessing, curse, command, affirmation). Perlocution is the effect of the utterance/act on its recipient.[9] Further, Austin points out that "it is always necessary that the *circumstances* in which the words are uttered should be in some way, or ways, *appropriate*, and it is very commonly necessary that either the speaker himself or other persons should *also* perform certain *other* actions, whether 'physical' or 'mental' actions or even acts of uttering further words" (8). Any performative utterance can be analyzed according to its locutionary existence, its illocutionary action, and its perlocutionary effect. And, more critical for the study of rhetoric, the result of any performative utterance (felicity/infelicity) can be determined through an understanding of the utterance's function in a larger rhetorical situation, which includes institutionalized conventions, appropriate participants, correct and complete procedures, and the full intent by all involved to behave in a manner appropriate to the institutional requirements of the utterance.

According to Austin, there are six "necessary conditions to be satisfied . . . for the smooth or 'happy' functioning of a performative" ([1962] 1975, 14), and violation of any one of these conditions threatens the felicity of the speech act in question:

- A.1. There must exist an accepted conventional procedure having a certain conventional effect, that procedure to include the uttering of certain words by certain persons in certain circumstances, and, further
- A.2. the particular persons and circumstances in a given case must be appropriate for the invocation of the particular procedure invoked.
- B.1. The procedure must be executed by all participants both correctly and
- B.2. completely.
- C.1. Where, as often, the procedure is designed for use by persons having certain thoughts or feelings, or for the inauguration of certain consequential conduct on the part of any participant, then a person participating in and so invoking the procedure must in fact have those thoughts or feelings, and the participants must intend so to conduct themselves, and further
- C.2. must actually so conduct themselves subsequentially. (15)

Austin continues, "Now if we sin against any one (or more) of these six rules, our performative utterance will be (in one way or another) unhappy" (15), and Austin calls unhappy performatives "infelicities" (16). There are two kinds of infelicitous performatives: misfires and abuses. Misfires are problems with the conditions of A and B. Austin writes, "If we, say, utter the formula incorrectly, or if, say, we are not in a position to do the act because we are, say, married already, or it is the purser and not the captain who is conducting the ceremony, then the act in question, e.g. marrying, is not successfully performed at all, does not come off, is not achieved" (16). Abuses are problems with the conditions of C. Austin explains that here "the act *is* achieved, although to achieve it in such circumstances, as when we are, say, insincere, is an abuse of the procedure" (16). Speech act theory is particularly useful for understanding ceremonial rhetoric because such discourse often prescribes conventionalized procedures for performative utterances, as the *Rule of the Community* does for the Yahad. In the next few pages, I explore some reasons, from the Essene community's perspective, that the speech acts performed in the Jerusalem Temple were infelicitous and the speech acts performed by members of the Yahad were felicitous.

INFELICITOUS SPEECH ACTS IN THE JERUSALEM TEMPLE

In the conduct of Temple rites and rituals, the correct or incorrect application of ceremonially prescribed speech acts and their associated material procedures determines whether or not a particular sacrifice or offering, for example, will have its desired effect (atonement, purification, etc.). In a dualistic ideology, such as the Yahad's, there is only success or failure; there is no middle ground. A felicitous ritual speech act transforms flesh and spirit to a state of purity or atonement. An infelicitous ritual speech act gives only the illusion of purity or atonement but leaves the spirit guilty and the flesh impure, just as they were before the ritual. The Yahad believed that Temple rituals were performed using incorrect or incomplete conventional procedures, were conducted by the wrong people, were arranged in the wrong circumstances, and were encouraged for the wrong motives. In other words, all of the priestly rites and rituals performed in the Temple by means of speech acts (and speech acts would be a critical component of *every* rite and ritual) were, according to the Essene community, infelicitous, unhappy, unsatisfied, and unfulfilled. These infelicitous ritual speech acts condemned all Israelites who participated in ineffectual Temple worship to the mere illusion of salvation, leaving them unaware of their own impending and inevitable damnation. Although the Yahad did not necessarily challenge the actual words spoken in Temple rituals, they did, nevertheless, challenge the *circumstances* that determine whether or not particular utterances are felicitous or infelicitous, and these challenges correspond to the six conditions of "happy" (felicitous) speech acts described above by Austin.

> A.1. Accepted conventional procedures for Israelite cultic worship are described throughout the Torah. The Yahad believed that the Temple priests misinterpreted or misapplied Torah law, thus violating accepted conventional procedures and invalidating the intended effects these procedures had (atonement, purity, etc.). For example, the Torah mandates that ritual sacrifices should be conducted "inside the camp" (Leviticus 17:1–7), meaning "inside Jerusalem." The Yahad believed that "Jerusalem" referred to the old city of David. However, the Hasmonean Jerusalem priests had incorporated a Hellenized neighborhood north of Jerusalem into the sacred city's boundaries and allowed sacrifices to be conducted there, in violation (as the Essene community believed) of Torah law.
>
> A.2. When Solomon succeeded David as king of the Israelites, Solomon decreed that all high priests henceforth should be born from the line of Zadok. In 171 BCE, the line of Zadok was deposed in the Jerusalem Temple with the installation of Menelaus as high priest. Many of the Essene community leaders were deposed Zadokite priests who believed they held the only rightful claim to the Jerusalem Temple's high priesthood, and all other claims to that office were illegitimate, making all rites and rituals performed by those priests also illegitimate.
>
> A.2. Menelaus and other non-Zadokite high priests changed Temple administration to an ancient lunar calendar, abandoning the solar calendar introduced by the Zadokites. According to the solar calendar, festivals requiring sacrifice and harvests always fell on the same day of the week, and thus could be arranged never to fall on the Sabbath. Conversely, according to the lunar calendar, festivals fell on different days of the week each year, and thus occasionally fell on the Sabbath, requiring work (harvests and sacrifices) on this day of sacred rest. Thus the circumstances for certain festivals, in the context of

the non-Zadokite lunar calendar, became a cause of sin rather than atonement.

B.1. The priests in Jerusalem executed ritual practices incorrectly. For example, Temple priests falsely assumed that pouring pure liquid from a pure vessel into impure liquid in an impure vessel would purify the impure vessel and liquid. The Yahad believed that this practice makes all vessels and liquids impure because impurity rushes up an unbroken stream.

B.2. The priests in Jerusalem executed ritual practices incompletely. For example, Israelites with leprosy were required by Torah law to ritually wash and shave a full seven days before consuming sacred food, but the Temple administration allowed lepers to consume food in the Temple before the close of the seventh day, thus making the sacred food they consumed impure for all others who subsequently consumed it.

C.1. The Yahad believed that the Jerusalem high priest and his administration acted upon motivations (thoughts and feelings) that were not directed toward the true goals of Temple practices (atonement and purity), but were directed instead toward fulfilling their own desires for money and political influence. With the wrong thoughts and feelings guiding their administration of sacred rituals, the Temple priests led into sin all Israelites who participated in Temple worship.

C.2. When, very early in its formation, the Essene community pointed out some of these legal and moral infelicities to the non-Zadokite Temple establishment (that is, in 4QMMT), this non-Zadokite administration not only rejected the Essenes' plea for renewed purification, but, as we find in the *Habakkuk Pesher*, the "Wicked Priest" also tried to have the Essene leader (the Teacher of Righteousness) killed on the Day of Atonement, which would have fallen on different days for the Yahad and the Temple establishment because of their use of different calendrical systems.

The *Rule of the Community* is a direct response to infelicitous speech acts performed by the priests in Jerusalem. If the ceremonial (cultic, ritual) speech acts of the high priest and his administration were infelicitous (invalid, unhappy, unfulfilled, etc.), then the Israelite people would be utterly lost, marked for eternal damnation in the end of days, unless a breakaway community of priests could establish themselves as a new (legitimate) authority over cultic worship.

The breakaway priests who formed the Essene sect and later occupied Qumran reformulated the Mosaic covenant that the Jerusalem priests had violated, and led other Israelites to violate, in the process gathering together a community of dedicated followers who would challenge the hegemony of the Jerusalem establishment. The Yahad viewed their settlement in the desert as a legitimate Temple, an alternative site for worship that was not defiled.[10] Ritual speech acts and practices performed at Qumran were felicitous because accepted conventional procedures were followed, ensuring the desired effects, atonement and purification (A.1), and these ritual speech acts and practices were performed by the right people (Zadokite priests) and in the right circumstances (according to the solar calendar) (A.2). The Yahad executed the ritual speech acts and practices correctly according to the strictest interpretation of Torah law (B.1), and they enforced the strict and proper timing of all ritual speech acts and practices, not allowing Israelites to consume sacred food until the full extent of their purification periods had elapsed (B.2). Both the Essene leaders and their community members had sincere thoughts and feelings, and they swore oaths and declared curses to reinforce those thoughts and feelings (C.1), and the Essene leaders and their community members conducted themselves according to their sincere thoughts and feelings (C.2), earning promotion or suffering demotion in the ranks of the community according to the righteousness of their deeds. All of these contextual matters made the Yahad's efforts at purification and atonement felicitous, not mere illusion.

Shifting the basis of membership in the community of the new covenant from national identity to personal choice required the institutionalization of *new* speech acts that would signify and thereby formally establish such membership. It was no longer sufficient simply to *be* an Israelite in order to participate in *felicitous* rituals of purification and atonement—that is, those that would actually achieve their intended effects. In order to consume pure food and to atone for sins (and not simply experience the *illusion* of purity and atonement), Israelites would now have to be initiated into the Yahad, the *only* community that would be marked for salvation in the end of days. According to the *Rule of the Community*, anyone who does not enter the new covenant "[plows] in the slime of irreverence" (column III, line 2) and "loathes the restraints of knowledge of just judgment" (column III, line 1). These non-Essenes are thus *never* in the right frame of mind to perform rituals and speech acts in a felicitous way, so their rituals and speech acts are *always* infelicitous: "He will not become clean by the acts of atonement, nor shall he be purified by the cleansing waters, nor shall he be made holy by the seas or rivers, nor shall he be purified by all the water of the ablutions. Defiled, defiled shall he be all the days he spurns the decrees of God, without allowing himself to be taught by the Community of his counsel" (column III, lines 4–6).

Within the Yahad, the emphasis of cultic worship shifts from the Temple's obsession with the technicalities of sacrifice and ablution, for example, to the spiritual frame of mind in which those acts are performed, and such a frame of mind can result only from instruction and judgment by the Instructor and the Community Council at Qumran: "For, by the spirit of the true counsel concerning the paths of man all his sins are atoned so that he can look at the light of life. And by the spirit of holiness which links him with his truth he is cleansed of all his sins. And by the spirit of uprightness and of humility his sin is atoned. And by the compliance of his soul with all the laws of God his flesh is cleansed by being sprinkled with cleansing waters and being made holy with the water of repentance" (column III, lines 6–9). Thus, it is not through ritual activities alone that atonement and purity are achieved; instead, it is only through the appropriate spiritual frame of mind (holiness, uprightness, humility, compliance, and repentance) resulting directly from the counsel and judgment of the Essene leaders that the felicitous effects of ritual speech acts (atonement, purity, and cleansing) are *genuinely* achieved.

Thus, all of the felicitous ritual speech acts and practices associated with daily Israelite worship would now, under the Zadokite leadership in Qumran, have to be preceded by speech acts that formally initiated new members into the community of the new covenant. Once initiates became members, the right to practice daily ritual speech acts would also have to be confirmed annually by speech acts that renewed dedication to the Mosaic covenant. These speech acts of initiation and renewal were the only means of validating the felicity of all other ritual speech acts traditionally associated with Temple worship; they were, in other words, the sine qua non speech acts of felicitous ritual practice in what the Yahad believed were the end of days.

Felicitous Speech Acts in the *Rule of the Community*

The rhetorical use of language throughout the *Rule of the Community* is clearly performative. As I have argued, the persuasive rhetoric of the Jerusalem priests had failed because their speech acts were infelicitous and their perlocutionary effects had led all other Israelites astray. The Yahad replaced the failed rhetoric of the Temple priests with performative rhetoric because it more fully enacted the values of personal commitment required by their new covenant. The Essene community believed that their identity as the remnant of Israelites who have established a new covenant was not innate (as was the identity of the Israelites in the old Mosaic covenant). Instead, Essene identity was performed, and the strategies of performative signification that constructed this Essene identity included the speech acts performed as part of the annual initiation and renewal ceremonies. In the next two subsections, I examine these speech acts in detail: first, analyzing the commissive speech acts of the initiation ceremony, and second, analyzing the verdictive speech acts of the renewal ceremony.

Speech Acts for Initiation into the Community of the New Covenant

According to the Yahad, the historical Mosaic covenant was broken and void, and national identity was not enough to claim a share in the material blessings associated with this covenant. In order to compensate for the loss of the historical covenant, the Yahad established a new eschatological covenant that required certain speech acts to be performed as part of the processes of initiation. This initiation ceremony is described in the most complete manuscript of the *Rule of the Community* (1QS, column I, line 16 through column II, line 18). In the initiation phase of the ceremony, commissive speech acts predominate. Commissives, according to Austin, "commit the speaker to a certain course of action" ([1962] 1975, 156), which, in this case, would include a commitment to the new covenant via total dedication and obedience to the letter of the Mosaic law. Here blessings transfigure the metaphysical and ontological status of material (people, food, etc.) from impure to pure; curses transform the metaphysical and ontological status of material from (potentially) pure to (assuredly) impure; confessions and acknowledgments recognize the reality of prior seductions into paths of darkness; oaths bind their speakers to a material and spiritual course of action (never straying from the paths of light) with consequences for its violation.

If these speech acts were performed correctly and completely, in the right context, by the right people, and with all involved in the right frame of mind, then the initiates would "establish a covenant before God in order to carry out all that he commands and in order not to stray from following him for any fear, dread, grief, or agony (that might occur) during the dominion of Belial" (column I, lines 16–18). This covenant is based primarily in the belief that obedience to Torah law is the path to righteousness and redemption. There are six specific speech acts required as part of the initiation ceremony.

The first speech act in the covenantal initiation ceremony is a *blessing* performed by Qumran priests and Levites and directed toward God, who has renewed his covenant with the Yahad (alone, presumably): "When they enter the covenant, the priests and the levites shall bless the God of salvation and all the works of his faithfulness and all those who enter the covenant shall repeat after them: 'Amen, Amen'" (column I, lines 18–20). This blessing may have functioned to gain God's favor (or, more mundanely, to get God's attention) before the initiation ceremony begins. Having been blessed in this way by the priests and Levites (and not by the nonpriestly members, who have no spiritual authority to bless such an undertaking), God will look favorably upon the initiation ceremony and admit into the new covenant those who perform the subsequent speech acts correctly, completely, and while in the right frame of mind.

The second speech act is a formal *acknowledgment* of God's greatness performed by the priests of the Essene community. This formal acknowledgment enumerates in dualistic fashion God's mighty works and the Israelites' sins and transgressions: "The priests shall recite the just deeds of God in his mighty works, and they shall proclaim all his merciful favours towards Israel. And the levites shall recite the sins of the children of Israel, all their blameworthy transgressions and their sins during the dominion of Belial" (column I, lines 21–24). This acknowledgment reinforces the difference between the divine perfection of God and the spiritual frailty of humans, establishing the need for a new covenant, a renewed promise of redemption in the end of days in exchange for a renewed dedication to overcoming the sins and transgressions of the Israelite nation, past and present. Without a covenant, or with one that is broken, there is no hope and thus no motivation to follow the paths of light; however, if the covenant is renewed, then the motivation to strive for redemption according to the constraints of the covenant is also renewed.

The third speech act is a *confession*, spoken by the initiates themselves. It is by virtue of the human condition, and its dualistic spirit, that all people sin and are seduced by the more pleasing paths of darkness. But only the righteous can recognize these worldly acts as sins, and confession is a formal speech act for recognizing fault:

> [And all] those who enter the covenant shall confess after them
>   and they shall say:
> "We have acted sinfully,
> [we have transgressed,
> we have si]nned, we have acted irreverently,
> we and our fathers before us,
> inasmuch as we walk
> [in the opposite direction to the precepts] of truth and justice
> [. . .] his judgment upon us and upon our fathers;
> but he has showered on us his merciful favour
> for ever and ever."
>
>   (column I, line 24, to column II, line 1)

One cannot be righteous and open to atonement without the recognition of sins committed under the influence of Belial. Acts are never neutral: they are either good or bad, righteous or sinful. Confession is a ritual act of recognition, a performative demonstration of the knowledge of good and evil and the differences between the two. Confession also implies awareness of guilt, and thus an understanding that those acts (and speech acts) that are listed fall into the metaphysical category of evil, which, recognized formally as such, is now to be energetically overcome.

The fourth speech act is another *blessing*, performed by the priests, and this time directed toward those hopeful initiates who have confessed their sins and chosen to enter the community of the new covenant:

> And the priests will bless all the men of God's lot who walk
>   unblemished in all his paths and they shall say:
> "May he bless you with everything good,

and may he protect you from everything bad.
May he illuminate your heart with the discernment of life
and grace you with eternal knowledge.
May he lift upon you the countenance of his favour
for eternal peace."

(column II, lines 2–4)

Once sins have been confessed, the initiates are then in the right frame of mind to receive this purifying blessing, atoning for past sins with the promise of strict observance of Mosaic law. Confession of sins is not enough; these sins (once recognized as such) must also be cleansed and forgiven through the intercession of the highest-ranking priests in Qumran. This blessing of the priests is one of the necessary speech acts devoted to the ritual cleansing of confessed sins.

The fifth speech act is a *curse* performed by the Levites and directed at all humanity, including wayward Israelites who have not entered the community of the new covenant:

And the levites shall curse all the men of the lot of Belial. They
   shall begin to speak and shall say:
"Accursed are you for all your wicked, blameworthy deeds.
May he (God) hand you over to dread
into the hands of all those carrying out acts of vengeance.
Accursed, without mercy,
for the darkness of your deeds,
and sentenced
to the gloom of everlasting fire.
May God not be merciful when you entreat him,
nor pardon you when you do penance for your faults.
May he lift the countenance of his anger to avenge himself
   on you,
and may there be no peace for you
in the mouth of those who intercede."
And all those who enter the covenant shall say, after those who
   pronounce blessings and those who pronounce curses: "Amen,
   Amen."

(column II, lines 4–10)

Since the initiates have now confessed their sins and been blessed by the priests, they have been at least partially transfigured from impure to pure and are not the intended recipients of this curse. Vengeance and the absence of peace are material consequences of this curse, much like the material consequences characteristic of curses found throughout the Torah, especially those listed in Leviticus that are directly associated with the Mosaic covenant. However, we also find here metaphysical and eschatological consequences of this curse that are not characteristic of Torah curses. In the *Rule of the Community* we find not material fire, but the "gloom of everlasting fire"—that is, a kind of metaphysical fire. The more general elements of the curse (lack of mercy, absence of pardon, and the presence of anger) also signal a move away from the specific materiality of the curses in Leviticus and toward universalized consequences associated with the impending end of days. This curse in the *Rule of the Community*, then, moves more in the direction of eschatological consequences, eternal consequences, thus also moving away from the more materially oriented curses in Leviticus, which formed the basis of the original (now broken) Mosaic covenant.

Speech Acts for Covenant Renewal

Although it is ambiguous in the text of the *Rule of the Community*, the initiation ceremony and the renewal ceremony appear to be sequential phases of the same general ceremony. In other words, every year new initiates were admitted into the community through the above sequence of blessings, curses, acknowledgments, and confessions. This same ceremony *then* turns to its next phase, the renewal of covenantal dedication of all those who are already members of the community, which would, presumably, now include all those who had just moments ago been formally admitted. While the initiation phase of the ceremony is based largely on commissive speech acts, the renewal phase of the ceremony is based on verdictive speech acts related to evaluation and judgment, and the determination from this process (re)establishes a specific hierarchy of community members.

Verdictives, Austin writes, entail "giving a finding as to something—fact, or value—which is for different reasons hard to be certain about" ([1962] 1975, 150), including "appraisals and assessments of character" (152). During the renewal phase of the ceremony, all members of the Yahad enter the meeting room strictly according to their spiritual rank in the community (1QS, column II, lines 19–23); members are then tested by the Instructor in order to assess their insight into the law and their deeds according to the law; and members are finally realigned into a revised hierarchy, reflecting their new assessment. No individual community members, at this point, have a right to adjust their own ranking in the community; such adjustments come only after careful assessment of insight and deeds according to the law: "And noone shall move down from his rank nor move up from the place of his lot" (column II, line 23). A shift in rank results only from the verdictive speech acts performed by the Instructor. As in the initiation phase, proclamations and oaths in the renewal phase of the ceremony bind their speakers to a material and spiritual course of action (never straying from the paths of light) with specific and dire consequences for its violation.

Since the human spirit consists of both light and dark, its character is dynamic, shifting with the tide of circumstances. This dynamic nature of the spirit, then, requires that all Yahad members go through regular (annual) and thorough reevaluation in order to determine the present (as opposed to eternal) quality of their spirits (Kvalvaag 1998, 175–76). The *Rule of the Community* states that both new initiates and established members alike will submit themselves to a process of evaluation and judgment: "They shall test their spirits in the Community (discriminating) between a man and his fellow, in respect of his insight and of his deeds in law, under the authority of the sons of Aaron" (column V, lines 20–21). And the purpose of this metaphysical test is clearly to establish or reestablish a hierarchy of members: "And their spirit and their deeds must be tested, year after year, in order to upgrade each one to the extent of his insight and the perfection of his path, or to demote him according to his failings" (column V, line 24). Thus, the general purpose of the verdictive speech acts in the covenantal renewal ceremony is to judge the spirit of each community member and to rank those members according to the qualities of their insight and deeds. There are many criteria by which the Instructor judges each community member, but the most critical for advancement or demotion are isolation from sin and obedience to Essene community leaders.

The first specific criterion of judgment in the verdictive speech acts of the renewal ceremony, then, is isolation from others who are marked by sin: to "keep apart from men of sin in order to constitute a Community in law and possessions" (column V, lines 1–2). Qumran community members then swear an oath in order to bind them, materially and spiritually, to remain separate from those who sin: "He should swear by the covenant to be segregated from all the men of sin who walk along paths of irreverence. For they are not included in his covenant since they have neither sought nor examined his decrees in order to learn the hidden matters in which they err by their own fault and because they treated revealed matters with disrespect" (column V, lines 10–12). One of the central reasons for this rule of isolation is that a state of sinfulness can be acquired by association. The *Rule of the Community* states that "no-one [from Qumran] should associate with him [a sinful person] in his work or in his possessions in order not to encumber him [from Qumran] with blameworthy sin; rather he should remain at a distance from him in every task" (column V, lines 14–15). Isolation, then, is a primary means to maintain the purity attained through life in the Qumran community.

The second specific criterion of judgment in the verdictive speech acts of the renewal ceremony is obedience to the authority of the Essene leaders (and thus not to the Jerusalem Temple priests) and other respected members of the community—that is, to "acquiesce to the authority of the sons of Zadok, the priests who safeguard the covenant, and to the authority of the multitude of men of the Community, those who persevere steadfastly in the covenant" (column V, lines 1–3). In order to bind them, materially and spiritually, to future acts of acquiescence, Qumran community members swear an oath to obey the Mosaic law and all that God has revealed about it to the sons of Zadok: "He shall swear with a binding oath to revert to the Law of Moses with all that it decrees, with whole heart and whole soul, in compliance with all that has been revealed concerning it to the sons of Zadok, the priests who keep the covenant and interpret his will and to the multitude of the men of their covenant who freely volunteer together for this truth and to walk according to his will" (column V, lines 8–10). All people who are not members of the Yahad must not be given any authority over a Qumran community member's deeds because non-Essenes "do not know the covenant," making their deeds, and the deeds they teach, futile (column V, lines 15–19). Authority over work and worship can be derived in Qumran only through knowledge of the new covenant revealed to the Essene leaders, making invalid all other claims to religious and secular authority.

Commissive and verdictive speech acts served different functions in each ceremony, with commissive speech acts ensuring the personal commitment to God's law of new community members, and verdictive speech acts determining the quality of commitment displayed during the year by established members. Yet, despite all of these performative rhetorical strategies, it was still possible for some Essene community members to be insincere in their performance of speech acts.

PREVENTING INFELICITOUS SPEECH ACTS
IN THE *RULE OF THE COMMUNITY*

Not only does the *Rule of the Community* outline appropriate speech acts for initiation into the Yahad and renewal of covenantal dedication, but it also provides curses and punishments for speech acts that are viewed as infelicitous in the institutional context of the Qumran community. In other words, despite all of their rhetorical efforts to manage the felicity of speech acts in Yahad discourse, the Essene leaders who conducted the initiation and renewal ceremonies recognized the possibility that some members may not always communicate appropriately and still others may not mean what they say. Harsh punishments and terrible curses were put in place for members of the Yahad whose speech acts were judged to be infelicitous.

The final speech act listed in the initiation ceremony, but which would have applied also to all members of the community seeking renewal, is a *curse* that functioned as a *warning* to those who enter into the covenant but do not accept all of its obligations, in particular the commandment not to worship false gods. This is a warning against initiates uttering infelicitous speech acts, entering the covenant without the full intent to abide by its principle conditions, for this kind of insincerity was the very exigency for the community's formation in the first place:

> And the priests and the levites shall continue, saying:
> "Cursed by the idols which his heart reveres
> whoever enters this covenant
> leaving his guilty obstacle in front of himself
> to fall over it.
> When he hears the words of this covenant,
> he will congratulate himself in his heart, saying:
> 'I will have peace,

> in spite of my walking in the stubbornness of my heart.'
> However, his spirit will be obliterated,
> the dry with the moist, mercilessly.
> May God's anger and the wrath of his verdicts
> consume him for everlasting destruction.
> May all the curses of this covenant
> stick fast to him.
> May God segregate him for evil,
> and may he be cut off from the midst of all the sons of light
> because of his straying from following God
> on account of his idols and his blameworthy obstacle.
> May he assign his lot with the cursed ones forever."
> And all those who enter the covenant shall begin speaking and
> shall say after them: "Amen, Amen."
>
> (column II, lines 11–18)

According to the Yahad, one of the central problems with the Hellenization of Israelites that was taking place late in the Second Temple period was that Greeks were polytheists, and some Hellenized Israelites believed that they could worship Yahweh as one god among many. But membership in the Yahad required strict obedience to the Mosaic law, which also forbade worship of idols and other gods. Thus, for the person who utters infelicitous speech acts in the context of Yahad discourse—the one who accepts initiation into the community of the renewed covenant but continues in private and in secret to worship another idol or god—for this person the most significant curses are reserved: an obliterated spirit, everlasting destruction, and isolation amid terrible evils. These are the initiates and community members who violate Austin's requirement that those who utter speech acts at Qumran should have "certain thoughts or feelings" and should "intend so to conduct themselves" ([1962] 1975, 15). The warning indicates that if one violates these requirements for felicitous speech acts, one's problems as a consequence will be eternal, not just immediate. Other speech acts that involve insincerity were not as reviled as those associated with the secretive retention of pagan values. Lying knowingly about small matters and speaking with deception result in six months of punishment, but lying knowingly about *goods* (presumably those that would be conferred to the community upon acceptance) results in one year of exclusion from pure food and one-quarter ration of bread. This latter punishment is harsh within the context of Essene ideology, since the consumption of impure food is a sin.

But not all infelicitous speech acts are infelicitous because they are spoken insincerely. Some speech acts may violate a conventional procedure or be spoken by inappropriate members. These infelicitous speech acts are punishable, but are also not worthy of the eternal curses associated with ideological insincerity. For example, while in the meeting place listening to the day's teachings, giggling inanely so that the voice is audible will result in thirty days of unspecified punishment. Being rude to (interrupting, retorting brusquely) and speaking against (complaining about or defaming) another community member carry punishments as small as ten days' and as great as one year's exclusion from pure food. Speaking against a community member is bad, but these same speech acts carry more severe penalties when they are directed toward Essene leaders. Speaking unintentionally against an Essene leader results in a six-month punishment (there is no punishment listed for speaking unintentionally against a community member), and speaking angrily against a priest results in one year's punishment and exclusion from pure food. Speaking against the community as a whole (whether defaming or complaining) results in permanent expulsion.

When words are spoken according to the procedures set out in the *Rule of the Community*, things happen, matter changes quality, states of existence transform, material access to resources and information shifts. Unlike in the Jerusalem Temple, where worshippers experience only the illusion of such changes, the Yahad established a counterinstitution in which only membership there, by means of the repeated performance of specified speech acts, resulted in true transfiguration from impure to pure, from sinful to atoned. Three assumptions, unique to the Qumran community, drove their desire to break ties with Jerusalem: a dualist construction of the psyche into good and evil spirits, the loss of the material blessings associated with the Mosaic covenant, and the impending apocalypse in the end of days. These assumptions are not merely technical matters; they are matters leading to salvation and damnation, and there was nothing more desired among the Essenes than eternal salvation.

In order to institutionalize their commitment to a new Mosaic covenant, one based in metaphysical blessings (to replace the material blessings characteristic of the broken covenant), the Essene leaders established and wrote down procedures for initiation into and renewal of membership in the community. Initiation into the Yahad was dominated by the recitation of commissive speech acts, including blessings, curses, acknowledgments, and confessions. Renewal of membership in the Yahad was dominated by verdictive speech acts designed to reestablish annually the social and religious hierarchy for all community members. Since infelicitous speech acts were, in part, the reason that cultic worship in the Jerusalem Temple was invalid, the Essene leaders included in their ceremonial process a final speech act, a warning against insincerity and false statements.

Performative rhetoric and speech act theory are useful methodologies for understanding the ceremonial purposes of the *Rule of the Community*. Once a community like the Yahad is formed and its values are solidified through salient discourses like the *Rule of the Community*, the next rhetorical task for such a community is to maintain its identity through dissociative rhetoric, which removes incoherent ideas that threaten the coherence of a community's ideal essence. This is the rhetorical purpose of the *Damascus Document* (the focus of the next chapter), which functions as a discursive complement to the *Rule of the Community*. While the *Rule of the Community* established the Yahad as a material entity, the *Damascus Document* preserves the Yahad's identity in the context of rampant iniquity.

CHAPTER 3

DISSOCIATION AS A RHETORICAL STRATEGY IN THE *DAMASCUS DOCUMENT* (CD)

Most scholars agree that the *Rule of the Community* was composed as a moral code and procedural guide for Zadokite priests and Essene leaders, and it emphasizes attaining and renewing membership in the new covenant of the Yahad through the repetition of specific speech acts as a form of material rhetoric. Like the *Rule of the Community*, the *Damascus Document* was also composed as a moral code and procedural guide, but not for an audience of Zadokite priests and Essene leaders. The *Damascus Document* was composed for common Essene sectarians living among outsiders throughout the Israelite territories, and it shares with the *Rule of the Community* the same rhetorical ecology, around 100 BCE.[1] This ecology was marked by the utter failure of historical institutions (the Temple and the monarchy) and by the incorporation of impure Hellenized populations into the nation of Israel and the city of Jerusalem. Since common Essenes were not geographically isolated like the residents of Qumran were, these sectarians constantly encountered impure Hellenistic and non-Essene beliefs and practices that the Essenes believed resulted in defilement. Thus, the *Damascus Document* seeks to limit the Essenes' exposure to impurity and defilement outside of Qumran by emphasizing rhetorical dissociation, the purging of impure concepts from the ideal Yahad. Through dissociation, the Essenes could maintain the material unity they achieved through the ceremonies described in *Rule of the Community*, and they could remove impure concepts from their group, making the Essenes the ideal remnant before the end of days, the true Israel.

Two fragments of the *Damascus Document* were known to scholars as early as 1910, when Solomon S. Schechter discovered two ancient Hebrew texts in a Cairo geniza (a storage place for worn-out or unused sacred texts) and published them as *Fragments of a Zadokite Work*. These fragments received little scholarly attention until the discovery of the Dead Sea Scrolls, among which were found ten more fragmentary copies of the same text.[2] In the context of the Dead Sea Scrolls, the Schechter discoveries were given the manuscript designation CD, or "Cairo Damascus," and the Qumran fragments were given the designations 4QD^{a-h}, 5Q12, and 6Q15. The Cairo and Qumran fragments are sometimes collectively called D. Most of the fragments found in the caves near Qumran during the 1950s duplicate text from CD, with only a few exceptions.[3] The sheer number of copies of the *Damascus Document* found near Qumran, and the fact that copies were found in three different caves, indicate that this text was of central interest to the Essene community (Davies 2000, 30). Throughout this chapter, I limit my discussion to CD, which is the most complete version of the *Damascus Document* as we know it, rather than the more fragmentary and redundant Qumran copies.[4] I hope to demonstrate that a primary rhetorical strategy employed throughout CD is *dissociation*.

Dissociation is an effective rhetorical strategy when a community's guiding principles and structuring concepts acquire incoherence because of shifting historical circumstances or new material conditions. Dissociation resolves incoherence by rhetorically carving away problematic ideas that are incompatible with the principles and concepts that guide the community. Throughout the *Damascus Document*, rhetorical dissociation maintains coherence among Essene concepts by removing from them incoherent ideas and practices that were characteristic of integrated Hellenistic pagans and competing Israelite sects. When an ideal guiding concept of a culture or community becomes incoherent and no longer serves adequately as a guiding concept, dissociation removes this incoherence by dividing the original ideal concept into a *real* aspect and an *apparent* aspect. The real aspect then becomes the new ideal guiding concept, and the apparent aspect is discarded.

There are three recognizable ways in which this sort of rhetorical dissociation happens, and they are not difficult to recognize in texts like the *Damascus Document*. First, the real aspect may retain the terminology of the original (incoherent) concept and simply redefine its referent in a more limited scope, excluding the meaning of the apparent aspect. Thus, without abandoning the term itself, the guiding concept *Israelite* may be redefined from a nationality to a voluntary orientation to the law, with nationalistic orientations to the covenants eliminated or dissociated from the semantic referent of *Israelite*. Second, the real and apparent aspects of a guiding concept may include modifying terms to signify their new dissociated relationship. Thus, *real* salvation may be opposed to *apparent* salvation, and *new* covenant may be opposed to *old* covenant. Third, the terminology of the original ideal concept may be abandoned entirely for a new pair of terms representing a dissociated conceptual (rather than purely linguistic) opposition. Thus, the Essenes become opposed to the congregation of wickedness. In each case, the rhetorical strategy of dissociation removes incoherence from the original ideal concept by replacing the original concept with a new and more coherent ideal concept.

There may be several reasons for using dissociation as a rhetorical strategy, especially in living texts like the *Damascus Document* that evolve in response to historical pressures. One reason is that language usage changes over time. The referent of the term "Israelite" surely changes from the Torah to the Prophets to the *Damascus Document*, and dissociation is a rhetorical strategy that can eliminate the semantic incoherence caused by such temporal shifts in usage. Additionally, changing material conditions, from independence to exile to vassalage, intensify in-group and out-group sensibilities, and dissociation can eliminate social incoherence caused by these changing circumstances. Finally, shifting ideological beliefs, even within the boundaries of a single community, can create incoherence in guiding concepts. As the Torah and the Prophets became more and more canonized, Second Temple Israelite belief systems shifted from obedience to the written Torah to the interpretation of a hidden Torah. In the context of isolated sectarian interpretation, Essene eschatology became more and more apocalyptic, requiring dissociative reformulations of guiding concepts like "covenant" into *real* new covenant and *apparent* old covenant.

DISSOCIATION

Much of Chaim Perelman and Lucie Olbrechts-Tyteca's *The New Rhetoric* (1969) discusses argumentation by means of association, including three fundamental techniques: quasi-logical arguments, arguments based on the structure of reality, and arguments establishing the structure of reality. According to Perelman and Olbrechts-Tyteca, "By processes of association we understand schemes which bring separate elements together and allow us to establish a unity among them, which aims either at organizing them or at evaluating them, positively or negatively, by means of one another" (1969, 190). Argumentation by means of association creates links among related ideas, resulting in more abstract conceptions that transfer an audience's adherence from the starting points of arguments to their conclusions. These abstract conceptions are not unified, however; they remain assemblages whose links may be broken through counterargument and rebuttal, especially when links result in assemblages that are considered incoherent from a particular perspective.

Perelman and Olbrechts-Tyteca are careful to explain that *dissociation* is not the same strategy as the breaking of connecting links. In dissociation, concepts are initially viewed as unified wholes, not assemblages, which means there are no connecting links to break.[5] Perelman and Olbrechts-Tyteca explain, "By processes of *dissociation*, we mean techniques of separation which have the purpose of dissociating, separating, disuniting elements which are regarded as forming a whole or at least a unified group within some system of thought: dissociation modifies such a system by modifying certain concepts which make up its essential parts" (1969, 190). Whereas the disbanding of an assemblage (the breaking of connecting links) may aid or hinder an argument, the dissociation of concepts has a more profound effect. Perelman and Olbrechts-Tyteca write, "The dissociation of notions brings about a more or less profound change in the conceptual data that are used as the basis of argument. It is then no more a question of breaking the links that join independent elements, but of modifying the very structure of these elements" (412). Thus, dissociation functions on a deeper level than the breaking of links; dissociation functions, instead, on an epistemological, ontological, and ideological level, as well as the level of pragmatic activity.

The dissociation of concepts is perceived as necessary when whole concepts begin to lose their sense of unity and coherence, especially when these concepts form the argumentative foundation of group identity. Dissociation is a rhetorical strategy that resolves incompatibilities in an ideal concept by dividing it into two related concepts, one real (thus valued) and one apparent (thus devalued). These complexities may signal incompatibilities in the whole, incompatibilities that may weaken an argument based on the ideal. In these cases, when an ideal concept becomes incoherent in reality, then in order to maintain the ideal concept as a basis for argumentation, the incoherent facets must be dissociated from the concept and invalidated, either discredited or shown to be irrelevant. As Perelman and Olbrechts-Tyteca explain, "While appearance may correspond to and merge with reality, it may also lead us into error concerning it. As long as we have no reason to doubt it, appearance is simply the aspect under which reality is presented to us, and we mean by appearance the manifestation of the real. It is only when, because of their incompatibility, appearances cannot all be accepted together that the distinction between the deceptive and the nondeceptive ones brings about the dissociation yielding the pair 'appearance-reality'" (1969, 416).

Dissociation centers upon a paradigmatic pair, appearance and reality, which are generative of other terms and dissociations. There is an extended passage in Perelman and Olbrechts-Tyteca's *The New Rhetoric* that explains the dynamic of the apparent and the real in dissociative argumentation:

> In order that our conclusions may be of general application, it will be convenient to make "appearance" term I and "reality" term II of the couple. . . .
>
> $$\frac{\text{appearance}}{\text{reality}} \quad \text{or, in general,} \quad \frac{\text{term I}}{\text{term II}}$$
>
> Term I corresponds to the apparent, to what occurs in the first instance, to what is actual, immediate, and known directly. Term II, to the extent that it is distinguishable from it, can be understood only by comparison with term I: it results from a dissociation

effected within term I with the purpose of getting rid of the incompatibilities that may appear between different aspects of term I. Term II provides a criterion, a norm which allows us to distinguish those aspects of term I which are of value from those which are not; it is not simply a datum, it is a *construction* which, during the dissociation of term I, establishes a rule that makes it possible to classify the multiple aspects of term I in a hierarchy. It enables those that do not correspond to the rule which *reality* provides to be termed illusory, erroneous, or apparent (in the depreciatory sense of this word). In relation to term I, term II is both normative and explanatory. After the dissociation has been made, term II makes it possible to retain or to disqualify the various aspects under which term I is presented. It makes it possible to distinguish, out of a number of appearances of doubtful status, those which are merely appearance and those which represent reality.

This point seems to us essential because of its importance in argumentation. While the original status of what is presented as the starting point of the dissociation is unclear and undetermined, the dissociation into terms I and II will attach value to the aspects that correspond to term II and will lower the value of the aspects that are in opposition to it. Term I, appearance in the strict sense of the word, is merely illusion and error. (1969, 416–17)[6]

Once a concept is selected for dissociation and thus split into term I and term II, a few different relationships may emerge among them. M. A. Van Rees explains, "The original term may have no part to play any more after the dissociation. That happens when the original term is given up and two new terms are introduced for the two concepts resulting from the dissociation" (2009, 6). Alternatively, Van Rees continues, "the original term can also be maintained, as denominator for one of the dissociated concepts, while for the other one a new term is introduced. In that case, of course, the original term receives a redefinition. The meaning of the original term is reduced, those aspects of the meaning of the original term that are subsumed under the new term being subtracted from the original meaning" (6). Whether term I becomes obsolete or is redefined, the new terms that emerge from dissociation are themselves, of course, subject to further dissociation.

Since dissociation is a rhetorical strategy, the intent of its use is to have some effect on an audience. Van Rees writes, "Dissociation serves to reconstruct the conception of the world of the audience and to do so in particular directions, serving certain interests and promoting certain views" (2009, 29). Further, Van Rees explains, "In order for dissociation to be successful, the views of the audience are of decisive importance. Ultimately, both the dialectical soundness and the rhetorical success of a particular dissociation depend on its acceptance by the audience. And this acceptance cannot be taken for granted; after all, dissociation involves a restructuring of our conceptions of reality" (114). Takuzo Konishi confirms Van Rees's understanding of dissociation's ontological and epistemological influence, explaining that "using dissociation, the arguer creates a new vision of the world, and persuades her or his audience to accept it. If the audience accepts the new version offered by dissociation, then a new reality will be established" (2003, 637).

Interestingly, Perelman and Olbrechts-Tyteca frame dissociation as an act of purification: "It is necessary to get rid of all impurity which causes disturbance and error. Purification is a process which makes it possible to separate term II from that which merely has its appearance, from that which is only its more or less imperfect approximation" (1969, 439). Term I, then, states an ideal that has become incoherent, containing impurities that require purification, which, in the present case, comes in the form of dissociative argumentation. Perelman and Olbrechts-Tyteca write, "The fragmentary, which is merely fugitive and accidental, is fated to disappear; on the contrary, that which is profound and durable, permanent and essential, is real. It is normal for all the activities that aim at isolating term II in its full purity to be regarded as a liberation, as a struggle against the obstacles accumulated by term I. In order to succeed, everything that has to do with term I must be treated as something foreign and hostile" (440).

Maxine L. Grossman explains that the drive toward rhetorical dissociation is a function of sectarianism generally. According to Grossman, "As products of a larger culture, sectarian movements partake of a common heritage of texts and traditions, even as they reject the larger culture's understanding of that heritage.... Members of a sect might claim to have exclusive textual knowledge, but they make that claim against the backdrop of a common culture in which other people might make very different claims with those same texts" (2008, 2). Grossman continues, "Members of an insider group are different from the people they think of as outsiders ... because they cultivate such differences" (2). I argue that rhetorical dissociation is one way in which such differences are cultivated, and it is the primary way differences are cultivated throughout the *Damascus Document*.

DISSOCIATION IN THE *DAMASCUS DOCUMENT*

The genre of the *Damascus Document* is best described as a moral code and procedural guide for Essenes living in Israelite territories outside Qumran, and it is usually divided structurally into two complementary sections, the Admonition (columns I–VIII and XIX–XX) and the Laws (columns IX–XVIII).[7] Its rhetorical intent is to persuade Essene citizens to preserve their purity in a context of institutionalized impurity and rampant iniquity. The strategies of dissociation that appear throughout the *Damascus Document* emphasize what Albert I. Baumgarten calls "boundary creation" (2000, 5). In-groups and out-groups are often defined by practices that are either idealized for the in-group or dissociated into the out-group: "All cultures employ boundary practices to distinguish insiders from outsiders.... These may include practices concerning food, dress, marriage, commerce, and worship, to name some of the most common examples" (5–6). Elsewhere, Albert I. Baumgarten writes:

> This dissent against the way of life of one's neighbor was expressed by sectarians through boundary-marking mechanisms—the classic methods employed by virtually all cultures to distinguish insiders from outsiders.... As opposed to a two-fold division of the world into insiders and outsiders, ancient Jewish sects organized humanity in a three-fold manner. On the inside were the sectarian brothers (or sisters, in those movements which had female members), around whom were other Jews, normally recognized as fellow insiders, but whom the sect treated as outsiders of a new sort. Finally, at the furthest remove, were the "real" outsiders, such as non-Jews, acknowledged as outsiders by all. (1998, 388)

Since the *Damascus Document* was a rule text for the Essenes who lived in the camps throughout Israel, some of their boundary-creation practices may have been challenged by other sects with competing ideologies and different practices. Thus, dissociation was a significant rhetorical strategy for creating boundaries that would define in-group membership and identify out-groups. According to Grossman, "At a most basic, narrative level, the *Damascus Document* distinguishes between righteous covenanters and the wicked who have gone astray" (2008, 5). The dissociations that structure the *Damascus Document* are based on a few key assumptions. God is the ultimate term that structures the hierarchy of values and the dissociations that occur within these hierarchies. Since God is perfect, without even the possibility for contradiction or incompatibility, the ultimate term "God," within the context of the *Damascus Document*, is not subject to dissociation.[8] However, any beliefs and practices that are anathema to God must be dissociated from the Essenes in order for this pious community to remain pure in the end of days. This is no simple task. Although God has sent anointed ones throughout history to teach the correct interpretation of Torah law, God's rival, Belial, has also tried, throughout history, to lead God's chosen people astray.

In a pesher on Isaiah 24:17, the author of the *Damascus Document* explains that Belial was sent against Israel in order to test its faith and obedience with a three-part entrapment: "They are Belial's three nets about which Levi, son of Jacob spoke, in which he catches Israel and makes them appear before them like three types of justice" (column IV, lines 15–17). Through avoiding entrapment in the three nets, Essenes who live throughout Israelite territories can "separate themselves from the sons of the pit" (column VI, lines 14–15), those who have given themselves over, body and spirit, to Belial's temptations. According to the *Damascus Document*, "The first net is fornication; the second, wealth; the third, defilement of the temple. He who eludes one is caught in another and he who is freed from that, is caught in another" (column IV, lines 17–19). The Essene leaders who lived in Qumran are said to have been celibate, but common Essenes who lived throughout Israelite territories were certainly not. The first net of Belial, then, does not refer to sex in general but to the acquisition of multiple wives at one time (column IV, line 20 to column V, line 6), or, more specifically, polygyny (Wassen 2005, 114–18).[9] The second net is wealth. Catherine M. Murphy explains that not all wealth was condemned by the Essenes, since some exchange of money or goods was permitted and regulated among community members and with the Temple administration (1991, 94). Instead, the author of the *Damascus Document* specifically implores Essenes "to abstain from wicked wealth which defiles, either by promise or by vow, and from the wealth of the temple and from stealing from the poor of the people" (column VI, lines 15–16). The *Damascus Document* explains that all economic transactions should occur under the jurisdiction of the Examiner in each enclave (column XIII, line 15). Murphy explains that "the examiner in the camp is given complete authority not only to reject or accept incoming members, but also to approve or prohibit all purchases and sales. The reason for this oversight is so that members will not err. Error in purchases and sales could include engaging with the wrong people (e.g., the sons of the pit), handling tainted funds (wealth gotten by violence), or contributing to institutions rejected by the community (the [defiled] Temple, perhaps the tax-farming system)" (1991, 103).[10] The third net, defilement of the Temple, occurred when worshippers entered the Temple having engaged in blasphemous speech against God's laws, having had sex with a menstruating woman, or having married and slept with a blood relative, all of which are affronts to God's purity and, once entered, defilements of his holy sanctuary (column V, line 6 to column VI, line 2) (Wassen 2005, 118–22).[11] Thus it is that each generation of Israelite remnants became ensnared in sin and marked for destruction; they "shifted the boundary" of the law "and made Israel stray" (column V, line 20).[12]

The Essenes interpret the law in the most stringent way in order to avoid being ensnared in Belial's nets, remaining pure in the end of days. And this was possible, not just at Qumran among the Essene leaders, but also in the Israelite territories generally, where certain practices such as marriage were allowed within the strict interpretations of Essene law. The author of the *Damascus Document* writes, "And if they reside in the camps in accordance with the rule of the land, and take women and beget children, they shall walk in accordance with the law and according to the regulation of the teachings" (column VII, lines 6–9). Each dissociation in the *Damascus Document* (whether historical and biblical, or sectarian and interpretive) emphasizes one or more of the evil traps set through the three nets of Belial.

Humanity: Apparent Humanity (Gentiles) and Real Humanity (Israelites)

The first dissociative rhetorical strategy in the *Damascus Document* is the division of the incoherent concept *humanity* into *apparent humanity*

(Gentiles, who are not parties in God's covenants and are thus marked for destruction) and *real humanity* (Israelites, or God's chosen people). Gentile nations (*goyim*) are dissociated from Israel, leaving only Israelites as a real humanity. This is a historical dissociation that long predates the Qumran community, yet it is also foundational to other dissociations made by the Essenes in the *Damascus Document*. As Collins points out, "The *Damascus Document* uses history for didactic purposes, to construct the identity of the movement" (2011, 296). Historically, the concept of humanity could have been maintained as the ultimate ideal, except that Adam and Eve sinned before God in the Garden of Eden, requiring subsequent covenants to be established in order for any sense of ideality to continue. Covenants with Abraham, Isaac, and Jacob distinguished the Israelites as God's chosen people, and the Mosaic covenant focused the conditions and provisions of the historical covenants on obedience to the law. Thus, the biblical covenants form the foundation of this first dissociation of the incoherent concept of *humanity* into *apparent* humanity (Gentiles) and *real* humanity (Israelites).

In the Hebrew Bible, the word "Gentiles" refers to foreign nations, heathens, and people occupying certain territories, and the *Damascus Document* demonizes Gentiles as those nations who are marked for destruction by pious Israelites. Gentiles are an obstacle, in other words, to the fulfillment of the Israelite covenants, and they must be overcome utterly, and with God's direct aid. The author of the *Damascus Document* writes that Israel will ultimately possess the nations of the Gentiles: "And what Moses says: Dt 9:5 'Not for your justice, or for the uprightness of your heart are you going to possess these nations, but because he loves your fathers and keeps the oath'" (the quotation is copied verbatim in column VIII, line 15 and column XIX, line 27). This passage makes it abundantly clear to an audience of Essenes that intermingling with Gentiles who are marked for destruction would be ill advised. The author of the *Damascus Document* writes, "Each one did what was right in his eyes and each one has chosen the stubbornness of his heart. They did not keep apart from the people and have rebelled with insolence, walking on the path of the wicked, about whom God says: Dt 32:33 'Their wine is serpents' venom and the head of cruel, harsh asps.' The serpents are the kings of the peoples and the wine their paths and the asps' head is the head of the kings of Greece, which comes to carry out vengeance against them" (column VIII, lines 7–12).

During the height of Hellenization, foreign nations would have been viewed by an apocalyptic sect, such as the Essenes, as rife with impurity. Associating with Gentiles is forbidden in Qumran literature: it is equated with stubbornness, insolence, wickedness, and vengeance. The *Damascus Document* makes it clear that any association with Gentiles and their cultures of wealth, hedonism, and power is fruitless and destructive, since the obedient and felicitous among the Israelites will no doubt ultimately reclaim power over the pagan nations. Yet the decision to associate with Gentiles is not necessarily an individual or personal one for each Israelite, since Israelites, and even the priests who administer the Temple, have been led astray. The author of the *Damascus Document* writes, "But all these things the builders of the wall or those who daub with whitewash, have not understood, for one who raises wind and preaches lies, has preached to them, the one against whose congregation God's wrath has been kindled" (column VIII, lines 12–13; this is clearly a reference to Ezekiel 13:10). Israelites, as a nation (its people and its priests), have been led astray by a high priest, a Hasmonean who builds a wall of the law where it does not belong by means of liberal interpretation (Wacholder 2007, 212–13), adorning it metaphorically with Greek architectural aesthetics. Here we see that the wicked high priest has led Israel astray, believing that Greek culture can be incorporated into the boundaries of Israelite law, leading liberal Israelites into the illusion of redemption and the reality of condemnation. In the *Damascus Document*, regulations against willful misdirection are relevant not only to the high priest who leads Israelites and other priests astray. Within the community of Essenes in general, any members who lead others astray will be dealt with as if they were Gentiles. The author of the *Damascus Document* writes, "Every man who gives a human person to anathema shall be executed according to the laws of the gentiles" (column IX, line 1).

In addition to associating with Gentiles who seduce Israelites into violating their covenant with God, there is also an element of impurity associated with Gentiles more generally. Charlotte Hempel writes, "Concern to avoid defilement through contact with Gentiles, particularly the pagan cult, is voiced in a number of passages in the laws of D" (2000, 79). The author of the *Damascus Document* writes, "No-one should stay in a place close to gentiles on the Sabbath" (column XI, lines 14–15). Further, stealing from and killing Gentiles appear to be sources of impurity, which are to be avoided. The *Damascus Document* explains, "He is not to stretch out his hand to shed the blood of the gentiles for the sake of riches and gain. Neither should he take any of his riches, so that they do not blaspheme, except on the advice of the company of Israel" (column XII, lines 6–8). And the sale of any sort of product to a Gentile that might be used in a pagan sacrifice must be avoided at all cost so that the Essene does not incur the guilt of a pagan sacrifice, however indirectly. The author of the *Damascus Document* writes, "No-one should sell an animal or a clean bird to the gentiles lest they sacrifice them. And he should not sell them anything from his granary or his press, at any price. And his servant and his maidservant: he should not sell them, for they entered the covenant of Abraham with him" (column XII, lines 8–11). Israelite purity is maintained by dissociating Gentile culture from everyday Israelite life. Those Israelites who obey the requirements of the historical covenants and dissociate Gentile culture from their beliefs and practices may be chosen, in the end, as a remnant to replace Israelites who have violated God's precepts. This dissociation of Gentiles from Israelites is achieved both symbolically and materially through the invocation of historical covenants and the declaration of Gentile bodies and culture as impure, limiting contact with Essene purity and influence over Essene destiny.

Israelites: Apparent Israelites (Nonremnants) and Real Israelites (Remnant)

The primary distinction between Israelites and Gentiles derives from the historical covenants that the Israelites alone (not Gentiles) have with their God, and these same covenants are also the foundation of the second dissociation in the *Damascus Document*: the dissociation of *apparent Israelites*, who abandon God's law in favor of the good or easy life and are condemned to destruction, from *real Israelites*, who obey God's precepts and are preserved as a remnant (*šar*). The author of the *Damascus Document* writes, "And thus is the judgment of the converts of Israel, who turned aside from the path of the people: on account of God's love for the very first who woke up after him, he loves those who come after them, because to them belongs the fathers' covenant. And in my hatred for the builders of the wall his anger is kindled. And like this judgment will be that of all who reject God's precepts and forsake them and move aside in the stubbornness of their heart" (column VIII, lines 14–19). Like the first dissociation (of Gentiles from

Israelites), this second dissociation (of nonremnants from remnant) is biblical, historical, predating the Qumran community, yet it is also foundational to other dissociations found throughout the *Damascus Document*. Historically, the concept of Israelites could have been maintained as an ultimate ideal, except that many Israelites, whether willfully or having been led astray, violate God's covenants by ignoring the precepts of the law. In this second dissociation, then, the concept *Israelites* has become incoherent, requiring the dissociation of incompatible notions in order to return to coherence and ideality. Thus, the author of the *Damascus Document* resolves incoherence in the concept *Israelites* by dissociating *apparent* Israelites (nonremnants) from *real* Israelites (remnant). In order to accomplish this dissociation, the *Damascus Document* uses the dissociative rhetorical strategies of moral history and violated covenants.

The *Damascus Document* tells a story of covenants, violations, and remnants as a cautionary tale, a moral history. The author of the *Damascus Document* writes, "For all those who walk according to these matters in perfect holiness, in accordance with his teaching, God's covenant is a guarantee for them that they shall live a thousand generations" (column VII, lines 4–6). However, the institutionalized and rampant violation of the Mosaic covenant among Israelites during the Second Temple period created the perception among Essenes that the ultimate term *Israelites* was no longer, or never was, coherent or unified. There were always Israelites who maintained their purity through strict interpretations of Mosaic law, and there were always Israelites who did not, opening up the entire nation of Israel to judgment and condemnation. The *Damascus Document* begins with a historical account of God's covenant with the Israelites and their subsequent iniquity, requiring the choice of a righteous remnant among Israelites to obey the requirements of the law and receive the blessings of the covenant. The author of the *Damascus Document* writes, "And now listen, all those who know justice, and understand the actions of God; for he has a dispute with all flesh and will carry out judgment on all those who spurn him. For when they were unfaithful in forsaking him, he hid his face from Israel and from his sanctuary and delivered them up to the sword. However, when he remembered the covenant of the very first, he saved a remnant for Israel and did not deliver them up to destruction" (column I, lines 1–5).

There had been individuals within each remnant who upheld God's precepts and maintained the correct path (Abraham, Isaac, and Jacob), and these individuals, though now perished, will reap the blessings of the eternal covenant in the end of days. The author of the *Damascus Document* writes:

> But with those who remained steadfast in God's precepts, with those who were left from among them, God established his covenant with Israel for ever, revealing to them hidden matters in which all Israel had gone astray: his holy Sabbaths and his glorious feasts, his just stipulations and his truthful paths, and the wishes of his will which man must do in order to live by them. He disclosed (these matters) to them and they dug a well of plentiful water; and whoever spurns them shall not live. But they had defiled themselves with human sin and unclean paths, and they had said: "For this is ours." But God, in his wonderful mysteries, atoned for their failings and pardoned their sins. And he built for them a safe home in Israel, such as there has not been since ancient times, not even till now. Those who remained steadfast in it will acquire eternal life, and all the glory of Adam is for them. (column III, lines 12–20)

In each generation, God provided wise teachers so that at least a few would remain who followed God's precepts with obedience and commitment. The author of the *Damascus Document* writes:

> For God did not choose them [historical remnants] at the beginning of the world, and before they were established he knew their deeds, and abominated the generations on account of blood and hid his face from the country, from ‹Israel›, until their extinction. And he knew the years of their existence, and the number and detail of their ages, of all those who exist over the centuries, and of those who will exist, until it occurs in their ages throughout all the everlasting years. And in all of them he raised up men of renown for himself, to leave as remnant for the country and in order to fill the face of the world with their offspring. And he taught them by the hand of the anointed ones through his holy spirit and through seers of the truth, and their names were established with precision. But those he hates, he causes to stray. (column II, lines 7–13)

Later, the author of the *Damascus Document* writes that Abraham, Isaac, and Jacob were among those men of renown who followed God's precepts and so were "written up as friends of God and as members of the covenant forever" (column III, lines 3–4). Historically, however, the Torah describes many historical remnants saved, and the result was always the same, eventual iniquity, resulting in a repeated process (destruction, remnant, iniquity; destruction, remnant, iniquity; . . . etc.).

These first two dissociations are historical, biblical, predating the rise of sectarianism and the establishment of the Essene community at Qumran. However, the next three dissociations are situated squarely in the late Second Temple world of sectarianism, and they function to distinguish one sect from another. These first two biblical dissociations represent the trajectory of history into the present and future of the sect. Albert I. Baumgarten writes, "What is important about the past for a sectarian was not some antiquarian interest, but the relevance of the past for present and future" (2000, 12). The most relevant lesson of the past for the Qumran community is that the old covenants based on national inheritance are void, and those who cling to them will be marked for death in the end of days. Thus, the Essenes "*exclude*" from membership in their community "all born Jews who have not made a conscious choice to enter the covenant" (Christiansen 1998, 97). These first two biblical dissociations thus project into the next several sectarian dissociations in fundamental ways.

Remnant: Apparent Remnants (Non-Essenes) and Real Final Remnant (Essenes, the Yahad)

Having dissociated impure Gentiles from Israelites and apparent Israelites from the status of remnant, the Essenes' third dissociative rhetorical strategy in the *Damascus Document* resolves incoherence in the concept *remnant* by dissociating apparent remnants (non-Essenes) from the real final remnant (Essenes, the Yahad). With advancing canonization of the Torah and many of the Prophets and Writings throughout the Second Temple period, covenantal fulfillment shifted from practicing the Torah as written to interpreting the Torah through sectarian lenses, and then practicing the interpretations. It is clear, for example, that the Essenes of the *Damascus Document* relied on their own stringent interpretations of Torah law as a dissociative rhetorical strategy to distinguish this sect from others of the time.[13] An emerging eschatology would lead the Essenes to believe that their interpretations of the law were the last and best interpretations before the end of days. In this third dissociation, then, the concept of *remnant* had become incoherent, with each sect interpreting the law and its eschatological context differently. Thus, the author of the *Damascus Document* resolves incoherence in the concept *remnant* by dissociating *apparent remnants* (non-Essenes) from the *real final remnant* (Essenes). In order to accomplish this dissociation of liberal sects from the Essenes, the author of the *Damascus Document* uses the dissociative rhetorical strategies of stringent interpretations of the law and the construction of an imminent eschatological context.

The Essenes, according to the *Damascus Document*, are the final remnant, selected 390 years after the Babylonian exile and just before the apocalyptic end of days. Even this final remnant, however, was not immune to the iniquities that doomed past remnants. So, with the end of days approaching, God aided this final remnant by delivering to them a Teacher of Righteousness who would keep them on the path toward purity and obedience. The author of the *Damascus Document* writes:

> And at the moment of wrath, three hundred and ninety years after having delivered them up into the hands of Nebuchadnezzar, king of Babylon, he visited them and caused to sprout from Israel and from Aaron a shoot of the planting, in order to possess his land and to become fat with the good things of his soil. And they realized their sin and knew that they were guilty men; but they were like blind persons and like those who grope for the path over twenty years. And God appraised their deeds, because they sought him with a perfect heart and raised up for them a Teacher of Righteousness, in order to direct them in the path of his heart. (column I, lines 5–11)[14]

The function of the Teacher of Righteousness was to interpret God's law as it was intended to be interpreted, in its most conservative sense, especially for the imminent end of days.

The Teacher of Righteousness is the salvation of the Essenes, since he alone perceives the correct procedural interpretation of Torah law and the accurate historical interpretation of the Prophets. Thus, the stringent sectarian interpretation of the law is a strategy for dissociation from contemporary sects that interpret the law in liberal ways. Israelites who do not follow the interpretations described by the Teacher of Righteousness "stray from the path" (column I, line 13), following the priest identified in Hosea as the scoffer,

> who scattered the waters of lies over Israel and made them veer off into a wilderness without path, flattening the everlasting heights, diverging from tracks of justice and removing the boundary with which the very first had marked their inheritance, so that the curses of his covenant would adhere to them, to deliver them up to the sword carrying out the vengeance of the covenant. For they sought easy interpretations, chose illusions, scrutinized loopholes, chose the handsome neck, acquitted the guilty and sentenced the just, violated the covenant, broke the precept, colluded together against the life of the just man, their soul abominated all those who walk in perfection, they hunted them down with the sword and provoked the dispute of the people. And kindled was the wrath of God against his congregation, laying waste all its great number, for his deeds were unclean in front of him. (column I, line 14 to column II, line 1)[15]

Just as the Teacher of Righteousness is the salvation of the Essenes, the scoffer is the damnation of the "congregation of traitors" (column I, line 12). He has "kindled the wrath of God against his congregation, laying waste all its great number, for his deeds were unclean in front of him" (column I, line 21 to column II, line 1). Even if the congregation of traitors is unaware of their transgressions and impurity, they are nevertheless guilty for following the scoffer and accepting the easy life over the righteous life. Despite being led astray, the congregation of traitors remains guilty and impure because God has provided both knowledge of the truth and council for understanding, yet they reject these, choosing sex, wealth, and defilement of the Temple as if these were acts of justice. Adopting a voice of authority, the author of the *Damascus Document* writes, "And now, listen to me, all entering the covenant, and I will open your ears to the paths of the wicked. God loves knowledge; he has established wisdom and counsel before him; discernment and knowledge are at his service; patience is his and abundance of pardon, to atone for persons who repent from wickedness; however, strength and power and great anger with flames of fire by the ‹hand› of all the angels of destruction against persons turning aside from the path and abominating the precept, without there being for them either a remnant or survivor" (column II, lines 2–7). Whereas other remnants in the history of the Israelites have misunderstood Torah law or interpreted it in easy or liberal ways, the Essenes believe that obedience to the most stringent interpretation of the law will result in their salvation as the real final remnant.

Essenes: Apparent Essenes (Fraudulent Members) and Real Essenes (Sincere Members)

Presumably, members of the Essene community at large meant well and kept their oaths as steadfastly as they could. However, throughout the Israelite camps, there were more temptations than there were at Qumran. Essene interpretations of Torah law are strict, and some common members' indiscretions may have led to certain punishments and even expulsion. These punishments served as another rhetorical strategy of dissociation. An oath to obey both Torah law and the Essenes' stringent interpretation of it was a crucial element for admission into the new Damascus covenant. Once admitted, any indiscretions among its members would endanger the salvation of the whole community, so the Essenes required rhetorical means to dissociate any *apparent Essenes* (fraudulent members) and their impure deeds from the *real Essenes* (sincere members) of the community, who considered themselves the true Israel. Albert I. Baumgarten writes, "To find those who disregarded the bounds of the Torah outside the covenant community would not have been surprising. For these villains to be *members* of the covenant community presented an especially difficult situation, requiring the drawing of new boundaries and the establishment of new refuges of purity" (2000, 6). In order to accomplish this dissociation, the author of the *Damascus Document* uses the dissociative rhetorical strategies of obedience to the new covenant (voluntary and metaphysical) and punishment (rebuke and exile) for violations.

It is clear from several passages in the *Damascus Document* that the covenants of old Israel have been repeatedly violated and are currently void and that a new covenant is necessary to reestablish metaphysical blessings in the end of days. The material blessings of the covenants of old Israel were assumed to be inherited through birth into the nation of Israel. However, with those old material covenants now void, the Essenes required a voluntary commitment to the new metaphysical covenant in the land of Damascus. Jintae Kim writes, "The new covenant in CD involves three divine blessings . . . : (1) the gift of knowledge of the 'hidden matters' [CD III.14] and diagnosis of the problem of the first generation; (2) knowledge of God [IV.22]; and (3) the gift of a safe home [III.19–20] and eternal life [VII.4–6 and XIX.1]" (2010, 105). This new covenant is not inherited but *chosen* and *earned* through strict obedience to the Essene interpretation of the law. Thus, there should be no excuse for the failure to obey. However, as I have explained, the Second Temple world of the Essenes was rife with impurity and temptation. Thus, some members of the Essenes may transgress and break the rules of the community or the law of God. In this case, there are procedures to determine whether the member should be forgiven and reinstated or ejected from membership forever. The author of the *Damascus Document* writes, "In accordance with his misdeed, all the men of knowledge shall reproach him, until the day when he returns to take his place in the session of the men of perfect holiness" (column XX, lines 4–5).

Swearing (or proclaiming oaths to ensure the truth of one's claims) was taken seriously by the Essenes, with regulations for swearing oaths clearly stated in the *Damascus Document*: "[He will not sw]ear by the Aleph or the Lamed ('EL = God) nor by the Aleph and the Daleth ('ADNOAI = The Lord), but by the oath of the youths, by the curses of the covenant" (column XV, lines 1–2). Swearing to a commitment and then breaking that oath was not just a lie in the context of the Essenes, it was a moral transgression that generated impurity, though apparently a relatively mild impurity. The *Damascus Document* continues, "And if he swears and transgresses, he would profane the name. And if he sw[ears] by the curses of the covenant [he should do it before] the judges. If he transgresses, he will be guilty and will have to confess and make amends but he shall not be liable [for sin and shall not] die" (column XV, lines 3–5). And "when he has imposed upon himself to return to the law of Moses with all his heart and all his soul [they will exact revenge] from him if he should sin. And if he fulfills all that has been revealed of the law [for the multitude] [of the camp], the Overseer should teach him and give orders concerning him which he should learn throughout a full year. And in accordance with (his) knowledge ‹he will approach›" (column XV, lines 10–15).

Here the method of dissociation is reproach; however, the *Damascus Document* clearly distinguishes between reproach, where the intent is to rehabilitate, and vengeance or resentment, where the intent is to inflict additional harm. The *Damascus Document* begins a discussion of ethical reproach with a pesher interpretation of Leviticus 19:18. The author of the *Damascus Document* writes:

> And what it says: *Lev 19:18* "Do not avenge yourself or bear resentment against the sons of your people": everyone of those who entered the covenant who brings an accusation against his fellow, *unless it is with reproach before witnesses*, or who brings it when he is angry, or he tells it to his elders so that they despise him, he is "the one who avenges himself and bears resentment." Is it not perhaps written that only *Nah 1:2* "he (God) avenges himself and bears resentment against his enemies"? If he keep silent about him from one day to the other, or accused him of a capital offense, he has witnessed against himself, for he did not fulfill the commandment of God which tells him: *Lev 19:17* "You shall reproach your fellow so as not to incur sin because of him." (column IX, lines 2–8)

The *Damascus Document* then continues to list further offenses against the community and its members that require reproach, including forced oaths, curses, theft, and claiming ownership of lost objects (column IX, lines 8–16). In the case of these laws requiring public reproach, Murphy points out that they are "more restrictive than biblical legislation" (1991, 98).

When property is stolen among the Essenes living in the camps, Kimberley Czajkowski explains, the owner of the stolen property swears an oath "adjuring anyone who knows anything about the whereabouts of the item to come forward. Those who do not do so 'shall bear the guilt.' This is often termed the 'oath of adjuration'" (2016, 92). These oaths must be pronounced publicly, since the guilty party must hear the oath in order to *not come forward* and thus incur guilt. The oath of adjuration may be ignored by non-Essenes and Gentiles who have not voluntarily entered into the new covenant with the Essenes, and thus are shunned as impure. However, actual members of the Essenes would take this oath very seriously. Theft of property violates the shared values of the Essenes, and "the whole concept of membership of the movement relies on the fact that people have opted in to these shared ideals" (100). Thus, "group beliefs or shared ideals are a key factor in the oath-curse's efficacy" (100). Murphy confirms the importance of ethical economic practices, noting that "the violation of communal rules regarding wealth is treated as the most serious trespass against the Torah. It is not only a capital matter, but an offence that by virtue of fewer witnesses is the easiest to prove" (1991, 101). All of those Essenes who are present during the oath and hear it "will believe in its efficacy because they (it is assumed) subscribe to the core ideals upon which that efficacy is founded. It therefore relies upon and enacts the 'faith' or group ideals of the movement. It has more than a purely administrative or practical function and becomes, in part, an affirmation of group-ideals and consequently an enactment of group identity" (100–101). Presumably, the guilt borne by the thief would be far more painful than any rebuke that might follow, and so, if the thief is a member of the Essenes, then rebuke and purification are the only tolerable courses of action.

Rebuke is one strategy of dissociation that helps to purify Essenes when transgressions cause impurities. But some transgressions cannot be purified, so the transgressors must be removed from membership in order for the Essenes to remain pure. The author of the *Damascus Document* writes, "And so is the judgment of everyone who enters the congregation of the men of perfect holiness and is slack in the fulfillment of the instructions of the upright. This is the man who is melted in the crucible. When his deeds are evident, he shall be expelled from the congregation, like one whose lot did not fall among the disciples of God" (column XX, lines 1–4). The *Damascus Document* continues:

> But when his deeds are evident, according to the exact interpretation of the law in which the men of perfect holiness walked, no-one should associate with him in wealth or work, for all the holy ones of the Most High have cursed him. And (proceed) according to this judgment, with all those who despise, among the first as among the last, for they have placed idols in their heart {and have placed} and have walked in the stubbornness of their heart. For them there shall be no part in the house of the law. They shall be judged according to the judgment of their companions, who turned round with insolent men, for they spoke falsehood about the holy regulations and despised the covenant {of God}. (column XX, lines 6–12)

Physical exclusion often accompanies rhetorical dissociation. The Essene community wished for purity in the end of days, and their constant dissociations of impurities led them toward a form of xenophobia. The author of the *Damascus Document* writes, "‹And no-one› stupid or deranged ‹should enter›; and anyone feeble[-minded and insane,] those with sightless [eyes, the lame or one who stumbles, or a deaf person, or any underage boy, none of these] should enter [the congregation, since the holy angels are in its midst]" (column XV, lines 15–17; see Hempel 2000, 76). This is the point at which rhetorical dissociation becomes xenophobic exclusion, a strange stance for a community on the brink of a metaphysical war between good and evil. With God on their side, the Essenes did not view numbers as a necessary military advantage.

Israel: Apparent Israel (Ephraim) and Real Israel (Judah) / Old Israel (Judah) and New Israel (Damascus)

When the twelve tribes of Israel split into the ten tribes of the Northern Kingdom (which retained the name Israel, but was called Ephraim by the Essenes) and the two tribes of the Southern Kingdom (which called itself Judah), the Zadokite priests, who would eventually evolve into the Essene sect, remained in the south, in Judah, and continued to administer the Temple in Jerusalem. However, it is clear throughout the *Damascus Document* that although Judah was preferable to Ephraim, Damascus, where the new covenant of the Essenes was established, was preferable to the Judah of the old covenants.[16] According to Ben Zion Wacholder, "Those who leave Judah will be the wise men who have the new covenant in the land of Damascus, a contract superior to the traditional Sinaitic covenant" (2007, 222). The Zadokite priests who eventually fled Judah for Damascus sought a new metaphysical covenant with God, one that would supersede not only the old covenants of liberal Israelite tribes, but also the covenants of Judah. Interestingly, although these Zadokite priests rejected the old Israel and the old Judah as having violated God's covenants, they preferred to refer to their own community, the Essenes, as the new *Israel*, perhaps preventing a complete rejection of national heritage.[17] John S. Bergsma writes that the sectarian scrolls, and especially the *Damascus Document*, demonstrate among the Qumran community "a marked preference for identifying themselves either as 'Israel' or 'Israelites,' rather than as 'Judah' or 'Judahites'" (2008, 172). In several passages throughout the *Damascus Document*, Judah is criticized, dissociating the Judahite commitment to the old biblical covenants from the commitment to the new covenant established in Damascus, thus reconstructing a new Israel to supersede the old Israel and its void covenants. Bergsma agrees, arguing that several references to Judah in the *Damascus Document* may, in fact, "express a desire [on the part of the Qumran community] to *dissociate* from Judah" (2008, 181; emphasis in original).[18] Thus, this final dissociation in the *Damascus Document* is actually a double dissociation of *apparent Israel* (Ephraim) from *real Israel* (Judah), and of *old Israel* (Judah) from *new Israel* (Damascus), returning Israel to its status as an ideal concept for the Essenes.

Although the Zadokites of the Essene community descended from the priests of Judah, they clearly preferred to call themselves Israelites, invoking the final remnant of a nation committed to God and moving beyond the divisiveness associated with Judah. In a lemma/pesher commentary, the *Damascus Document* author writes, "[Ezekiel 44:15] 'The priests and the levites and the sons of Zadok who maintained the service of my temple when the children of Israel strayed far away from me, shall offer the fat and the blood.' The priests are the converts of Israel who left the land of Judah; and the ‹levites› are those who joined them; and the sons of Zadok are the chosen of Israel, 'those called by name' who stood up at the end of days" (column III, line 21 to column IV, line 3). And in a later lemma/pesher commentary, the *Damascus Document* author writes, "[Numbers 21:18] 'A well which the princes dug, which the nobles of the people delved with the staff.' The well is the law. And those who dug it are the converts of Israel, who left the land of Judah and lived in the land of Damascus, all of whom God called princes, for they sought him, and their renown has not been repudiated in anyone's mouth" (column VI, lines 3–7). In both of these passages, Israel is the chosen name of the Qumran community and Judah is rejected as a past identity, perhaps now associated with the iniquities of division. Bergsma writes, "The leaving of the land of Judah indicates dissatisfaction with the 'path' the people in Judah were following," and thus also "indicates dissociation from Judah" (2008, 181, 182). And in the second passage, Damascus, not Judah, is the location of the community of the new covenant.

It is clear that the righteous Zadokites left Judah, and thus the Temple, because a powerful faction of priests had begun to abuse their power, leading Judahites astray. This faction is referred to in the *Damascus Document* as the "princes of Judah." According to the author of the *Damascus Document*,

> Thus will be the judgment of all those entering his covenant but who did not remain steadfast in them; they will have a visitation for destruction at the hand of Belial. This is the day when God will make a visitation. The princes of Judah are those upon whom the rage will be vented, for they hope to be healed but it will cleave to them; all are rebels in so far as they have not left the path of the traitors and have defiled themselves in paths of licentiousness, and with wicked wealth, and avenging themselves, and each one bearing resentment against his brother, and each one hating his fellow, and each one despising his blood relative; they have approached for debauchery and have manipulated with pride for wealth and gain. Each one did what was right in his eyes and each one has chosen the stubbornness of his heart. (column VIII, lines 1–9)[19]

Both fornication and wealth are emphasized in this passage. Regarding wealth, Murphy writes, "The central portion of the passage mentions wealth as one of the two ways in which these princes of Judah erred.... The pursuit of wealth is characterized as a means of exacting vengeance on neighbors for grudges long borne. The wickedness of these actions is described as self-centered, wanton, and vicious" (1991, 89). Just as the nets of Belial are linked (if you escape one you fall into another), so are wealth and fornication linked in this passage. Murphy writes, "The pressure to err after the wantonness of one's heart is apparently being brought to bear by Hellenistic kings and Hellenizing Jewish 'princes.' The pressure is specifically associated with new sexual/marital customs and profiteering at the expense of one's kin and neighbors" (89). Murphy concludes, "The practice of economic liberation [among Essenes] thus functions to legitimate the community's claim to uphold the true covenant" (94).

These princes of Judah have interpreted God's precepts in liberal ways, moving the boundary of the law to include practices that are impure or incorrect, yet easy for the priests and palatable for their congregation. The author of the *Damascus Document* writes, "This is the day when God will make a visitation, as he says: *Hos 5:10* 'The princes of Judah will be like those who move the boundary, upon them he will pour out his fury like w[ater]'" (column XIX, lines 15–16). Although the Zadokite priests remained in Judah during the split with the northern tribes of Ephraim, it is clear that even Judah strayed, and a remnant of faithful Zadokites fled the iniquity to Damascus in order to establish a new covenant. Since many of these foundational documents are eschatologically oriented, it makes sense that the Qumran community would be interested in putting aside past divisions and unifying the nation (or at least the pure and pious of the nation) again in preparation for the end of days. Bergsma writes, "The *Yahad* endeavors to become the functioning, restored twelve-tribe entity of Israel," and the Essenes view themselves "as the vanguard of the eschatological restoration of Israel. In fact, in the eschaton the *Yahad* and Israel will be one" (2008, 179, 182; see also 187). Thus, in this double dissociation, Israel begins as an incoherent concept for the Essene community, but it ends as a reconstituted ideal concept through its association with the metaphysical covenant established at Qumran.

In the Essene camps amid the Israelite territories, it was the role of each camp's Inspector to materialize all of these dissociations by judging each member's quality, quality determined by the extent to which a member's life and practices reflect the dissociations promoted throughout the *Damascus Document*. First, the Inspector "shall instruct the Many in the deeds of God, and shall teach them his mighty marvels, and recount to them the eternal events with their solutions. He shall have pity on them like a father on his sons, and will heal all the strays like a shepherd his flock. He will undo all the chains which bind them, so that there will be neither harassed nor oppressed in his congregation" (column XIII, lines 7–10). Following instruction, the Inspector then judges each community member's strength of character as it relates to the dissociations described throughout the *Damascus Document*. The author of the *Damascus Document* writes, "And everyone who joins his congregation, he should examine, concerning his actions, his intelligence, his strength, his courage, and his wealth; and they shall inscribe him in his place according to his condition in the lot of light. No-one of the members of the camp should have the authority to introduce anyone into the congregation against the de[cision] of the Inspector of the camp" (column XIII, lines 11–13). Thus, the rhetorical strategy of dissociation is institutionalized in the interactions among Essenes and between themselves and the communities they viewed as wicked and as sources of wickedness.

The rhetoric of dissociation in the *Damascus Document* removes incoherent concepts from the community of the new covenant until all that remains are sincere Essenes, the final remnant, the new (true) Israel. However, dissociative rhetoric is not sufficient to maintain the strict level of purity required by the new, and annually renewed, metaphysical covenant of the Essenes, especially since some impurities were inevitable (resulting from natural bodily functions, for example), and since most members of the sect lived among converted and Hellenized Israelites (who were impure but behaved as if they were pure). Dissociation in the *Damascus Document* creates an ideal community, but material rhetoric (embodiment, entitlement, and erasure) in the *Purification Rules* and the *Temple Scroll* creates a corporeal community free from impurities of flesh and a physical Temple free from impurities of sin. The purification of the Essenes (final remnant, true Israel) and the purity of the eschatological Temple (final, true) were not merely desires; they were the divine requirements of the new metaphysical covenant for the end of days. And the Essenes took purity and purification very seriously, since the metaphysical curses of their new covenant (the punishments for impurity) were far worse than the material curses of the violated Mosaic covenant. In the next chapter, I discuss the Essenes' rhetorical approach to purity, impurity, and purification from the perspective of material rhetoric.

CHAPTER 4

IMPURITY AND PURIFICATION AS MATERIAL RHETORIC IN THE *PURIFICATION RULES* (4QTOHOROT A AND B) AND THE *TEMPLE SCROLL* (11QT)

In the last two chapters, I discussed performative rhetoric in the *Rule of the Community* and dissociative rhetoric in the *Damascus Document*, all in the context of the rhetorical ecology around 100 BCE. This rhetorical ecology is marked especially by the hegemony of the Hasmonean family, who usurped both the Zadokite line of high priests and the Davidic dynasty of Israelite kings, putting an end to historical traditions in these two central Israelite institutions. With historical institutions in shambles under Hasmonean rule, deposed Zadokite priests exiled themselves to Qumran and wrote procedural guides and moral codes that created a new sect, the Essenes. The Essenes were a separatist group who understood themselves as the Sons of Light, the final remnant and the true Israel, and all others (Greeks, Romans, and Egyptians, yes; but *especially* the Hasmonean high priests and their followers) comprised the Sons of Darkness. The central criterion God would use in the impending apocalypse to distinguish the Sons of Light from the Sons of Darkness would be their purity (*ṭohorah*).

Several documents among the Dead Sea Scrolls address purity, impurity, and purification, but two in particular represent the Essenes' obsession with the topic under the Hasmonean dynasty, the *Purification Rules* (4QTohorot A and B) and the *Temple Scroll* (11QT).[1] In this chapter, I emphasize certain specific events that occurred within the more general rhetorical ecology surrounding 100 BCE as a context for the material rhetorics in the *Purification Rules* and the *Temple Scroll*, which were likely composed late in the second century or early in the first century BCE.[2] In particular, during that time, two Hasmonean high priests, John Hyrcanus (134–104 BCE) and Alexander Jannaeus (103–76 BCE), expanded the land of Israel from the isolated province of Judea out into the surrounding Hellenized territories, exposing Israelites to pagan impurities and the seductions of Greek culture. These two Hasmonean high priests also committed willful sins that polluted the nation of Israel and the Temple sanctuary, making all of their rites and rituals ineffectual.

Early Hasmonean high priests (Jonathan and Simon) were deeply concerned with purifying the Temple of Hellenistic defilement and returning the Temple cult to its function of purifying individual Israelites and atoning for the sins of the nation of Israel. In *Heritage and Hellenism*, Erich S. Gruen explains, "The persecutions of [Seleucid king] Antiochus IV [around 167 BCE] posed an awesome challenge to the Jews. Royal policy aimed at eradication of Jewish worship, traditions, and religious way of life. The defiling of the Temple and its rededication to Zeus Olympios, with the concomitant compulsion of Jews to participate in pagan sacrifices and rituals, represented a campaign to repress Judaism forcibly and to impose Hellenic institutions upon Jerusalem" (1998, 1). However, Gruen continues, "the resistance of Mattathias and his sons turned back the challenge. Judas Maccabeus' victories and Seleucid preoccupations elsewhere enabled the [Hasmonean] Jews to regain and cleanse the Temple, restore ancestral practices, and eliminate the abominations perpetrated by the Hellenistic king" (1). Hellenization, at least in this instance, would have caused the end of Israelite monotheism if not for the resistance led by the Hasmonean family.

Although later Hasmonean high priests (including John Hyrcanus, Aristobulus, and Alexander Jannaeus) would continue to fight for "an autonomous Jewish state, with religious and political authority centered upon the Temple and in the hands of the High Priest" (Gruen 1998, 2), they also embraced other aspects of Hellenism wholeheartedly. Gruen writes, "The Hasmoneans themselves, in the course of the century that followed the Maccabean revolt, engaged regularly in diplomatic dealings with Greek kings, adopted Greek names, donned garb and paraded emblems redolent with Hellenic significance, erected monuments, displayed stelai, minted coinage inspired by Greek models, hired mercenaries, and even took on royal titulature" (2). Levine agrees, explaining that "Jewish and Hellenistic features were incorporated into many facets of Hasmonean life and [were] viewed as complementing one another" (2002, 97).

During the first half of the second century BCE, according to Eric M. Meyers and Mark A. Chancey, Judea "remained more or less encircled by Hellenistic settlements" (2012, 24). However, by the end the second century BCE, John Hyrcanus had begun a campaign to conquer those Hellenistic settlements and integrate them into the nation of Israel, forcing their pagan citizens to convert to Israelite monotheism and participate in the Jerusalem Temple cult. And at the turn of the century, Alexander Jannaeus continued this Hasmonean campaign of expansion until the newly Hellenized Israel matched its historical boundaries under David and Solomon. In the process of expansion, these two Hasmonean high priests and rulers disturbed the relative isolation of Judea, threatening the purity of its culture and religion. Although the Hasmoneans would force conquered populations to convert to Israelite monotheism, their resulting conversion was more a negotiated integration than an utter transformation. For example, after John Hyrcanus conquered the Greek city of Samaria, new Israelite "settlements began appearing, perhaps due to the arrival of Hasmonean colonists. The subsequent population would be a diverse mixture of Samaritans, Jews, and pagans" (Meyers and Chancey 2012, 33). This would be the case with each conquest outside of Judea, and all of these new Hellenistic Israelites would periodically travel to Jerusalem to practice integrated rites and rituals, defiling the Temple and all true Israelites who came into contact with them. Converted Israelites might not understand, for example, menstruation and corpse contact as sources of ritual impurity, visiting the sacred Temple in an impure state and inadvertently making all they touched impure. This Hellenistic liberality under the Hasmoneans drove the Essenes to reformulate ritual purity in more and more conservative ways, and the *Purification Rules* records this sectarian effort.

In addition to exposing pious Israelites to ritual impurities caused by territorial expansion, John Hyrcanus and Alexander Jannaeus also committed willful sins related to wealth and fornication that caused the nation of Israel and the Temple itself to become irreversibly defiled (recall the three nets of Belial described in the *Damascus Document*). Following the Babylonian exile, Israelites who lived in Samaria (the region, not the city) split from the Israelites in Jerusalem and constructed their own temple on Mount Gerizim, complete with its own high priest and full courses of attending priests and Levites. The original Samaritan temple, modeled after the architecture of the Jerusalem Temple, was constructed in the fifth century BCE and expanded around 200 BCE. The Samaritans believed that their temple was God's only residence on earth, and they paid temple tax and tithes to the priests who administered it throughout the year. When John Hyrcanus marched his troops (only about thirty miles) north to the region of Samaria, he destroyed the temple on Mount Gerizim and refused to allow its reconstruction. There may have been several different motivations for destroying the Samaritan temple, but wealth and power were certainly among them. The Samaritan temple was administered by priests of the historically legitimate Aaronide line, who clearly threatened the authority of the Jehoiarib Hasmoneans (Bourgel 2016, 520). Thus, John Hyrcanus destroyed the Samaritan temple in order to centralize Israelite worship in the Jerusalem Temple and to eliminate the struggle for credibility with Aaronide priests. But it is also clear that John Hyrcanus destroyed the Samaritan temple so that all of the taxes and tithes that had been paid at the Samaritan temple would now be paid in Jerusalem, accessible to John Hyrcanus for military and architectural enterprises. Bourgel writes, "It is also likely that John Hyrcanus expected substantial economic benefit from destroying the sanctuary on Mount Gerizim, in the anticipation that the offerings and tithes that had formerly been sent to Mount Gerizim would henceforth be redirected to the Jerusalem Temple" (2016, 520).

With funds generated through conquest and taxation, John Hyrcanus constructed a Hasmonean state palace in Jericho (which Alexander Jannaeus later expanded), violating Joshua's curse against any who might rebuild Jericho, and incurring its wrath (two dead sons, the oldest and the youngest). After Moses died, Joshua led the Israelites across the river Jordan and into the promised land, where their first obstacle was Jericho, a walled pagan city. Joshua and the Israelites followed God's instructions in their siege, causing the city's walls to crumble and its inhabitants to succumb to the sword. Following the victory, Joshua swore an oath, which is quoted and interpreted in 4QTestimonia: "At the moment when Joshua finished praising and giving thanks with his psalms, he said (Joshua 6:26), 'Cursed be the man who rebuilds this city! Upon his first-born will he found it, and upon his Benjamin [youngest] will he erect its gates!' And now /an/ accursed /man/, one of Belial, has arisen to be a fowler's trap for his people and ruin for all his neighbours. [. . .] will arise, to be the two instruments of violence. And they will rebuild [this city and ere]ct for it a rampart and towers, to make it into a fortress of wickedness [a great evil] in Israel, and a horror in Ephraim and Judah. [. . . And they wi]ll commit a profanation in the land and a great blasphemy among the sons of [. . . And they will shed blo]od like water upon the ramparts of the daughter of Sion and in the precincts of Jerusalem" (lines 21–30). The accursed man, the one of Belial, is John Hyrcanus (Eshel 2008, 75), whose firstborn son, Antigonus, was killed by the bodyguards of John Hyrcanus's youngest son, Aristobulus, who then died a short time later under mysterious circumstances. Hyrcanus rebuilt Jericho as a monument to the wealth and power of the Hasmonean theocratic state, in direct violation of a famous biblical curse, and he suffered the wrath of the curse exactly as it was described in Joshua 6:26. It must have taken some arrogance to willfully violate a biblical curse in order to construct monuments to Hasmonean wealth and power. Destroying temples, violating curses—these are the sins of the Israelite high priest at the end of the second century BCE. Unfortunately, Alexander Jannaeus, another of John Hyrcanus's five sons, was even worse.

Alexander Jannaeus continued his father's drive for territory, wealth, and power, but his most grave sin related to fornication, or, in this case, the sin of forbidden marital relations. When king and high priest Aristobulus (104–103 BCE) died an untimely and mysterious death in 103 BCE, his queen, Salome Alexandra, married Aristobulus's younger brother, Alexander Jannaeus, securing for him the titles of king and high priest. Like his father, Alexander Jannaeus favored the Sadducees, who supported his military campaigns and his cultic leadership. According to Kamm, however, the Pharisees were "incensed at his breaking the Law (Leviticus 21:14) which expressly states that no priest, let alone the High Priest, should marry a widow" (1999, 154). Israelite resentment over the cost of constant wars and the sinful marriage of their defiled high priest reached the breaking point around 96 BCE. Kamm writes, "At the Feast of Tabernacles (Sukkot), the congregation pelted [Alexander Jannaeus] with lemons, which they were carrying as part of the seasonal ritual, and hurled insults at him. According to Josephus, he retaliated by massacring six thousand of his own people, and built a wooden partition around the altar as a defense against further missiles when he was performing the sacrifice" (1987, 154–55). Many of the Israelites Alexander Jannaeus murdered were Pharisees, who objected to his willful violation of Torah law and his greedy pollution of the nation of Israel and the Temple sanctuary. Both John Hyrcanus and Alexander Jannaeus committed sins of wealth and fornication, causing the nation of Israel and the Temple they administered to be polluted with moral impurity. For the Essenes, all of these sins required a more conservative approach to purification and atonement for the nation of Israel, including a plan for a new and pure Temple in the eschaton. This is the function of the *Temple Scroll*.

Purity is a central theme throughout the Dead Sea Scrolls. In *The Purity Texts*, Harrington writes, "The majority of the [Qumran] community's laws recorded in the extant manuscripts deal with matters related to the cult and purity," and the "Qumran texts seem to oppose anything but full purification of impure persons before participation in community activities" (2004, 7, 20). In this chapter, I move beyond the importance of purity in general to a more detailed analysis of the discursive materialization (embodiment, entitlement) of impurities and their material erasure through specific ritual practices as they are described in the *Purification Rules* and the *Temple Scroll*. Since impurities *exist*, embodied in flesh and materialized in nation and sanctuary, material rhetoric enables a complex understanding of the rhetorical means by which impurities are both acquired and subsequently erased, ensuring the sanctity of God's chosen people in the end of days.

MATERIAL RHETORIC

Material has always been rhetorical, but "material rhetoric" is a relatively new feature in the communication theory landscape. One central problem with articulating a theory and practice of material rhetoric is that, throughout their disparate histories, materialists and rhetoricians have viewed themselves as fundamentally opposed, making it difficult for them to integrate their interests. Carole Blair laments rhetoric's persistent antimaterialist "symbolicity," which "has become stiflingly dominant in relation to rhetoric," and "when we have theorized rhetoric, the 'material' or 'real' most often has been understood as characteristic of the rhetorical context—the physical setting, or sociocultural environment, of the rhetorical text—rather than of the text itself" (1999, 20, 16). Hence, "materiality . . . has rarely been taken as a starting point or basis for theorizing rhetoric" (18). Other rhetoricians agree with Blair's assessment. Ronald Walter Greene says that "the problem with an attempt to build a rhetorical materialism is that [rhetoric] is unable to break free from the logics of representation" (1998, 38). Michael Calvin McGee asserts that in order to articulate an effective conception of material rhetoric, "a fundamental alteration of perspective is necessary to counterbalance the overwhelming influence of idealism in rhetorical theory" (1982, 45). Dana L. Cloud agrees, suggesting that "we ought not sacrifice the notions of practical truth, bodily reality, and material oppression to the tendency to render all of experience discursive, as if no one went hungry or died in war" (1994, 159). And Jack Selzer quips, where rhetoric is concerned, "words have been mattering more than matter" (1999, 4).

Just as rhetoricians have tended to avoid materialism as a theoretical grounding, so materialist Marxists have also tended to avoid language and rhetoric. In *Rhetoric and Marxism*, James Arnt Aune suggests that "Marxism as a conceptual system," which includes a rigorous commitment to materialism, "has tended to ignore problems of communication," especially "that form of strategic communication known in Western culture as 'rhetoric'" (1994, ix). In general, materialists agree that language and rhetoric have not been preoccupations in their critical methodologies. In *Marxism and the Philosophy of Language*, V. N. Vološinov writes that "to date, there is not yet a single Marxist work on the philosophy of language" (1973, xiii). Louis Althusser and Etienne Balibar suggest in *Reading Capital* that "only since Marx have we had to begin to suspect what, in theory at least, *reading* and hence writing *means*" (1979, 16). Further, when the subject of language *is* discussed in conjunction with materialism, however briefly, it is very often treated with enmity: in *Language and Materialism*, Rosalind Coward and John Ellis point out that "Marxist thought has only been capable of negative formulations of language" (1977, 78).

Unfortunately, Karl Marx and Friedrich Engels themselves do not offer much help. In the entire corpus of writing produced by Marx and Engels (literally tens of thousands of pages), there is little direct theoretical treatment of *language* and no discussion of *rhetoric*.[3] The problem is that Marx and Engels most often viewed language either as a meaningless material object ("agitated layers of air, sounds") or as a representation of false consciousness ("*language* is the immediate actuality of thought") ([1846] 1976, 44, 446). However, the whole point of dialectical materialism is to descend "from the world of thoughts to the actual world" and thus to descend "from language to life" (446). Dialectical materialism is "a question of revolutionizing the existing world, of practically coming to grips with and changing the things found in existence" (38), but neither "language-as-material-object" nor "language-as-false-consciousness" has any potential to revolutionize the world or change existence. Thus, for Marx, Engels, and generations of materialist Marxists to follow, the term "material rhetoric" would have been viewed as an oxymoron.

Writing in 1982, McGee explained, "With the possible exception of Kenneth Burke, no one I know has attempted formally to advance a material theory of rhetoric" (1982, 38). Since then, however, some rhetorical theorists (influenced by new communication technologies, visual rhetorics, and theories of discourse) have begun to challenge both materialism's exclusive *pragma*-centrism and rhetoric's exclusive *logo*-centrism, integrating the concerns of both into a powerful synthesis called new material rhetoric.[4] Communication is always embodied in some medium; new material rhetorics explore the (social) semiotic force of each medium and the actual affordances that each offers in any given situation. The objects and images that surround us every day communicate complex meanings; new material rhetorics interpret these meanings and consider ways to communicate using both material itself and visual representations of material. Language does more than just generate mental effects (instruction, conviction, persuasion); new material rhetorics consider the tangible results of rhetorical acts and the linguistic effects of corporeal conditions.

Although new material rhetorics emphasize communication phenomena that are increasingly enabled by recent networked technologies, some of the lessons learned from explorations of new material rhetorics pertain to the study of ancient texts, including the Dead Sea Scrolls.[5] According to Laurie E. Gries (2015), the rhetorical agency of nonhuman entities interacting with humans (or thing-power) and the consequentiality of rhetorical circulation (or futurity) are hallmarks of new material rhetorics. In new material rhetorics, things derive power when Cartesian oppositions such as subject/object are deconstructed and all matter, human and nonhuman, acquires equal ontological status in relational contexts. Even individual thinkers lose Cartesian control ("I think; therefore, I am") when cognition is distributed across multiple entities in variable contexts and heterogeneous assemblages. New material rhetorics critique the limitation of instrumentalist views of rhetoric (author, purpose, delivery, audience, etc.), suggesting that rhetorical performances acquire their most profound effects in cycles of distribution beyond the scope of the exigent occasion. Once rhetorical performances circulate outside the occasion of their production, authors lose power over their rhetorical effects, thus leaving the material products of rhetoric to acquire a kind of agency of their own. As these material products circulate from context to context, they enter into relationships with other entities, both human and nonhuman, and all entities contribute equally to the construction of rhetorical meaning. In new material rhetorics, since meaning is generated in the intra-action of multiple entities in various contexts, more traditional concepts like individual authors and intended purposes become distributed into heterogeneous assemblages and unpredictable effects.

If thing-power (ontological agency), distributed cognition (heterogeneous assemblages), and futurity (consequential circulation) are salient qualities of new material rhetorics, versus old material rhetorics, then new material rhetorics are just as useful for studying the Dead Sea Scrolls as they are for studying the Internet. In both the *Purification Rules* and the *Temple Scroll*, sources of impurity have agency to transform Israelite flesh and the Temple sanctuary from a status of purity to a status of impurity, not just impressionistically so, but *materially* so. There is thing-power in a *miqveh*'s water, in pure food, and in the implements of ritual purification. In the assemblage of Essenes and in the institutional context of Qumran, material objects and humans intra-act with shared agency. While the Essenes at Qumran shared a particular procedural interpretation of Torah law, their rhetorical intentions could not be fulfilled without agential participation among humans and objects, a kind of distributed cognition throughout every aspect of the ritual process. In Qumran, traditional concepts like rhetorical exigencies and purposes are only the beginning of a subsequent flow of rhetorical consequences related to holiness and salvation, the fulfillment of the Mosaic covenant, which the Essene community was reestablishing through ritual practices every day. And these ritual practices employed both words and things interacting with humans in ritual contexts as rhetorical means to purify acquired impurities. Both the materialization of impurities and their ritual erasure have deeply meaningful consequences for the Essene community, and these future consequences are just as rhetorically salient as the actual performance of the rituals themselves.

Since there are myriad ways in which rhetoric is material and material is rhetorical, each individual articulation of material rhetoric selects salient aspects of this integrated approach and applies them situationally. In order to theorize the discursive materialization and ritual erasure of impurities as material symbolic actions, I draw from two perspectives that directly challenge, and offer alternatives to, the representational model of the linguistic sign in which words represent things and concepts. First, Kenneth Burke's theory of entitlement reverses the traditional structure of the linguistic sign, arguing that words inspirit things with meaning, so that things represent words, not the other way around. In the *Purification Rules* and the *Temple Scroll*, entitlement explains how sacred texts inspirit flesh and objects with material conditions of impurity. Second, J. L. Austin's speech act theory describes utterances as intentional actions, not arbitrary representations, that create material effects in the world. In the *Purification Rules* and the *Temple Scroll*, speech act theory explains how actions and utterances in purification rituals erase material impurities. These two material symbolic actions, inspiriting and erasure, treat language as a materializing (not representational) force, thus opening up the possibility for a powerful theory and practice of material rhetoric.

As I will explain, the Israelites' status as either pure or impure was high stakes, since this status actually determined their fate in the end of days. Material purity of sacred objects and Israelite bodies was a condition of the Mosaic covenant, and purity guaranteed inheritance of covenantal blessings. The presence of material impurity was a violation of the Mosaic covenant, which could result in subjection to covenantal curses, and it required ritual erasure as a means of material purification. Since inspiriting and erasure are both verbal *and* physical processes, material rhetoric is the best method available for explaining their effects throughout the Dead Sea Scrolls, but especially in the *Purification Rules* and the *Temple Scroll*.

PURITY AND COVENANT

As Fredric Jameson (1972) suggests in his preface to *The Prison-House of Language*, it is important to understand any particular practice or set of related practices in the larger context of the thought-models that both enable the very conception of these practices and also constrain them within a particular discursive domain. In *The Logic of Practice*, Pierre Bourdieu calls this discursive domain a "habitus," and he defines habitus as a "system of structured, structuring dispositions . . . , which is constituted in practice and is always oriented towards practical functions" (1990, 52).[6] Jonathan Klawans (2000), too, recognizes the importance of understanding particular practices, such as ritual purification, in the context of larger discursive domains and structuring dispositions. Ritual impurity, moral impurity, and practices of purification among the ancient Israelites must be understood, according to Klawans, as "part of a larger sacrificial system," which is in turn part of an even larger system, "Israelite religion as a whole" (2000, 38). For the Essene community, perhaps the most critical discursive contexts or structuring dispositions were the covenants described in the Torah, and it was the very *telos* of the Essenes to receive the blessings of these covenants in the end of days.

A covenant is a conditional promise between God and another entity (usually an individual, such as Abraham, or a collective, such as the nation of Israel), and this promise comes with blessings if the conditions of the covenant are upheld, and curses if they are neglected or violated. According to Edward F. Campbell Jr., the theological ideology of Judaism during the First Temple period (from Solomon's death to the Babylonian exile) was "effectively covenantal. Based in divine gift, human gratitude, and mutual trust, the covenant demanded exclusive loyalty to the deity and human responsibility in communal relations" (1998, 209). After the Babylonian exile and the reconstruction of the Temple, thus inaugurating the Second Temple period, the centrality of covenantal theology in ancient Judaism was reaffirmed and deepened with a renewed commitment to the divine promise and an increased emphasis on the legal requirements of the covenant (Bright 2000, 356–58, 430). John Bright explains that "the religion of the postexilic period is marked by a tremendous concern for the keeping of the law. This is, indeed, its distinctive character and that which, more than anything else, distinguishes it from the religion of preexilic Israel" (2000, 430). Thus, as the Second Temple period progressed, the integral relationship between covenant and law increasingly became the discursive context and system of structuring dispositions around which the Israelite faith centered, and the cult of the Jerusalem Temple was responsible for administering this faith by organizing traditional legal observances and conducting ritual purifications. In the case of the Mosaic covenant, God promised Moses that he would be Lord to the Israelite nation, conferring upon them material blessings, in exchange for their purity by means of the strict observance of Torah law.

But obedience was not itself the goal of this covenant. The goal of the Mosaic covenant was a pure people and a holy nation, worthy of doing God's will in the end of days. None of this would be possible without strict adherence to the purity laws and procedures for purification that God provided to Moses and Aaron on Mount Sinai. The Essene leaders viewed the Torah as the literal word of God, infallible and true. If the word of God describes moral conditions or physical states as impure, then the bodies or objects that exhibit those conditions or states *are* impure, not conceptually, not hypothetically, but *materially*, in fact. These bodies and objects, then, become inscribed with the material status of impurity. The discursive description of impurity in the Torah serves to materialize impurity in Israelite bodies, their nation, and their sanctuary. The function of the Mosaic laws (or commandments) was to ensure purity, since impurity is anathema to God. However, according to the Essenes, the Temple establishment under the Hasmoneans was not following the strictest interpretations of the Mosaic laws. Thus the Essenes believed that the Temple establishment was leading all Israelites who worshipped in Jerusalem into a perpetual state of impurity.

In order to ensure their own purity in the face of rampant defilement, the Essenes became more strict in the observance of Torah law than even the Torah itself required (Harrington 2004, 12). According to Harrington, "Among all of the Jewish groups of the Second Temple era, the Qumran community was the most rigorous in the maintenance of purity. The laws of purity and impurity were a central concern for the authors of the Dead Sea Scrolls" (2004, 7). If the community at Qumran could succeed in remaining pure, then upon God's return to earth in the end of days, they would stand with God against the forces of evil, and once these forces are defeated, they would live forever with God in everlasting glory and redemption. But if they were impure upon God's return, they would be destroyed along with all other wickedness in the world. To say the least, the stakes were high to remain pure, but unfortunately the ancient Israelite world was absolutely rife with sources of impurity. Klawans (2000) distinguishes between two kinds of impurity, both of which have already been mentioned but not fully explored: ritual impurity and moral impurity.

Ritual impurity is not the consequence of sin but is a natural by-product of everyday life in ancient Israel. It is embodied in individual Israelites, and it is erased by situational rituals such as isolation, bathing, and sprinkling with *me niddah*. Klawans explains, "The term 'ritual' is particularly useful in this regard because this kind of impurity affects the ritual status of the persons stricken by it. Ritually impure persons are excluded from participation in certain ritual acts and barred from entering sacred precincts. In certain cases, such persons may affect the ritual status of those around them as well. Moreover, ritual purity is achieved, at least in part, *ritually*, that is by means of sacrifices, sprinklings, washings, and bathings" (2000, 22–23). Ritual impurity is acquired through experiencing or contacting signs associated with the cycle of birth and death, the condition of human existence after Adam and Eve were expelled from Eden. Such signs include semen, menstrual fluid, and corpses. Not only were most of these sources of ritual impurity unavoidable, but also some of the most important legal injunctions necessitate exposure to ritual impurities. The commandment to be fruitful and multiply requires contact with semen and a woman who experiences a menstrual cycle, and the traditional practice of burying the dead requires contact with corpses.

Since ritual impurities are not the consequence of sin, the erasure of ritual impurities is relatively simple, requiring isolation, bathing, laundering, and waiting till sundown, for example. Despite being relatively simple, however, the erasure of ritual impurities is crucial, since these impurities are highly contagious. Thus, refusing to purify ritual impurities becomes a sin and converts ritual impurities into moral defilements (Klawans 2000, 25). For example, if a ritually impure Israelite knowingly enters the Temple grounds or touches sacred food, the land and all of its inhabitants become defiled as a consequence. Thus, refusing to purify ritual impurities is a sin resulting in moral defilement. Throughout the Dead Sea Scrolls, and particularly in the *Purification Rules*, discursive embodiment inscribes material impurities onto Israelite flesh, and ritual erasure purifies Israelite flesh through specific utterances and material practices, transfiguring impure bodies back to a state of purity. In both of these cases, discursive embodiment and ritual erasure, the effect of rhetoric is material and the force of material is rhetorical.

Unlike ritual impurity, moral impurity is acquired through sin. It is embodied in the nation of Israel and its sanctuary, and it is erased by execution, exile, and/or the ritual performance of required festivals and sacrifices. Moral impurity is an abomination, not just an inconvenience. It results from "what are perceived to be immoral acts" (Klawans 2000, 26). The sins that cause moral impurity include incest, adultery, idolatry, and murder, and the impurities resulting from these serious sins are materialized discursively in the nation of Israel and the sanctuary. There are no individual rituals (bathing, laundering) that can purify moral impurities in part because the consequences of moral impurities are suffered by the entire community. Klawans writes, "The impurity that is contracted by the performance of sin is conveyed to the land" (2000, vi). Thus, individual means of ritual erasure are insufficient to remove moral impurity, which requires direct punishment, atonement, and festivals and sacrifices that erase moral impurity from the nation of Israel and its sanctuary.

Moral impurity was certainly a known phenomenon, and leaving it unchecked or unpurified resulted in grave consequences for the entire Israelite nation. Klawans writes, "The ultimate result of this [moral] defilement, if it remains unchecked, is the exile of the land's inhabitants" (2000, 30). So there must have been some way to deal with moral defilement, beyond just prevention. In the case of a relatively minor sin, such as adultery, the morally impure individual remains in the community despite the impurity incurred through this individual on the nation of Israel and the sanctuary. This sinner is restricted from certain sacred activities but is not expelled or executed. In the case of more serious sins, such as murder and idolatry, the morally impure individual cannot remain among the community of Israelites, leaving execution or exile as the only means to rid the Israelites of the source of moral impurity. However, exile and execution alone do not purify the Israelite nation or the sanctuary. It is the purpose of the Day of Atonement, for example, to purify the nation of Israel and the sanctuary of moral impurity. But if rampant sin causes moral impurities to accumulate (because they are not officially recognized, not sufficiently punished, or not correctly atoned), thus permanently defiling the nation and sanctuary, then the entire community of Israelites must be exiled or put to the sword.

DISCURSIVE EMBODIMENT, RITUAL IMPURITY, AND RITUAL ERASURE IN THE *PURIFICATION RULES*

The *Purification Rules* describes the discursive embodiment of ritual impurity in individual Israelites and the ritual erasure of embodied impurities through purification.

Discursive Embodiment of Ritual Impurity

Sacred discourses (the scriptures, especially the Torah, and the Essene sectarian writings, such as the *Purification Rules*) inscribe material qualities of purity and impurity onto physical bodies. Discursive embodiment results from what Burke calls entitlement, a process through which material things come to stand for words and their related concepts, reversing the traditional structure of the linguistic sign in which words stand for things. Burke talks about entitlement in *The Rhetoric of Religion* (1970) and in his essay "What Are Signs of What?" (1966), which appears in *Language as Symbolic Action*. In "What Are Signs of What?" Burke wonders what would happen if we rejected the traditional semiotic view that "words are the signs of things" and tried "upholding instead the proposition that 'things are the signs of words'" (1966, 360, 361). Burke asks, "Might words be found to possess a 'spirit' peculiar to their nature as words? And might the things of experience then become in effect the materialization of such spirit, the manifestation of this spirit in visible tangible bodies?" (361). This spirit of words emerges from "the forms of language" themselves and from "the group motives that language possesses by reason of its nature as a social product" (361).

According to Burke, entitlement includes both abstracting and inspiriting. In the process of entitlement, terms are repeatedly abstracted from increasingly wide ranges of discourses and their situations until an ultimate term (or a god term) is reached. These god terms then become abstract titles for collections of discourses. But god terms are not the signifiers of the things they name, as traditional semiotics would have it. Instead, the things named by god terms become the signifiers of all of the discourses that have been abstracted in the process of entitlement. According to Burke, "In mediating between the social realm and the realm of nonverbal nature, words communicate to things the spirit that the society imposes upon the words which have come to be the 'names' for them. The things are in effect the visible tangible material embodiments of the spirit that infuses them through the medium of words" (1966, 362). Thus, the discourses that are abstracted through the process of entitlement actually inspirit material things with meaning, so that these things become the signs of words.

Entitlement, at Qumran, is a form of material rhetoric in which physical bodies are inscribed with social meanings through powerful terms, such as "pure" and "impure." Material impurity is inscribed on Israelite bodies through a process of discursive embodiment in which the flesh is recognized to have met the conditions of ritual impurity described in sacred texts, especially the priestly books of the Torah and the purity texts among the sectarian Dead Sea Scrolls (including the *Rule of the Community*, the *Damascus Document*, the *Temple Scroll*, and, of course, the *Purification Rules*). Discursive embodiment occurs when powerful discourses inspirit flesh with qualities that are understood as materially present when certain conditions arise. One function of material rhetoric is to reconnect objects in the physical world with the discourses that inspirit them.

Although God is the ever-present god term throughout the entire corpus of the Dead Sea Scrolls, there are other terms that are nearly as universal, though they result from the abstraction of a smaller number of discourses through entitlement. I call these demigod terms, since they float between the most abstract god terms and the less abstract terms whose descriptive capacities are limited to concrete situations. In the *Purification Rules*, although God is the universal god term, purity and impurity are demigod terms that describe the material condition of Israelite bodies, signifying their value to God in the end of days. Thus, all of the discourses in the priestly books of the Torah and in the purity texts among the Dead Sea Scrolls actually inspirit Israelite flesh as either pure or impure, and materially so.

For Israelites of the Second Temple period, the world was a treacherous place, rife with sources of impurity, but purity (by means of obedience to the law, or purification when the law is transgressed) was the mandate of the Mosaic covenant. There are four primary sources of ritual impurity described throughout the *Purification Rules*: menstruation, seminal emission, gonorrhea, and corpse contact. The texts that were sacred to the Essene community inscribe (entitle, embody) ritual impurities onto Israelite flesh, and this inscription requires ritual purification.

Unfortunately for the women associated with the Essene community, their monthly flow of menstrual blood was associated with bloodshed more generally conceived, and "Qumran texts exclude the menstruant from society" (Harrington 2004, 101). As a general form of bloodshed, then, menstrual flow was viewed as a source of impurity that required both isolation and purification. This understanding of menstrual blood as a potent source of impurity by its association with other forms of bloodshed is borne out in 4QPurification Rules A (4Q274). Like other ritual impurities, the impurity caused by menstruation is extremely contagious (Harrington 2004, 20). In fact, menstrual blood is such a potent impurity that direct contact with it is considered to cause the same level of defilement as the direct experience of one's own discharge: "And the one who counts (their seven days), whether male or female, should not to[uch . . .] at the onset of her menstruation, unless she is pure of her mens[truation, for behold, the blood of menstruation is considered like a discharge [for] him who touches it" (4Q274, fragment 1, column I, lines 7–8). In other words, contact with menstrual blood does not result in an indirect impurity; it results in the equivalent of a direct impurity, as if the ones who touch a menstruating woman or her menstrual blood had experienced a discharge of their own.

Not only is a woman's own menstrual flow contagious, but she can also increase the level of her own impurity during menstruation by coming into contact with others who are impure with discharges. According to 4QPurification Rules A (4Q274), "She who has a discharge of blood, during the seven days shall not touch the man with gonorrhea or any of the utensils which the man with gonorrhea has touched, <upon which he has lain>, / or/ upon which he has sat" (fragment 1, column I, lines 4–5), and she shall not "touch any woman [with a discharge] of blood of several days" (fragment 1, column I, line 6). If a menstruating woman comes into contact with another menstruating woman or a man who is experiencing gonorrhea, her level of impurity increases, and she is not allowed access to communal resources, such as food and formal worship, until she undergoes additional purification procedures that return her to purity.

In the Torah, the Hebrew word *zera* takes on three related meanings: botanical seed, human offspring, and semen. The use of *zera* to signify botanical seed and offspring appears frequently through the entire Torah, but the use of this term to signify semen is specific only to a limited section of the Levitical laws (Leviticus 15–27, but especially chapter 15, which focuses on seminal and menstrual discharges). Neither Leviticus nor the *Purification Rules* explains why seminal discharge is a source of impurity; however, many scholars, such as Harrington, believe that semen represents a life-giving, vital force that is lost (Harrington 2004, 35). The *Purification Rules* describes semen as a highly contagious source of ritual impurity, and, in keeping with other aspects of Essene approaches to impurity, it "regards semen as more defiling than a straightforward reading of Scripture would suggest" (Harrington 2004, 104). According to 4Q*Purification Rules A*, "Whoever [has an em]ission of semen contaminates through contact" (4Q274, fragment 1, column I, line 8; see also 4Q274, fragment 2, column I, lines 1–9), either making the pure impure or raising the impurity level of the temporarily impure. In fragment 2 of 4Q*Purification Rules A*, we find that whoever touches semen or any objects defiled by semen becomes impure and must undergo purification, including the defiled objects themselves.

In the Torah, the Hebrew word *zab* refers to many different kinds of discharge from the body (or a person who experiences such discharges), one of which may be caused by gonorrhea. The general kind of discharge described in the Torah is treated with the same level of impurity characteristic of seminal and menstrual discharges. In the *Purification Rules*, however, *zab* refers specifically to the unclean discharge resulting from gonorrhea, and here *zab* becomes a more potent source of ritual defilement than it is in its biblical treatment. Because gonorrhea may result from sexual misconduct, it is viewed as an extremely potent source of impurity, and, according to Harrington, "Anything the *zab* touches becomes impure and contaminating to other persons" (2004, 95).

Even more contagious than the impure person is the impure discharge itself. 4Q*Purification Rules B^c* explains that "everyone who touches [. . .] [. . .] his discharge [. . .] in the water [. . .] [. . .] will be impure [. . .] his be[d and his] dwelling [. . .] they touched his discharge, like he who touches the impurity of [a corpse]" (4Q277, fragment 1, lines 10–12). According to the *Purification Rules*, then, touching the impure discharge of the person with gonorrhea carries the same level of ritual impurity as corpse contact, which is the highest level of ritual impurity. The Essene treatment of gonorrhea as a source of ritual impurity is clearly an intensification of the Levitical treatment of the same condition.

Many purity laws function to eliminate or isolate semiotic signs of death, the lot of human existence since Adam and Eve's transgression in Eden. There can be no more direct semiotic sign of death than the lifeless corpse itself, which is the most potent and contagious source of ritual impurity discussed in both the Torah and the Qumran scrolls (Harrington 2004, 20, 71). So strong was the impurity caused by corpse contact that the person affected was not allowed to partake of communal meals (72). Harrington points out that, like their laws regarding other sources of impurity, "the Qumran laws regarding the corpse are derived from the Torah but represent a very stringent interpretation" (72). The nature of impurity acquired through corpse contact is not directly described in the *Purification Rules*, but there is extensive treatment of the rituals required to purify the flesh of this defilement in *Purification Rules B^b* (4Q276) and *Purification Rules B^c* (4Q277), which I will discuss later.

Since impurity is anathema to God, and since impurity is highly contagious, all forms of ritual impurity, especially the most potent ones, needed to be purified through ritual erasure as soon as possible. And ritual erasure, like discursive embodiment, is a form of material rhetoric because its effects are derived from the dialectical integration of verbal and physical signification.

Ritual Erasure Through Purification

Although not a formal symbolic aspect of the purification process, the first speech act following the discursive embodiment of ritual impurity is to entitle oneself as impure, since many ritual impurities are not marked by outwardly visible signs (one cannot see corpse contamination). So that there would be no doubt about their status, impure members of the Essene community were required to declare their impurity publicly and loudly: "For this is what it says: [Leviticus 13:45–46] 'Unclean, unclean, he will shout, all the days that [the con]dition la[sts] him'" (4Q274, fragment 1, column I, line 4). Here we have an intentional act of self-entitlement in which impure Israelites shout out the title of their affliction so that other Israelites will not become impure by contact or association, and through this symbolic act, all of the discourses that are abstracted in the process of entitlement inspirit the Israelite with a material quality of impure flesh.

Once physical bodies become materially impure by means of entitlement or discursive embodiment, only specific ritual acts of purification, correctly and completely performed, can erase this inscription. These ritual acts are both verbal and physical processes that result in material changes, transfiguring impure Israelite flesh into pure flesh by means of material rhetoric. In *How to Do Things with Words*, Austin ([1962] 1975) describes speech acts as a kind of material rhetoric in which words make things happen in reality. Although Austin himself did not apply his theory of speech acts to nonverbal communication, it is not difficult to describe nonverbal ritual acts as locutions, illocutions, and perlocutions. For example, ritual locutionary acts are the material performances of the ritual purification procedures themselves, including prescribed periods of isolation, methods of bathing and laundering, and requirements of sprinkling with purifying fluid (*me niddah*). Ritual illocutionary acts (again, isolation, bathing, and sprinkling) carry the force of intent to purify the impure, and these acts, carried out correctly and completely, actually transfigure impure flesh into pure flesh. Ritual perlocutionary acts account for the material and behavioral effects that these ritual procedures have on those who are newly purified, such as a renewed access to communal meals, worship, and study.

The discursive embodiment (entitlement, inscription) of material impurities onto Israelite flesh requires material rituals of purification in order to erase these discursive inscriptions, and the ritual acts intended to purify ritual impurities have a relatively limited range: first, isolation; second, bathing in a *miqveh* (or purification pool), laundering contaminated clothes, and waiting until sunset on a prescribed day; and third, sprinkling with *me niddah*. Most of these procedures are biblical in origin; however, the Essene community interpreted these procedures in a strict way. According to Harrington, "The many purity texts found at Qumran reveal an approach to purity which is stringent. The biblical prescriptions for purity are often increased and impurity is regarded as a more potent force than it is by any other ancient Jewish group in antiquity" (2004, 12). It is also clear that these three basic means of purification are intended to cleanse individual Israelites, not the nation of Israel, since isolation, bathing and laundering, and sprinkling with *me niddah* are inherently individual acts, not acts performed by or for the nation as a whole.

At Qumran, isolation and repentance were prescribed to "anyone suffering from any form of ritual impurity" (Toews 2003, 81), and they served two primary functions. First, isolation separates impure people from pure people and objects (especially food), limiting the contagion of impurity. Second, isolation provides the opportunity for impure Israelites to confess their sins and repent, even sins that may have been committed unknowingly, and even if sin was not the direct source of the ritual impurity in question. The purification rituals prescribed by the Essene leaders would only take effect, in other words, if the heart was willing to reject sin and commit itself again to future purity. The opening lines of 4Q*Purification Rules A* highlight the critical importance of initial isolation following the acquisition of impurity: "He shall begin to lay down his [re]quest; he shall lie down in the bed of sorrows, and in the residence of lamentation he shall reside; he shall reside apart from all the impure, and far from the pure food, at twelve cubits; he shall dwell in the quarter reserved for him, to the northeast of every dwelling, at the distance of this measure" (4Q274, fragment 1, column I, lines 3–4). The request is, of course, to receive purification from God, not just from the conduct of the ritual alone, which is preceded with sorrow and lamentation in addition to physical isolation "at twelve cubits" in a house reserved specifically for the impure among the community. Physical isolation of impure community members was important as a means to prevent the spread of contagious impurities, as in the isolation of a woman experiencing menstruation: "And she must not mingle in any way during her seven days, so that she does not contaminate the camps of the holy [ones of] Israel" (4Q274, fragment 1, column I, lines 5–6). The purpose of this isolation is to prevent contagious intensification of impurity in those who are temporarily impure (presently undergoing purification) and to prevent the contagious defilement of the community's pure food. Isolation was a precursor to purification but was not itself an active form of ritual erasure. As performative material rhetoric, then, isolation was certainly a locutionary act, but it lacked illocutionary and perlocutionary force.

Following isolation and repentance, bathing in a *miqveh*, laundering impure clothes, and waiting until sunset on a prescribed day are the most basic means of purification among the Essenes (Harrington 2004, 22), and all of these ritual acts have the full complement of locutionary, illocutionary, and perlocutionary forces, the building blocks of performative material rhetoric. The least potent ritual impurities, such as contacting someone who has experienced seminal emission or menstruation, can be completely erased from the flesh by this process in just one day, allowing the newly purified Essene to subsequently eat pure communal food and participate in communal worship. According to 4Q*Purification Rules A*, "Every man of the impure who [touches] him (who is also impure), shall bathe in water and wash his clothes, and afterwards he will eat" (4Q247, fragment 1, column I, line 3). Further, a menstruating woman who touches a man with gonorrhea is now so impure that she cannot consume any food at all, but 4Q*Purification Rules A* states that "if she does touch, she shall wash her clothes and bathe, and afterwards, she will eat" (4Q247, fragment 1, column I, line 5).

Recent excavations at Qumran reveal an aqueduct connecting ten *miqva'ot*, one of which was located just outside of the compound and may have been used for purification following routine, though impure, activities (Magness 2002, 134–62). Other ritual impurities required a more extended time for purification, such as the process required to erase the impurity caused by the direct experience of seminal emission or menstruation. In these cases, isolation, bathing, laundering, and waiting until sunset were required each day for seven days. While bathing and laundering can be used to reduce one's level of impurity during the purification process, it is also used as a way of ending the purification process, providing one final purification to ensure that there is no incorrect assumption about one's status. These performative ritual acts of purification transfigured Israelite flesh from impure to pure, in keeping with the primary condition of the Mosaic covenant, and this performative material rhetoric enabled the Qumran community to engage in certain everyday activities that were impure but also necessary and inevitable.

Not all sources of impurity were acquired in the course of everyday life in the Second Temple world. Corpse contact was a particularly potent source of ritual impurity that required potent material rhetoric for purification. Like the purification of everyday impurities, corpse contact also required seven days of ritual erasure in order to achieve purification. The seven days required to purify corpse contact included the same rituals of erasure that were used to purify other impurities (isolation, bathing, laundering, and waiting till sunset on the last day), with one important addition. On the third and seventh days, those undergoing ritual erasure for corpse impurity were sprinkled with *me niddah*. According to Torah law, *me niddah*, or the ash of a red heifer sin offering mixed with pure water, red wool, and hyssop, is sprinkled on people made impure by contact with a corpse (Numbers 19:17–21; Joseph M. Baumgarten 2000, 481; Harrington 2004, 22). 4Q*Purification Rules B^b* describes part of the process for creating *me niddah*: "And slaughtered shall be [. . .] the heifer before him, and he shall place its blood in a new vessel which [. . .] on the altar, and sprinkle some of the blood with his finger. Seven [. . . times] at the entrance of the tent of meeting. And he shall cast the cedar, [the hyssop, and] scarlet into the midst of its fire. . . . and he who col[l]ects the ashes of the heifer [. . .] . . . as a reserve [for the lustral water . . .]" (4Q276, fragment 1, lines 1–9).[7] Joseph M. Baumgarten points out that in 4Q*Purification Rules B*[c] (4Q277), the Essene community adds further requirements to the Torah specifications, including that the priest who gathers ashes from the red heifer purification offering must be pure and of mature age, and the recipient of this potent purification ritual must bathe before sprinkling in order to reduce the level of impurity present and allow the *me niddah* to purify all impurities, even those of which the impure/purifying Israelite may not be aware (2000, 481). I do not believe that the Essenes considered it a sin to come into contact with a corpse, since a cemetery was excavated just outside of the compound, and some members of the community must have buried their dead and must not have been exiled for doing so. However, the fact that *me niddah* was made from the ashes of a sin offering indicates that a certain level of guilt may have been involved, though perhaps only indirectly, as a condition of human existence in the cycle of life and death after Eden, not as the direct result of corpse contact. Harrington explains that "the association of guilt and corpse impurity is found . . . nowhere else in early Jewish sources" (2004, 83). Either way, the discursive embodiment of corpse contamination is a potent impurity requiring an equally potent means of ritual erasure.

Although in Torah law, the impurity caused by gonorrhea and sexual intercourse was purified by isolation, bathing, and laundering, the Essenes may have believed that the sexual act associated with the acquisition of gonorrhea, and the impurity caused by sexual intercourse, required an additional sprinkling with *me niddah* for full purification (Joseph M. Baumgarten 2000, 482), equating it with the severity of corpse contact (Harrington 2004, 98). Thus, not only did the Essenes require preparatory purifications before the sprinkling of *me niddah*, but they also generalized the use of *me niddah* and its preparatory rituals to other kinds of defilement, including gonorrhea and sexual intercourse (Joseph M. Baumgarten 2000, 483). In "The Use of *me niddah* for General Purification," Joseph M. Baumgarten goes so far as to suggest that *me niddah* may have been used at Qumran for the purification of all impurities (2000, 484–85). I find this claim convincing, since even those among the Essenes who indirectly contact impure individuals must sprinkle with *me niddah* in order to be purified. Further, it is entirely possible that *me niddah* purified not only material contaminations but also contamination from metaphorical corpse contact. According to Harrington, at Qumran, "it is very likely that corpse purification, with its special purgation water, was used to mark the very entrance of a candidate to the sect: he passed from death to life by his entrance into the community" (2004, 83). The Essene community appears to associate blood and semen with death, or at least with the loss of life-force, and have thus associated the rituals of purification, reserved in the Torah for corpse contamination only, to other forms of impurity that appear to have their origins in death or exhibit signifiers associated with death, such as blood and discharge.

As a form of material rhetoric, ritual performative utterances and acts erase impurities from Israelite bodies, transfiguring impure flesh back to pure flesh, which was one of the primary conditions of the Mosaic covenant. Bathing, laundering, and waiting for a prescribed period before reengaging in communal activities were not only persuasive acts (changing minds) but were also material acts (changing reality), together forming a complex practice of material rhetoric.

DISCURSIVE ENTITLEMENT, MORAL IMPURITY, AND RITUAL ERASURE IN THE *TEMPLE SCROLL*

The *Temple Scroll* describes sources of moral impurity, their discursive materialization or entitlement in the nation of Israel and the sanctuary, and the ritual erasure of discursive entitlement through required festivals and sacrifices.[8] Although it is difficult to date the *Temple Scroll* (because 11QT is a copy of an older text and may be a composite of several different versions), it is clear that the purity regulations described there are more stringent than those described in the Torah, a hallmark of Essene sectarian ideology.[9] The *Temple Scroll* begins with a detailed description of the altar, the sanctuary, and the court. These dimensions, designs, and materials are not selected for aesthetic reasons but for metaphysical reasons, since the structure of God's Temple in heaven served as the blueprint or prototype for the Temple on earth (Price 2005, 49–52). Since the earthly Temple was a place for God literally to abide, it was imperative that this Temple remain pure and undefiled, just as the heavenly Temple was pure and undefiled. Unfortunately, the Israelites were human, not divine, and moral impurity was a condition of their very existence since the moral transgression of Adam and Eve. Moral impurity resulting from sin did not defile individual Israelites, as ritual impurity did; rather, moral impurity defiled the entire nation of Israel and the sanctuary that was their God's residence on earth, making moral purity (in addition to ritual purity) critical to the continuation of the biblical covenants.

Discursive Materialization of Moral Impurity

Like ritual impurities, moral impurities are materialized through what Burke calls entitlement, a process in which material objects acquire meaning through their associations with specific discourses. In entitlement, language acquires a kind of spirit from its social uses, and words about things inspirit these things with meaning. Thus, things become the signs of words (not the other way around). Throughout the biblical texts, specific details are abstracted until a few salient objects take on all of the various meanings throughout the discourses of the Torah, the Prophets, and the Writings. In the case of moral impurity and the discourses that describe it, those salient objects are the nation of Israel and the sanctuary. The demigod term that inspirits the nation and sanctuary of the Israelites with moral impurity is *sin*, and the term "sin" is an abstraction of biblical discourses about various actions that are abominations to God. The Torah describes numerous different sins that cause moral impurity: unjust treatment of other Israelites, sexual deviance, murder, polytheism, idolatry, swearing against God, apathy toward God, profaning a commandment, refusing to rebuke an Israelite sinner, and reneging on a vow made before God. Although the word "sin" appears throughout the Torah, its use is concentrated in the Priestly (P) literature, and especially in Leviticus and Numbers, which together contain about three-quarters of the Torah's uses of the word "sin," and many of those uses (about three-quarters) are part of the phrase "sin offering." In the communal language of the Torah, each individual sin becomes part of a larger abstraction, conceptual *sin*, now a demigod term.

On two occasions, the *Temple Scroll* refers to abstract sin (column XVIII, line 7 and column LVIII, line 17) with no further explanation. Elsewhere, two particular sins are mentioned in the *Temple Scroll*. The first, which also appears in Numbers (23:21), relates to fulfilling promises when a vow is made: "If you make a vow, do not delay in fulfilling it, because I shall certainly demand it from your hand and it shall become a sin to you" (column LIII, lines 11–12). It is important to note that the sin is not in the broken promise; it is in the unfulfilled vow before God, since a broken promise without a vow is not a sin: "But if you refrain and do not make a vow you shall not have a sin" (column LIII, line 12). The second particular sin mentioned in the *Temple Scroll* refers to bribery, which is not mentioned in the Torah as a source of moral impurity. The author of the *Temple Scroll* writes, "In all your cities you shall install judges and magistrates who judge the people with correct judgment, not show partiality in judgment, and accept no bribe, and not pervert justice, because a bribe perverts justice, corrupts the words of the just person, blinds the eyes of the wise, commits a serious offence and defiles the House with the wickedness of sin" (column LI, lines 11–15). The designation of bribery as a sin and a cause of moral impurity is unique to the Essenes and the Dead Sea Scrolls, which may indicate that bribery had become a serious problem for Israelites in the late Second Temple period. It is also further evidence that the Essenes held more stringent purity requirements than other sects. The abstract sin and particular sins of unfulfilled vows and bribery mentioned in the *Temple Scroll* entitle and inspirit the Israelite nation and the sanctuary with moral impurity. And this moral impurity must be erased through rituals requiring confession and sacrifice lest the Israelites incur the wrath of God in the end of days.

Ritual Erasure Through Purification

Once sins are committed, the demigod term that erases moral impurity from the nation and sanctuary is "atonement." The term "atonement" is an abstraction of various discourses about confession, sacrifice, and forgiveness. In order to erase moral impurity from the nation and the sanctuary, God provided the Israelites with a calendar of required festivals in which priests and Israelites confess their sins and perform various sacrifices and offerings for atonement. Unfortunately, an Israelite who commits a sin knowingly and willfully, but does not confess or repent, is not eligible for purification and risks the permanent materialization of moral impurity on the Israelites and their sanctuary. In this case, in order for priests and Israelites to atone for sin and thus purify the nation and sanctuary of willful transgression, the unrepentant sinner, a potential source of permanent moral impurity, must be exiled or executed, removed entirely from the community of God's covenant. However, even sins that are committed knowingly can be downgraded to "unintentional" status through repentance and confession prior to sacrificial atonement (Bautch 2012, 34; Falk 2007, 135; Milgrom 1976, 119). All sins committed unintentionally, unknowingly, or through ignorance (including intentional sins that have been downgraded to unintentional) are collectively eligible for ritual erasure through confession and sacrifice.

The *Temple Scroll* describes at least eleven different required festivals and sacrifices in the Israelite ritual calendar.[10] Although rhetorical purposes overlap among all the festivals and sacrifices, the *Temple Scroll*'s description of the Day of Atonement (Yom Kippur) is the most detailed, not just about the technical procedures of the ritual itself, but also about the material exigencies and rhetorical purposes of the ritual. While individual sins do contribute to abstract sin, the priests of the *Temple Scroll* seek to purify abstract sin, sin that materializes in the nation and sanctuary, rather than individual Israelites. The exigency for the rituals on the Day of Atonement is moral impurity, and the material-rhetorical purpose of the Day of Atonement is purification of the sanctuary and the nation of Israel. The biblical account of the Day of Atonement ritual is found in Leviticus 16, and it is recounted in the *Temple Scroll*, with some sectarian inflections.

Leviticus 16 details three specific sacrifices whose purposes are the purification of the sanctuary and the atonement of the nation of Israel. According to Leviticus 16, Aaron (or, later, the high priest) sacrifices a bull for his own purification and atonement and sprinkles the blood of the bull over the sanctuary in order to purify it from the pollution of his sins, thus preparing himself and the sanctuary for the next stage of the ritual. Once the blood of the bull has atoned for the high priest's sins and purified the sanctuary from his pollution, a second set of two sacrifices continues the process. Next, the high priest brings two goats and draws lots, choosing one for Yahweh and one for Azazel. He then sacrifices the goat designated for Yahweh and sprinkles its blood on the sanctuary, along with more blood from the bull sacrificed earlier, in order to purify the sanctuary from the pollution of Israelite sin (*generally*, not just the high priest's) and atone for "all their sins" (Leviticus 16:16; Abegg, Flint, and Ulrich 1999, 94). Once the sanctuary is purified of the moral impurity caused by the sin of the high priest and the Israelites, a final goat receives the guilt of sin for the nation, and it is sent into the wilderness to die by the wrath of God or at the hand of Azazel. Throughout all of these sacrifices associated with the Day of Atonement, David Volgger explains, the emphasis is not on any individual sin but rather on "the totality of offences" (2006, 258). Thus, the rhetorical purpose of the Day of Atonement is purification of both the sanctuary and the Israelite nation of moral impurity.

According to Jacqueline C. R. de Roo, in the Levitical context, the etymology of Azazel may refer to the "wrath of God." However, in the *Temple Scroll*'s gloss of the Levitical Day of Atonement, Azazel is spelled Asael, a clear reference to a demon mentioned in Enoch (Roo 2000, 238). Enoch describes Asael as suffering utter destruction on the day of judgment for inciting evil among the Israelites, which may indicate that the purpose of the scapegoat sacrifice is to return to Asael (a demon) the sin that is his own, isolating it for extermination in the end of days. Summarizing relevant passages in Enoch, Roo writes, "Azazel [or Asael] and his hosts will be consumed, destroyed by fire on the day of judgment. Ascribing the sins of the people to Azazel and punishing him and his followers for them on the day of judgment will get rid of iniquity and injustice and cleanse the land. So the destruction of the cause and symbol of evil, that is, Azazel, will destroy sin and its detrimental effects" (2000, 239). William K. Gilders agrees, writing, "The members of the Qumran sect viewed the Azazel of Lev 16 as a fallen angel, a demonic figure, who had been the leader of the Watchers, before his confinement [in the wilderness]. Sending the nation's sins out to him (as indicated by the *Temple Scroll*) returned them to their source, so to speak. This sending away of sin to the demonic realm prefigures the eschatological triumph over sin" (2012, 71).

The *Temple Scroll* provides an extended description of the exigencies and rituals associated with the Day of Atonement:

> The tenth of this month is the day of atonement. On it you shall afflict your souls, because anyone who does not do penance on this same day will be expelled from his people. On it you shall offer a holocaust for YHWH: a bullock, a ram, seven yearling lambs {. . . } and a he-goat for the sin-offering. Besides the sin-offering of the day of atonement and its offerings and libations according to the prescription for the bullock, the ram, the lambs, the he-goat, and the sin-offering of the day of atonement, you shall offer two rams for the holocaust. One the High Priest will offer for himself and for the house of his father. [. . .] The High Priest [will cast lots] [concerning the two he-goats:] one will fall by lot [to YHWH, the other

to Azazel,] [and] he will slaughter the he-goat which [has fallen by lot to YHWH and will take] its blood in the golden sprinkling bowl which he has in his hand and will treat [its blood as he treated the blood] of the bullock which was for himself, and with it he will atone for all the people of the assembly. Its fat and the offering of its libation he will burn on the altar of holocausts; but its flesh, its hide, and its entrails they shall burn together with his bullock. It is the sin-offering for the assembly and they shall be forgiven. He will wash his hands and his feet from the blood of the sin-offering and will go to the live he-goat and will confess over its head all the sins of the children of Israel with all their guilt together with all their sins; he shall place them upon the head of the he-goat and will send it to Azazel, to the desert, from the hand of man indicated. And the he-goat will take with itself all the sins. (column XXV, line 10 to column XXVI, line 13)

While the *Purification Rules* describe individual sources of ritual impurity, each with its own corresponding method of erasure, the *Temple Scroll*, on the other hand, describes abstract sin as the source of moral impurity, with the sin offerings on the Day of Atonement as the method of erasure. The only sense of individuality comes in the threat that those who do not do penance or afflict their souls will be exiled from the nation of Israel, since without this prior individual act, the sins of the nation will not be erased.

One Essene sectarian inflection present in the *Temple Scroll*'s description of the Day of Atonement, but absent in the Leviticus description, is the emphasis on forgiveness resulting from the day's rituals and sacrifices. Gilders explains that the *Temple Scroll*'s description of the Day of Atonement emphasizes "forgiveness as a result of atonement" (2012, 68); thus, "in this particular passage the Temple is not the major focus of concern. Rather, the focus is on the atonement of the people and the forgiveness of their sins" (68). Since the Essenes had rejected the Jerusalem Temple as impure, the *Temple Scroll*'s shift of emphasis from Temple purification to national (or at least that community's) forgiveness serves their sectarian interests.

Like the Torah, the *Temple Scroll* assumes that sin is endemic to the human condition, but also that sin is a violation of the covenants God made with the historical Israelites. Thus, at the end of the section of the *Temple*

Scroll on festivals and sacrifices, the author of the *Temple Scroll* relates all of these rituals back to the covenants. The *Temple Scroll* says:

> These are [. . .] for your holocausts and your libations [. . .]. In the house above which I shall make my name reside [they shall offer] the holocausts, [each day that corresponds to] that day according to the ruling of this precept, continually, from the children of Israel, besides their freewill offerings. All that they offer me, all their libations and all the presents which they bring me for acceptance, I shall accept them. They shall be for me a people and I will be for them forever and I shall establish them forever and always. I shall sanctify my temple with my glory, for I shall make my glory reside over it until the day of creation, when I shall create my temple, establishing it for myself for ever, in accordance with the covenant which I made with Jacob at Bethel. (column XXIX, lines 2–9)

The historical covenants were crucial to the Qumran Essenes, and these conditional promises had to be reestablished among the community of the new covenant because other Israelites had utterly violated them, ensuring God's wrath in the end of days. Eyal Regev notes, "Total triumph over evil and moral impurity would be won only on the eschatological day of judgment" (2004, 396). However, even the Essenes knew that sin is an endemic condition of human existence and that the only hope of salvation in the end of days was to purify material impurity through ritual erasure.

Ritual and moral purity are central conditions of the historical covenants, and they define Israelites as God's chosen people among all others who do not maintain purity and are thus not holy. Harrington writes, "According to the Torah, the combination of a proper moral and ritual status separates Israel from pagan nations and allows God's holiness to be active among his people (Lev 19:2, 20:20–24; Deut 23:13–15)" (2011, 329), and the Essene community's ever more stringent emphasis on purity corresponds to its increasingly apocalyptic worldview. According to Harrington, "Purity is necessary for holiness, and holiness fights wars" (2004, 39). But the Hasmonean expansion of Israel into pagan territories exposed Israelites to increasing ritual impurities, since converted pagans did not necessarily understand menstruation, seminal emissions, gonorrhea, and corpses as sources of defilement. Their participation in the Temple cult was a source of defilement (even if only indirect) for all other Israelites. And the Hasmonean high priests' willful sins (of wealth and fornication) exposed the nation of Israel and the Temple sanctuary to increasing moral impurities, since immoral high priests did not successfully atone for sins attributed to the collective nation. Their infelicitous administration of the Temple cult led all Israelites who followed them into a state of moral impurity. Thus, the Essenes used material rhetoric to establish new, more stringent procedures for purifying ritual and moral impurities.

Material rhetoric is a useful methodology for exploring the covenantal demand for ritual and moral purity and the Qumran community's procedures for purification because material rhetoric accounts for the communicative nature of physical bodies and the persuasive functions of material practices. Throughout the Dead Sea Scrolls, material practices, ritual procedures that take material form, are rhetorical, and the rhetorical effects they have are material. In fact, throughout the sectarian scrolls, the noun *tohorah* (purity) is used in both an abstract sense, the absence of impurity, and also a concrete sense, the ritually purified food and drink consumed during communal meals (Harrington 2004, 23). Successful and complete purification erases ritual and moral impurities and reinscribes (or reembodies) the material status of purity in flesh and sanctuary, making the purity texts in general vital to a complex understanding of the Dead Sea Scrolls. And Burke's theory of entitlement and Austin's speech act theory contribute to an understanding of the discursive embodiment and ritual erasure of impurity as crucial aspects of a material rhetoric that is relevant to the Dead Sea Scrolls.

While purity was a central concern among the Essenes around 100 BCE, events would take a turn for the worse after the Roman invasion of Judea in 63 BCE, turning the Essene community's attention from the possibility of purification to full-blown apocalypse. With the loss of access to genuine prophecy shortly after the return from Babylonian exile, the Essenes began to reinterpret biblical prophecies as relevant (again) in their own time. These reinterpretations are called *peshers*, and the subject of the next chapter is the Essenes' reinterpretation of the book of Habakkuk in the *Habakkuk Pesher* (1QpHab).

CHAPTER 5

HERMENEUTICS/RHETORIC IN THE BOOK OF HABAKKUK AND THE *HABAKKUK PESHER* (1QPHAB)

I began this book with a discussion of *Miqṣat Ma'aśeh ha-Torah* (4QMMT), which is one of the founding documents of the Essene community, composed around 150 BCE. I end this book with a discussion of the *Habakkuk Pesher* (1QpHab). The *Habakkuk Pesher* was probably composed between 63 and 31 BCE (Eshel 2008, 178), though the copy found in Cave 1 dates between 30 and 1 BCE (Lim 2002, 21). The rhetorical ecology of Judea in the final decades of the first century BCE was marked by Roman occupation and oppression, and the *Habakkuk Pesher* represents an advanced evolutionary stage in the Essenes' apocalyptic worldview under Roman control. With the divine annihilation of the material world surely just around the corner, the Essenes developed new rhetorics that would help them interpret older biblical prophesies for the end of days (which were long overdue by now). Interpretation is a common persuasive *topos* throughout the sectarian Dead Sea Scrolls. However, in the *Habakkuk Pesher*, interpretation is not just a persuasive *topos*; it represents the entire substance and structure of the text. The *Habakkuk Pesher* is a passage-by-passage commentary on the book of Habakkuk, now considered one of the canonical Minor

Prophets, and these interlinear interpretations represent the Essenes' understanding of the relationship between biblical prophecy and their own historical context. The *Habakkuk Pesher*, one of the first scrolls discovered in 1947, exemplifies a genre that was previously unknown to scholarship on Second Temple Judaism. Although other *pesher* scrolls were discovered in later searches of the caves near Qumran, the *Habakkuk Pesher* is the most materially complete and methodologically representative *pesher* found so far.[1]

Throughout this chapter, I examine the book of Habakkuk and the *Habakkuk Pesher* as specialized examples of hermeneutics/rhetoric, or rhetoric that employs interpretation as its central mode of persuasion.[2] In the book of Habakkuk, the prophet offers up a complaint to Yahweh based on his own prejudices, and he receives a divine oracle in response. Oracles received during the First Temple period were conveyed in divine signs and symbols that had to be interpreted by the prophets in human terms and then communicated as contextualized prophecies for different audiences, including kings, priests, and Israelites. These prophetic interpretations, as hermeneutics/rhetoric, relate Yahweh's abstract oracles to the concrete context of First Temple tradition, making the divine oracular messages meaningful and persuasive to the prophets and their human audiences. The prophetic interpretation of Yahweh's oracle is what Habakkuk (or later scribes) wrote down in his eponymous book, leaving the true character of the original oracle inaccessible to later audiences. Prophetic writing in this period was an inherently hermeneutic process representing a fusion of horizons (a fusion of prejudices and traditions, which I will explain shortly), and the book of Habakkuk is no exception.

While the prophetic interpretation in the book of Habakkuk represents a hermeneutic process, the revelatory reinterpretation of Habakkuk recorded in the *Habakkuk Pesher* represents a *double* hermeneutic process, or a process of interpreting interpretations. In the *Habakkuk Pesher*, the Essenes begin their double hermeneutic process with the original prophetic interpretation itself (that is, the text of Habakkuk). They then receive mysteries from Yahweh that reveal the meaning of Habakkuk's prophecy, not for the late First Temple period, but instead for the tradition of the late Second Temple period. By means of these mysteries, the Essenes atomistically replace Habakkuk's prejudices with their own, eventually arriving at a holistic and coherent meaning based on the narrative structure of the book of Habakkuk.

The mysteries received by the Essenes are not the same as the oracles that Habakkuk interpreted: they are new revelatory reinterpretations of prior prophetic interpretations of original oracles from Yahweh, which are lost forever. The Essenes understood these mysteries in human terms and then reinterpreted them as recontextualized *pesher* revelations for an audience of Essene community members in the end of days. These new prophetic reinterpretations, as hermeneutics/rhetoric, fuse the horizons of Habakkuk's late First Temple interpretation of Yahweh's oracle (event by event, person by person, passage by passage) to the new apocalyptic tradition of late Second Temple Judaism.

Before I proceed to a more detailed analysis of the book of Habakkuk and the *Habakkuk Pesher* as specialized examples of hermeneutics/rhetoric, I would like first to explore what exactly hermeneutics/rhetoric is, since there is little agreement in scholarship on the matter and since I use the term in a specialized way. Following a discussion of hermeneutics/rhetoric, I turn to the book of Habakkuk and the *Habakkuk Pesher*, examining each author's use of hermeneutics/rhetoric to understand and interpret oracular and mysterious discourse and convey its meaning to particular audiences. In each case, although the context of interpretation is different, the process of hermeneutics/rhetoric remains consistent: an articulation of each author's *prejudices*, a divine oracle or mystery that articulates the *traditions* within which their prejudices must be understood, and the interpretive *fusion of horizons* between the authors' respective prejudices and their contextual traditions. In the case of the *Habakkuk Pesher*'s double hermeneutic process (the Essenes's interpretation of Habakkuk's interpretation), the reinterpretation for a new tradition leaves Habakkuk's interpretation a relic of the past, giving new life to the original oracle through its reinterpretation by means of divine mysteries.

HERMENEUTICS/RHETORIC

Although the practice of interpretation is old (Aristotle and Augustine wrote about it), the art and science of hermeneutics, as we know it, is relatively new. Before the nineteenth century, the practice of interpretation was unsystematic, with methods varying from critic to critic and from context to context, including law, theology, and philology. During the early nineteenth century, Friedrich D. E. Schleiermacher transformed interpretation's early incoherence into a systematic theory and practice of understanding and interpretation called hermeneutics. Schleiermacher's romantic notion of hermeneutics as the recovery of an author's intentional meaning in texts would appeal to Wilhelm Dilthey, who applied Schleiermacher's hermeneutics to the newly emerging academic discipline of history. During the early twentieth century, Edmund Husserl and Martin Heidegger applied systematic hermeneutics to phenomenology and existentialism, and by midcentury Hans-Georg Gadamer had generalized the application of hermeneutics to philosophy broadly conceived. Later, Jürgen Habermas and Paul Ricoeur faulted philosophical hermeneutics for its foundation in hegemonic traditions, calling for a new critical hermeneutics that would (or at least could) challenge the status quo.[3]

Unlike hermeneutics, rhetoric is not new (it is old), and for millennia rhetoric had been getting along just fine without hermeneutics. When rhetoric needed another art to fill in some of its gaps, it always had its trusty counterpart, dialectic, close at hand. "Unfortunately," Michael Leff writes, "modern rhetorical critics, who have concentrated almost exclusively on the technical lore of classical rhetoric, have failed to appreciate the way interpretation and production interact in the full program of traditional rhetorical education" (1997, 200). The fact is, there are times when hermeneutics contributes important functions to the larger rhetorical enterprise, functions that dialectic cannot always fulfill. When rhetoricians appropriate hermeneutics, they usually view the pair of arts in one of three relations: either hermeneutics and rhetoric are counterpart arts (*hermeneutics and rhetoric*), or hermeneutics is an inventional tool situated within the art of rhetoric (*hermeneutical rhetoric*), or rhetoric justifies certain interpretive strategies and grounds them in historical trajectories (*rhetorical hermeneutics*). Later, I will explain a fourth relationship, *hermeneutics/rhetoric*, in which interpretation constitutes both the substance and structure of argument and persuasion. It is this fourth relationship, hermeneutics/rhetoric, that I see at work in the book of Habakkuk and the *Habakkuk Pesher*.

Hermeneutics and rhetoric are often framed as counterpart arts that occupy opposite sides of the same metaphorical coin: with hermeneutics, speakers and writers understand and interpret situations through analytical methodologies; with rhetoric, speakers and writers enter and alter situations through effective speech and writing. This view of the relationship between hermeneutics and rhetoric originates in the hermeneutic theories of Schleiermacher and Ricoeur. In "General Hermeneutics," Schleiermacher writes, "Hermeneutics and rhetoric are intimately related in that every act of understanding is the reverse side of an act of speaking, and one must grasp the thinking that underlies a given statement" (2006, 74). Like dialectic in the rhetorical tradition, according to Schleiermacher, hermeneutic understanding both precedes and presupposes rhetorical expression. And in "Rhetoric—Poetics—Hermeneutics," Ricoeur argues that hermeneutics and rhetoric "are irreducible to one another" so that "each discipline speaks for itself" (1997, 71). For Ricoeur, then, "hermeneutics remains the art of interpreting texts," and "rhetoric remains the art of arguing with a view to persuading an audience that one opinion is preferable to its rival" (71). Nevertheless, despite their obvious differences, it is not difficult to "locate the noticeable points of intersection" between the disciplines (71). For both Schleiermacher and Ricoeur, hermeneutics and rhetoric are fundamentally different, yet each remains useful to the other as a counterpart art.

There are also several more recent articulations of the same idea, that hermeneutics and rhetoric are distinct yet counterpart arts, by scholars based in rhetoric and communication studies. Richard E. Palmer, like Schleiermacher, argues for a "rhetoric informed by hermeneutics" (1997, 108 and passim), which "recognizes that listening and understanding go with, indeed should precede, every act of speaking well. If speaking is usually a response to something, there is no escape from the task of understanding" (127). Charles Altieri, like Ricoeur, views the function of hermeneutics as independent from the art of rhetoric, preferring to focus instead on the differences between hermeneutics and rhetoric (1997, 95–96), though recognizing their usefulness to each other. Calvin O. Schrag writes, "Surely there is a close connection between hermeneutics and rhetoric. Yet the one cannot be simply analyzed into the other. They overlap, they interconnect, they supplement each other; but one cannot be reduced to the other" (1997, 136). Finally, Michael J. Hyde and Craig R. Smith explain, "Meaning is derived by a human being in and through the interpretive understanding of reality. Rhetoric is the process of making-known that meaning" (1979, 348). For Hyde and Smith, then, "if the hermeneutical situation is the 'reservoir' of meaning, then *rhetoric is the selecting tool for making-known this meaning*" (354). In all of these cases, hermeneutics and rhetoric are separate but counterpart arts, similar in relation to the classical arts of dialectic and rhetoric.

In *hermeneutical rhetoric*, hermeneutics and rhetoric are not separate counterpart arts; instead, they are integrated and articulated, with hermeneutics serving a specialized function within rhetoric. In hermeneutical rhetoric, according to Leff, "interpretive processes become inventional resources in texts that purport to address extraverbal reality"; thus, "hermeneutical strategies enter into the production of political rhetoric" (1997, 198). For Leff, the rhetorical strategy, both classical and modern, that best illustrates the fusion of interpretation and persuasion in hermeneutical rhetoric is *imitatio*, or imitation. Leff explains that "*imitatio* is not the mere repetition or mechanistic reproduction of something found in an existing text. It is a complex process that allows historical texts to serve as equipment for future rhetorical production" (201). For example, Leff writes, "imitation of the structure and language of an old text may help introduce radically new ideas. Even more broadly, historical texts may serve as political and moral as well as artistic paradigms—paradigms that embed themselves deeply into the rhetorical performance and help constitute the persona of the rhetor" (203). Here "*imitatio* functions as a hermeneutical rhetoric that circulates influence between past and present. As the embodied utterances of the past are interpreted for current application, their ideas and modes of articulation are reembodied, and old voices are recovered for use in new circumstances" (203). According to Leff, hermeneutical rhetoric "focuses upon interpretation as a source of invention and suggests how traditions can be altered without destroying their identity. It offers a view of community as a locus of deliberating subjects who change themselves and one another by renewing and revaluing moments in their history" (203–4). In the case of hermeneutical rhetoric, then, hermeneutics functions as an inventional tool or *topos* for the development of political rhetoric.

Rhetorical hermeneutics also does not view hermeneutics and rhetoric as separate counterpart arts; instead, they are integrated and articulated, with rhetoric serving a specialized function within hermeneutics. Steven Mailloux offers rhetorical hermeneutics as a remedy to "Theory with a capital *T*" (1985, 627). Rhetorical hermeneutics, Mailloux explains, recognizes, first, that "validity in interpretation is guaranteed by establishing norms or principles for explicating texts" (1985, 621), and these norms and principles are established rhetorically. Rhetorical hermeneutics views interpretive strategies as "historical sets of topics, arguments, tropes, ideologies, and so forth, that determine how texts are established as meaningful through rhetorical exchanges. In this view, communities of interpreters neither discover nor create meaningful texts. Such communities are actually synonymous with the conditions in which acts of persuasion about texts take place" (1985, 629; also see 2006, 41). "Interpretive work," then, "always involves rhetorical action, attempts to convince others of the truth of explications and explanations" (1985, 630). Although rhetorical hermeneutics can shed light on any critical practice, it is most powerful when it does so in historical context. Mailloux writes, rhetorical hermeneutics "should also provide histories of how particular theoretical and critical discourses have evolved . . . [since] acts of persuasion always take place against an ever-changing background of shared and disputed assumptions, questions, assertions, and so forth. Any full analysis of interpretation must therefore describe this tradition of discursive practices in which acts of interpretive persuasion are embedded. Thus, rhetorical hermeneutics leads inevitably to rhetorical histories" (631). While hermeneutical rhetoric incorporates hermeneutics within the scope of rhetoric as a strategy for invention, rhetorical hermeneutics "incorporate[s] rhetoric at the level of literary theory and its analysis of critical practice" (637). Rhetorical hermeneutics, then, grounds interpretive practices within historical trajectories, and rhetoric is used to justify the use of some practices over others.

Hermeneutics/rhetoric, the fourth relationship between hermeneutics and rhetoric, has not yet been developed in scholarship, perhaps simply because there has been no particular exigency for it. Here both hermeneutics and rhetoric are understood as nouns, and they form a single compound noun when joined by a slash (rather than an adjective-noun hierarchy or two nouns linked by a conjunction). In hermeneutics/rhetoric, hermeneutics is the substance and structure of argument and persuasion. My articulation of hermeneutics/rhetoric derives in part from Gadamer's work on philosophical hermeneutics, where he discusses the roles of tradition and history in the processes of understanding, interpreting, and communicating. In *Philosophical Hermeneutics*, Gadamer writes, "The rhetorical and hermeneutical aspects of human linguisticality completely interpenetrate each other. There would be no speaker and no art of speaking if understanding and consent were not in question, were not underlying elements; there would be no hermeneutical task if there were no mutual understanding that has been disturbed and that those involved in a conversation must search for and find again together" (1976, 25). Here hermeneutics does not precede or complement rhetoric as a counterpart art, hermeneutics does not serve as a means for rhetorical invention, and hermeneutics is not a critical method that is justified by rhetoric. For Gadamer, hermeneutics and rhetoric, together, mediate cognition and communication, *both* critically and *both* productively.

Although Gadamer is not always as enlightened about rhetoric as rhetoricians would like him to be, I do believe that some of the key concepts he uses to articulate his theory of philosophical hermeneutics are extremely useful in the development of hermeneutics/rhetoric, even if Gadamer himself didn't recognize these ideas as *rhetorical* concepts.[4] These ideas include prejudices, traditions, and the fusion of horizons. For Gadamer, prejudices, traditions, and the fusion of horizons integrate into a simultaneous and cyclical hermeneutic process that challenges both objectivist positivism and subjectivist romanticism, resulting in social epistemologies and ontologies that are productive for the human sciences. Although I treat each idea (prejudices, traditions, and the fusion of horizons) separately here, Gadamer explains that their function in hermeneutics is dialectical. In other words, prejudices would have no meaning outside the context of traditions, and traditions would be oppressively deterministic without the constant pressure of prejudices. Further, the fusion of horizons prevents hermeneutic stagnation, forcing change and opening up the possibility for new meaning. In this dialectical process, horizons fuse, creating possibilities for complex meaning; traditions expand, accommodating new prejudices; and prejudices bond together, enabling interpretations to support the broadening scope of traditions. In the remaining pages of this section, I will explain *prejudices, traditions,* and the *fusion of horizons*, in turn, as a way of articulating hermeneutics/rhetoric in general, and I will apply them later both to the book of Habakkuk and to the *Habakkuk Pesher*.

In Gadamer's hermeneutic dialectic, since we are always more than just observers in the world, *prejudices* represent the stakes each person has in the process of experience. Prejudices are also, according to Jeffery L. Bineham, "grounded in language," so they are inevitably "social or communal in nature," not subjective or objective (1995, 7). Prejudices are the starting points of interpretation, the exigencies of hermeneutic inquiry and rhetoric. The ongoing hermeneutic process produces prejudices, presumptions that are present to us in our experience of the world and that help us initiate interpretations of new experiences and communication about them. But while prejudices are always productive of meaning, they do not always produce the best meaning. At least initially, Gadamer admits in *Truth and Method*, interpreters are not always "able to separate in advance the productive prejudices that make understanding possible from the prejudices that hinder understanding and lead to misunderstandings" (1975, 263). The process of hermeneutics, then, is not the elimination of prejudices in general, but the elimination of only those prejudices that cause misunderstanding.

For Gadamer, the encounter with tradition and its texts provides a kind of temporal distance that makes prejudices visible to the critical eye. Gadamer writes:

> It is only this temporal distance that can solve the really critical question of hermeneutics, namely of distinguishing the true prejudices, by which we understand, from the false ones by which we misunderstand. Hence the hermeneutically trained mind will also include historical consciousness. It will make conscious the prejudices governing our own understanding, so that the text, as another's meaning, can be isolated and valued on its own. The isolation of a prejudice clearly requires the suspension of its validity for us. For so long as our mind is influenced by a prejudice, we do not know and consider it as a judgment. How then are we able to isolate it? It is impossible to make ourselves aware of it while it is constantly operating unnoticed, but only when it is, so to speak, stimulated. The encounter with a text from the past can provide this stimulus. (1975, 266)

Here different prejudices encounter each other as *others*, opening up the possibility for critical distance and the qualitative judgments that become visible as a result of it. Thus, a prerequisite to ethical hermeneutics, and the rhetoric that emerges dialectically with it, is an openness to other prejudices and a corresponding willingness to expand our own prejudices and perceptions in light of other, stronger perspectives.

In Gadamer's hermeneutics, *tradition* is a collective force of historical values and interpretations that condition our experience of the world and our understanding of the present, and traditions are the historical products of rhetorical activity. Values and interpretations are established as tradition through hermeneutics/rhetoric, and hermeneutics/rhetoric employs tradition as a rhetorical context within which prejudices are ultimately understood as meaningful. Although tradition is the framework (or the medium) within which the hermeneutic processes of understanding and interpretation operate, Gadamer never defines tradition as *this* or *that* because it is always multivocal. Gadamer writes, "Our historical consciousness is always filled with a variety of voices in which the echo of the past is heard. It is present only in the multifariousness of such voices; this constitutes the nature of the tradition in which we want to share and have a part" (1975, 252–53). As history moves forward, elements of tradition acquire new meanings from encounters with new perspectives (both temporal and cultural), and all of these meanings and perspectives become a complex and multivoiced assemblage that can never be fully unified.

Tradition is made up from texts (the products of rhetorical activity) that speak to the present as clearly as they once spoke to the past, which challenges the subjectivist romantic notion that interpretation should reveal the creative genius of the individual author and the meaning received by the author's original audience. Gadamer writes, "Every age has to understand a transmitted text in its own way, for the text is part of the whole of the tradition in which the age takes an objective interest and in which it seeks to understand itself. The real meaning of a text, as it speaks to the interpreter, does not depend on the contingencies of the author and whom he originally wrote for. It certainly is not identical with them, for it is always partly determined also by the historical situation of the interpreter and hence by the totality of the objective course of history" (1975, 263). Gadamer continues, "Not occasionally only, but always, the meaning of a text goes beyond its author. That is why understanding is not merely a reproductive, but always a productive attitude as well" (264). Just as tradition is not an objective or subjective notion, according to Gadamer, neither is the present interpretation of tradition objective or subjective, based, as it is, on prejudices.

Gadamer's notion of hermeneutic understanding requires a *fusion of horizons*, the fluid intersection at which historical tradition meets the prejudices of immediate experience. It is in the dialectical workings of this fusion of horizons where the real work of hermeneutics/rhetoric is accomplished. Gadamer explains, "Understanding is not to be thought of so much as an action of one's subjectivity, but as the placing on oneself within a *process* of tradition, in which past and present are constantly fused" (1975, 258; emphasis added). A horizon, Gadamer explains, "is the range of vision that includes everything that can be seen from a particular vantage point.... A person who has no horizon is a [person] who does not see far enough and hence overvalues what is nearest to him. Contrariwise, to have an horizon means not to be limited to what is nearest, but to be able to see beyond it" (269). Since horizons, based on traditions and prejudices, are constantly engaged in a dialectical process of fusion, horizons are never closed. Gadamer writes, "The closed horizon that is supposed to enclose a culture is an abstraction. The historical movement of human life consists in the fact that it is never utterly bound to any one standpoint, and hence can never have a truly closed horizon. The horizon is, rather, something into which we move and that moves with us. Horizons change for a person who is moving. Thus the horizon of the past, out of which all human life lives and which exists in the form of tradition, is always in motion" (271). It is within the scope of this integrative motion that historical and modern horizons fuse into one, "a single horizon that embraces everything contained in historical consciousness. Our own past, and that other past towards which our historical consciousness is directed" (271). This fusion of horizons is a constant (not occasional) activity, the activity of understanding, interpretation, and rhetoric in the practice of everyday life, and the interpretive and rhetorical activities that result in and from the fusion of horizons, keep traditions alive.

One means to create a fusion of horizons is in the application of historical texts to present rhetorical situations, and this application is most powerful when the object representing the horizon of tradition is a *written* text. Gadamer writes, "The full hermeneutic significance of the fact that tradition is linguistic in nature is clearly revealed when the tradition is a written one. In writing, language is detached from its full realization. In the form of writing, all tradition is simultaneous with any present time" (1975, 351). And, later, Gadamer explains, "Everything that is set down in writing is to some extent foreign and strange.... The interpreter of what is written, like the interpreter of divine or human utterance, has the task of overcoming and removing the strangeness and making its assimilation possible" (487). Once they have become textualized, traditions then enter into what Gadamer and others call the hermeneutic circle in which prejudices, traditions, and fusions of horizons mediate understanding in ever-widening spheres and new contexts. Gadamer describes the hermeneutic circle not as a consciously applied methodology, but as a fundamental experience of understanding in context. For Gadamer, prejudices represent partial meanings centered in the present, traditions represent holistic beliefs deriving from the past, and the fusion of horizons mediates their cyclical interaction until prejudice and tradition, part and whole, present and past, all become harmonized through interpretation (258–67), through hermeneutics/rhetoric.

The fusion of horizons locates and emphasizes similarities between prejudices (present, partial) and traditions (past, holistic), enabling interpretation via hermeneutics/rhetoric to overcome the strangeness of new experiences and new texts. In order to illustrate the importance of textualization, application, and cyclical mediation, Gadamer hearkens back to the "forgotten history of hermeneutics," when "it was considered obvious that the task of hermeneutics was to adapt the meaning of a text to the concrete situation to which it was speaking. The interpreter of the divine will, who is able to interpret the language of the oracle, is the original model for this" (1975, 275). The interpretation of oracles, according to Gadamer, is the prototype of what I call hermeneutics/rhetoric, and, although Gadamer does not explain his comment on oracular interpretation any further, it will be the task of the next few sections of this chapter to do so, first in the context of the book of Habakkuk (complaint, oracle, interpretation, and redaction), and second in the context of the *Habakkuk Pesher* (prophecy, mysteries, revelation, and interpretation). In order to understand hermeneutics/rhetoric in the *Habakkuk Pesher*, we must first understand it in the book of Habakkuk.[5]

HERMENEUTICS/RHETORIC IN THE BOOK OF HABAKKUK

Hermeneutics/rhetoric in the book of Habakkuk is grounded in the cyclical process of complaint, oracle, interpretation, and redaction (see fig. 1), and this process occurs in the hermeneutic context of prejudices, traditions, and the fusion of horizons.[6] Interpretation is the substance and structure of the book of Habakkuk's rhetorical message, making it a paradigm case of hermeneutics/rhetoric. Habakkuk's own prejudices, or his situated perception of present rhetorical exigencies, result in his complaints to Yahweh regarding internal Judean injustice and external Chaldean oppression. Yahweh's oracles, communicated in response to Habakkuk's complaints, invoke the ancient tradition of the Mosaic covenant as the context within which Habakkuk's prejudices should derive meaning and significance. Habakkuk then interprets his complaints (or prejudices) in the context of Yahweh's

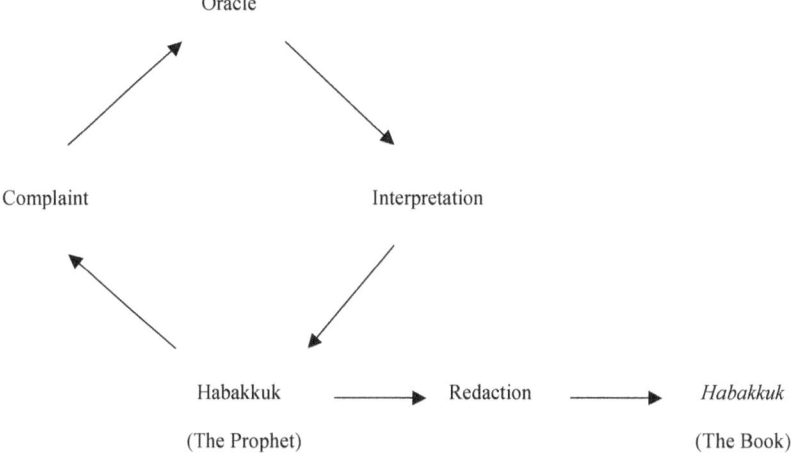

FIG. 1 | The hermeneutics/rhetoric process in the book of Habakkuk.

oracular invocation of covenantal tradition, resulting in a complex fusion of horizons. Scribes later (perhaps much later) redacted Habakkuk's hermeneutics/rhetoric, situating it within the larger tradition of biblical prophecy, resulting in an additional fusion of horizons that we now recognize as the book of Habakkuk.

Prejudices: Complaints and Oppressive Circumstances in the Book of Habakkuk

In terms of hermeneutics/rhetoric, Habakkuk's prejudices are the exigency for his complaint (*tôkaḥat*) regarding present circumstances that are perceived as unjust, and these prejudices are likely shared among his audience.[7] Since the circumstances of Habakkuk's complaints relate to internal strife and external oppression, the dates of Habakkuk's complaints may safely be placed during the reign of Jehoiakim (608–598 BCE), since the earlier reign of Josiah (639–609 BCE) would not have provoked such concern from a prophet.[8]

Internal Strife
Scholars generally agree that Habakkuk's first complaint (Habakkuk 1:2–4) regards internal strife within Judean society caused by Jehoiakim's late monarchic disregard of Josiah's prior reforms (Sweeney 1991; Thompson

1993, 34–35). In his first complaint, Habakkuk cites six causes of internal strife (violence, injustice, wrong, destruction, strife, and conflict), all of which are fully evident in the final decades before the exile. After the fall of Israel to Assyria in 722 BCE, Judah, under the reign of King Ahaz (735–715 BCE), became a vassal to Assyria in exchange for oppressive "protection" that lasted just over a century, committing Judah to a system of taxes and tributes that would financially devastate the monarchy and its people (Cogan 1998, 242). King Hezekiah (715–698 BCE) upheld this oppressive subservience to Assyria in exchange for continued tribute-insured military protection in part because the relationship did not require the monarchs or citizens of Judah to worship Assyrian gods or defile the Temple (255). However, Hezekiah's successor, King Menasseh (698–642 BCE), became deeply invested in Assyrian religion, far more than was required by the historical vassal relationship. In fact, as Kamm points out, Menasseh "shock[ed] conservative Yahwists with the intensity of his active encouragement of, as well as participation in, pagan cults, including the sacrifice of his own children, necromancy, and other mediumistic measures" (1999, 101). Free to worship Yahweh in his own way, and not required to worship Ashur in any way, Menasseh, nevertheless, actively pursued idolatry, polytheism, ritual prostitution, divination, magic, and human sacrifice, all in direct and willful violation of the Mosaic covenant that required obedience to the law. He also decentralized the worship of Yahweh to localized shrines throughout Judah, decreasing consistency and oversight in ritual practices (Bright 2000, 312). Following Menasseh's death, his son Amon (642–639 BCE) ruled Judah for two years but was assassinated during a revolt, after which Menasseh's younger son Josiah (639–609 BCE) was declared king at only eight years of age (Bright 2000, 316; Cogan 1998, 256).

As he grew into his reign during his early teen years, Josiah became weary of Judah's subservience to Assyria, and Assyria had weakened so much in the region that Josiah ended his tribute obligation and began to annex land in Samaria, Megiddo, and Gilead (Bright 2000, 317). As a consequence of Josiah's newfound political independence, he also sought to free the worship of Yahweh from Assyrian and other pagan influences (318). During his eighteenth year, Josiah thus began to institute a series of nationalistic and religious reforms, including renovating and purifying the neglected Temple and recommitting the people of Judah to strict adherence to the law and its required monotheistic worship of Yahweh. During his renovation of the

Jerusalem Temple, workers discovered a lost "book of the law" (probably a portion of the book of Deuteronomy) that guided some of Josiah's reforms and encouraged (and legitimated) a focused recommitment to the Mosaic covenant (Cogan 1998, 260). These and other reforms, including centralizing the worship of Yahweh in the Jerusalem Temple itself, were met with popular respect. This was a time of redemption for the kingdom of Judah, which had fallen into idolatry and injustice under Menasseh.

During the last quarter of the seventh century, Assyria's power in the region faded, largely because of the rise of Babylon in alliance with Chaldea. Although the Assyrians had invaded Egypt earlier in the century, the Egyptians viewed Assyrian rule in the region of Judah as preferable to rule by the much stronger and now more ambitious Babylonians. During the final decades of Josiah's reign, the Egyptian pharaoh Psammetichus marched north through Judah, allowing Josiah to reign unimpeded. With the death of Psammetichus in 610 BCE, however, his successor, Pharaoh Neco II, took over Egyptian advances into formerly Assyrian territories, killing Josiah in battle near Megiddo in 609 BCE. According to the usual rules of succession, Josiah's oldest son, Eliakim, should have become the next king of Judah; however, the Judean people viewed Eliakim as unreliable, so they passed him over for his younger stepbrother, Jehoahaz. Jehoahaz was committed to his father's anti-Assyrian and anti-Egyptian foreign policies, which did not sit well with Pharaoh Neco II, who summoned Jehoahaz to a meeting in Riblah. According to Kamm, Neco II "deposed Jehoahaz, who had presumably refused to submit to Neco's authority, and sent him as a prisoner to Egypt, appointing Eliakim (now to be named Jehoiakim) king of Judah in his place" (1999, 102). Jehoiakim (608–598 BCE) was now king of Judah, a vassal of Egypt, and he began to reverse many of Josiah's reforms, returning to ambivalence toward pagan worship, allowing impure sacral practices in the Jerusalem Temple, and taking the Mosaic covenant for granted, regardless of Judean misbehavior in relation to the law. Jehoiakim was, according to Bright, "a petty tyrant unfit to rule" (2000, 325; see also Holladay 2001, 127), and Josephus writes that Jehoiakim "was of a wicked disposition, and ready to do mischief, nor was he either religious toward God, or good-natured towards men" (1987, 271).

Two of Jehoiakim's activities in particular were affronts to Josiah's social and religious reforms. First, Jehoiakim was required to pay massive tribute to Egypt in order to prevent total conquest, so he instituted an unjust land tax on Judeans in order to fund his ill-advised alliance, forcing many of his people into poverty (Kamm 1999, 102). As Kevin G. O'Connell suggests, "Unjust government and heavy taxes encourage all members of the community to oppress and rob one another" (1979, 228). Second, Jehoiakim enslaved his own Judean citizens, forcing them to build a luxurious palace for him (Bright 2000, 325; Kamm 1999, 102). Despite the prophet Jeremiah's appeal to return to the "covenant demands for justice and righteousness in public life" (Cogan 1998, 262), Jehoiakim continued his evil ways. In general, Bright writes, "pagan practices crept back and public morality deteriorated," and prophets and priests who rebuked Jehoiakim and his immoral acts were confronted with "harassment and persecution, and in some cases death" (2000, 326). These circumstances, all occurring under Jehoiakim's reign, are the objects of Habakkuk's first complaint, in which he lists six social conditions that cause internal Judean dysfunction (violence, injustice, wrong, destruction, strife, and conflict), paralyzing the law, perverting and preventing justice, and inhibiting righteousness.

External Oppression
Scholars generally agree that Habakkuk's second complaint (Habakkuk 1:12–17) regards external oppression by the Chaldeans, whose militant attacks were exacerbating the internal strife referenced in the first complaint (Sweeney 1991; Thompson 1993). Having established that internal strife is rampant in Judea, Habakkuk turns his complaint to the Chaldeans and their role in the collapse of Judean society.[9]

By 605 BCE, Nebuchadnezzar II had forced Neco and the Egyptians out of Assyria and Judah, and Jehoiakim arranged a new alliance with the successful Babylonians. However, one year later, the Egyptians defeated the Babylonians in Carchemish, and Jehoiakim withheld his tribute to Babylon and realigned with Egypt, unsure of where power in the region would lie. Egypt moved its border north into the Sinai Peninsula, but it offered no assistance to Jehoiakim against the refreshed Babylonian armies. Without resistance from Egypt, however, Nebuchadnezzar felt no need to destroy Judah immediately, so the Babylonians simply kept Judah weak by "sending contingents of Babylonian, Aramaean, Moabite, and Ammonite commandos" to abuse the Judeans and weaken their will to resist (Kamm 1999, 103–4). Bright agrees, explaining that during the time when Nebuchadnezzar was preparing his armies for a battle in Judah, he "dispatched against her such

Babylonian contingents as were available in the area, together with guerilla bands of Arameans, Moabites, and Ammonites, to harry the land and keep it off balance" (2000, 327). This process of orchestrated harassment lasted for eight years, until Jehoiakim died. According to Marvin A. Sweeney, "The intent and setting [of Habakkuk's second complaint] center around an attempt to explain the rise of the oppressive Neo-Babylonian empire in the late-7th century B.C.E. as an act of YHWH which does not contradict divine righteousness and fidelity to Judah" (1993, 81). Although Habakkuk was a prophet, he was also a human, and his experience of present circumstances generated prejudices that he was unable to interpret without divine guidance. Thus, the unjust experiences of his time were the exigency leading him to request oracles from Yahweh explaining the greater meaning behind his experiences.

Traditions: Oracles and the Mosaic Covenant in the Book of Habakkuk

Habakkuk was weary of the internal strife and external oppression he witnessed and experienced under Jehoiakim's reign in Judah, so he requested oracles (*maśśā'*) from Yahweh to explain their meaning and purpose. According to O. Palmer Robertson, Habakkuk "will not attempt to reconcile in his own mind the apparent contradiction between the election of Israel by God as the object of his special love and the devastation of Israel at the hands of the rapacious Chaldeans as ordered by the Lord himself. He will not resort to the resources of human wisdom. Instead, he will watch for an answer that can come only from the Lord. Habakkuk knows that, in accordance with the nature of the prophetic office in Israel, revelation from God alone can answer his perplexity" (1983, 53). Although the actual language of Yahweh's oracles to Habakkuk has probably been lost in the process of prophetic interpretation and editorial redaction, we can assume that the kernel messages in Habakkuk's accounts of Yahweh's oracles at least resemble the content of the original divine messages. Yahweh's oracles place Habakkuk's complaints (prejudices) within the *tradition* of the Mosaic covenant.

Oracles
The book of Habakkuk begins by declaring the generic form of prophecy Habakkuk received or saw: oracle. Thus, in order to understand the book of Habakkuk, we also have to understand the nature of ancient oracles,

especially Judean oracles. Oracles are short, abstract, oral statements from a god (such as Yahweh) to a prophet (such as Habakkuk), packed with meaning and power. According to Robert R. Wilson, "The word *maśśā'* designated a specialized oracle that was peculiar to Judah.... *Maśśā'* [oracle] is a nominal form of the verb *naśā'*, 'to lift up,' 'to bear,' 'to carry.' In a number of contexts *maśśā'* clearly means 'burden,' and for this reason it has been argued that the term was secondarily applied to prophetic oracle because it was both a 'burden' laid on the prophet and a 'burden' laid by the prophet on the people. Alternatively, *maśśā'* is said to refer to an oracle that the prophet 'lifts up' or 'calls out'" (1980, 258). Later, Wilson concludes, "the term *maśśā'* may have been used to designate some sort of characteristically Judean oracle" (262). Oracles were a common form of prophetic communication throughout the ancient Levant; however, Judean oracles in particular imply that such communication from Yahweh was considered a burden, probably because of the connection of Judean oracles to the strict legal requirements of the Mosaic covenant, which I will explain shortly.

Oracles are usually short and abstract. Sigmund Mowinckel explains that oracles are originary prophetic utterances: "The relatively brief—complete and circumscribed, independent, separate—saying (the oracle) is the original and genuine form of prophetic speech and message" (2002, 53). Since oracles are short, abstract messages from deities, they are thus neither immediately comprehensible by humans nor directly applicable to human situations. In other words, they require interpretation.[10]

Only a few statements in each of Yahweh's responses to Habakkuk's complaints qualify as oracles. Since oracles are short and abstract, the extended passages Habakkuk presents as oracles are probably not pure oracular statements but are oracles interpreted by the prophet. In order to identify oracular messages amid Habakkuk's situational interpretations, we must seek short statements that articulate abstract truths. There are two such oracular statements. In response to Habakkuk's first complaint (prejudice) about internal strife in Judean society and leadership, Yahweh replies with the following oracle: "Look [at] the nations, and [obser]ve, and be amazed! W[ond]er! For I am wor[king] a work [in] your [day]s [which you will] n[ot believe though you] were [told]" (Habakkuk 1:5; Abegg, Flint, and Ulrich 1999, 459). This first oracle is unusual in its negativity. According to Walter E. Rast, "Usually an oracle in response to a lament was one containing a promise of deliverance, the so-called priestly oracle of salvation. In this first oracle the divine response is just the opposite" (1983, 171).

Yahweh's oracular response to Habakkuk's second complaint is equally abstract yet more uplifting in its outlook: "Beh[old] the proud one, his soul is not right [within him; but the rig]hteous shall liv[e] by his faith" (Habakkuk 2:4; Abegg, Flint, and Ulrich 1999, 460).[11] O'Connell explains, "It is probably best to take the [second] oracle as a general statement, intended to encourage the worshipers or auditors with the assurance that righteousness will finally prevail. In terms of Habakkuk's complaint, the implication would be that the haughty and sinful Babylonian [or Chaldean] will not ultimately enjoy the success of the righteous" (1979, 230), a blessing reserved only for those faithful to the covenant. Both of these oracles given by Yahweh in response to Habakkuk's complaints are short and abstract; however, together they clearly connect Habakkuk's prejudices (internal injustice and external oppression) with Judah's covenantal tradition.

The Mosaic Covenant
According to Kamm, "Arguably the most influential event in the history of the Israelites occurred about three months into the journey" known as the exodus (1999, 19), in which Yahweh lays the groundwork of the Mosaic covenant. A covenant is a mutual and conditional promise. In the Mosaic covenant, the Israelites promise to obey Yahweh's laws in exchange for favored status among nations, and these laws were first inscribed on stone tablets in Sinai, and inscribed again during annual covenant renewal ceremonies. The specifics of the Mosaic covenant's conditionality are described in Deuteronomy 28, where Yahweh (via Moses) describes blessings for obedience and curses for disobedience.[12] The ultimate punishment for Israelite iniquity in violation of the Mosaic covenant is conquest (Deuteronomy 28:49–50). Throughout ancient covenant theology, Yahweh uses "the nations" as a force of punishment for the Israelites' disobedience to the law and disregard for the covenant, though these nations are not intended to thrive for long, their own iniquities causing their eventual downfall. Only the righteous among Judahites will survive the curse of conquest as a remnant due to their faith amid infidelity.

Having witnessed the Assyrian destruction of the northern tribes of Israel in 722 BCE, preexilic Judean prophets understood their mission as realigning Judean religious practices with the requirements of the biblical covenants, the constant violation of which may have caused, in their minds, the fall of the Northern Kingdom. When the prophets reassured their people, it was always in the context of their covenantal selection as Yahweh's chosen people, and when the prophets criticized their people, it was always in the context of their iniquities and infidelities in relation to their covenants with Yahweh. Ronald E. Clements writes, "It is to this tradition of a covenantal code of conduct that the great prophets of the eighth and seventh centuries appealed when they accused their nation of disloyalty to Yahweh" (1965, 23). The preexilic prophets, according to Clements, achieved "the awakening of a deeper awareness of what the covenant meant, so that, with the experience of defeat and exile, there might arise a new community, penitent of its past sins, and eager to receive the fulfillment of the gracious promises of a restored covenant" (26). In this respect, as we will see, Habakkuk is no different from any other biblical prophet.

The language of the Deuteronomic covenantal curses bears a striking resemblance to the language of Habakkuk's complaints, since both Deuteronomy and the book of Habakkuk invoke violence, injustice, wickedness, and destruction as retribution for iniquities. This is no surprise since preexilic prophets were deeply concerned with upholding the Mosaic covenant, a concern that would have been inherited by Habakkuk as a guiding tradition from his eighth-century predecessors.[13] In fact, Yahweh's injunction for Habakkuk to "write the vision, and make it plain [on tablet]s" (Habakkuk 2:2; Abegg, Flint, and Ulrich 1999, 460) is, according to Robertson, a direct correlation to the inscription "of the original 'ten words' of the book of the covenant" (1983, 55) given to Moses on Mount Sinai. Although Yahweh's oracles are short and abstract, Habakkuk interprets the oracles in the context of Judahite covenantal tradition, since Deuteronomy obviously would have been very familiar to Habakkuk (Johnson 1985, 262–63). Thus, Yahweh's oracles, invoking "the nations" as punishment for iniquity, and righteous fidelity as a means to redemption, would have moved Habakkuk to understand his prejudices in a specifically covenantal context.

Fusion of Horizons: Prophetic Interpretation and Canonical Redaction in the Book of Habakkuk

There are two ways to understand Habakkuk's interpretations of Yahweh's oracles as hermeneutics/rhetoric: as an immediate application of Yahweh's short and abstract oracles to present concrete circumstances in an intentional act of prophetic interpretation (*pathar*), or as a later editorial (or scribal) redaction, interpreting circumstances that followed the oracles but were not yet present at the time, applying scribal tradition in persuasive interpretation.

Prophetic Interpretation
Having complained to Yahweh based on his own prejudices, and having received short and abstract oracles from Yahweh contextualizing Habakkuk's prejudices within the covenantal tradition, it remains for Habakkuk to interpret the intersections among his prejudices and Yahweh's oracles, resulting in an interpretive fusion of horizons. Habakkuk receives Yahweh's oracles as visions that require interpretive application. As Martti Nissinen explains, "A prophecy means nothing unless it is understood, interpreted, and applied in a specific socio-religious and linguistic environment, whereby interpretation is not a matter of perverting the original words but making the message significant" (2004, 29). As Sweeney points out, in addition to receiving and repeating Yahweh's oracles, "it is the role of the prophet to explain the meaning of YHWH's statement" (1991, 72; see also Clements 1996, 225), and this interpretive explanation was enabled by writing. Hans Walter Wolff explains that the work of the classical prophets (one of whom was Habakkuk) was "purely and simply *collections of sayings*," and that narrative elements were added in the writing process with "the sole function of making individual sayings understandable" (1978, 18). Clements adds, however, that dire historical circumstances would also have been a powerful exigency for recording prophecies in writing: "It was the impact of Assyrian and Babylonian imperial expansion upon Israel, with Israel's consequent loss of national freedom and national identity, which provided the primary stimulus for preserving prophecies dealing with these events" (1996, 203). Yet the very act of preserving these prophecies in writing was also an act of interpretation.

Although Habakkuk's first complaint is about internal Judean injustice, Habakkuk's first interpretation understands Yahweh's "Look at the nations" oracle as an indication of future punishments for present iniquities. Habakkuk interprets Yahweh's oracle by continuing the prophecy in Yahweh's voice, but applying Yahweh's short, abstract, divine oracle to human contexts that would be recognized by Habakkuk's audience. This adaptation is achieved by converting Yahweh's abstract oracle into metaphors that Habakkuk's audience would recognize. Ancient Hebrew prophecy begins, in a sense, where argumentative discourse fails, where communities neglect to adhere to the way of life described in the Torah and the Temple liturgies. Margaret D. Zulick explains that Hebrew prophecy recognizes that "argument alone neither moves nor convinces" (1998, 483), but metaphors lend an emotive effect to prophetic arguments, increasing their potential to persuade, to change minds and incite action. As Galen L. Goldsmith explains, "Ancient Israelite rhetoric," or what I call hermeneutics/rhetoric, "drew metaphors of which most people had first-hand experience to create sayings that would be easily understood by non-literate listeners on the first proclamation" (2011, 18).[14] And Benjamin L. Merkle explains, "The Old Testament prophets used metaphorical language to describe truths that otherwise would not have been intelligible to their audience" (2010, 22–23).

During the late seventh century BCE, the nation in the Fertile Crescent that warranted utter amazement was Chaldea. The Chaldeans were self-centered, not Yahweh-centered, and they established their own personal laws, ignoring those derived from external (divine) sources. In order to make Yahweh's short and abstract oracle meaningful, Habakkuk employs metaphors to secure concrete understanding: horses faster than leopards and fiercer than wolves during peak hunting activity. They devour other nations like vultures devour carrion. They are silent like the wind and accumulate innumerable prisoners, like grains of sand. Thus, through metaphors, Goldsmith explains, "the inconceivable is told with chilling clarity" (2011, 11). When Yahweh says, "Look [at] the nations, and [obser]ve, and be amazed" (Habakkuk 1:5; Abegg, Flint, and Ulrich 1999, 459), the Judeans of Habakkuk's generation would naturally turn east toward Chaldea and anticipate divine punishment for present iniquities, and the metaphorical embellishment of Yahweh's abstract oracle, a function of written interpretation, would have enhanced the rhetorical effect of the prophecy.

The second oracle Yahweh gives (Habakkuk 2:4) in response to Habakkuk's second complaint is interpreted by Habakkuk in 2:5–20. Immediately following Yahweh's abstract oracle that the wicked man is "puffed up" but "the righteous man is rewarded with life for his fidelity," Habakkuk relates this abstract message to his own human context, including drunkenness, arrogance, and greed among the nations. However, although the treacherous and arrogant man goes unpunished for now, he will not for long. The constant rise and fall (and rise and fall) of nations, such as Egypt and Assyria, attest to the likelihood that surviving nations will plunder the oppressor, all in time. The false idols of conquering nations give false confidence in dumb wood, and their worship of idols will ensure their demise.

Editorial Redaction

Like all oracles and prophecies in the Judean tradition, Habakkuk's were likely oral in origin and written down only later, when their meaning became of interest to new audiences in new circumstances. In addition, as the Bible was undergoing a process of canonization, all of the prophetic books were revised to reflect the new constraints of a coherent collection of related works. Clements argues that biblical redactors, concerned with canonical coherence, wrote new material into the oral prophecies that removed them from their situated specificity and connected them to other prophecies through related themes (1996, 211). Philip Whitehead calls this process decontextualization, which "certainly permits, and perhaps even invites, later readers to relate situations contemporary with themselves to the text, as the Qumran community did in 1QpHab" (2016, 267).

Not only did certain themes emerge across prophetic texts in the process of editorial redaction, but, Clements explains, so did certain structures. In other words, written prophecy enabled "the formation of paradigms, or patterns, so that prophecy relating to one set of historical circumstances came to be adapted to apply to others" (1996, 176). Thus, books like Habakkuk, whose prophecies were surely fulfilled with the Babylonian exile, continue (well after the exile) to have prophetic relevance by virtue of their redaction as canonical books in an emerging Hebrew Bible. Further, the redactors of works that would become the Hebrew Bible must have focused their energies on books that spoke to them as an audience as well. Zulick writes, "Prophetic texts must not only be seen to conform to one another and to history as a harmonious record of God's dealings with Israel, but they must also continue to speak prophetically to readers who are also compositors, charged with bringing these accounts together into a unified narrative" (2003, 201). And Mark E. Biddle explains, "A purely historical reading fails to credit 'already-fulfilled' prophecy with any ongoing canonical authority" (2007, 154). In fact, Biddle continues,

> the "canonical impetus" that produced the prophetic corpus required the curators of this corpus to shape it such that it would function as more than a mere historical record of prophetic activity. In order to serve authoritatively beyond the historical moment,

> it must include varieties of positions on certain questions; it must permit and even exemplify the transposition of literally fixed material onto new situations; it must transform situation-bound prophetic oracles into open-ended sayings applicable to changing and unforeseen historical contingencies; and it must reflect a sophisticated theory of prophecy and fulfillment that anticipates the varying needs of changing times. These editorial principles, in turn, define for subsequent interpreters a hermeneutical approach to the corpus they produced. (155)

Thus, interpretive readings of prophetic writings, such as the *Habakkuk Pesher*, emerge from nonhistorical or transhistorical readings of written texts, which recognize the continuing relevance of all biblical prophecies, even those that have already been fulfilled by recognizable historical circumstances.

All of this revision constitutes a fusion of horizons in which the prophets' original prejudices and traditions are worked and reworked into new traditions, some more remote from the original circumstances than others. Mowinckel writes, "Between the origin of the saying and its recording in the book, there is a long period of traditions, history of tradition, and development of tradition.... We can see how tradition—consciously and unconsciously—has arranged the sayings in groups. Sayings have come to form tradition complexes because they share the same catchword, have similar content, have the same addressee, or are from the same period in the prophet's work. These tradition complexes have also been arranged according to different principles" (2002, 44). Whereas each prophecy was intended to apply to a particular situation, the redaction of prophetic books as a collection of related texts enabled intertextual correlations and future applications that would not have been possible in each prophecy's original iteration.[15] Part of this process of revision and redaction includes placing Habakkuk's localized prejudices into the larger context of a biblical prophetic tradition.

HERMENEUTICS/RHETORIC IN THE *HABAKKUK PESHER*

While the book of Habakkuk represents the cyclical process of hermeneutics/rhetoric, the *Habakkuk Pesher* represents a double cyclical process that

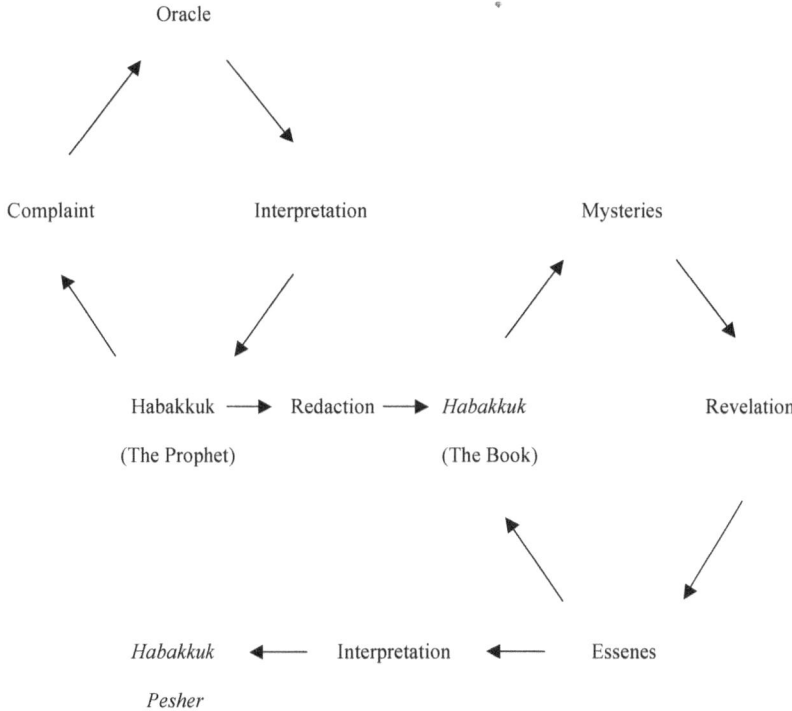

FIG. 2 | From prophecy to pesher: the (double) hermeneutic process in the *Habakkuk Pesher*.

begins its interpretive journey where the book of Habakkuk left off (see fig. 2). In other words, the hermeneutic substance and structure of the *Habakkuk Pesher* is a reinterpretation of the prejudices, traditions, and fusions of horizons in the book of Habakkuk based on a new cyclical process of updated prejudices (written prophecy and apocalyptic circumstances), traditions (mysteries and a new covenant), and the fusions of horizons (pesher method). This double hermeneutic reinterpretation, known as pesher, substitutes the book of Habakkuk's historically obsolete hermeneutics/rhetoric with a new hermeneutics/rhetoric that accounts for late Second Temple prejudices, traditions, and fusions of horizons. Since the book of Habakkuk was delivered and perhaps written near the end of the seventh century BCE, and the *Habakkuk Pesher* was written near the end of the first century BCE (Fabry 2003, 252), about six hundred years of historical activity passed between these interpretations. However, since the preexilic period of genuine prophecy had ended, and since the Essenes had essentially the same complaints as Habakkuk (internal injustice and external oppression), there was no reason for the Essenes to seek a new oracle from Yahweh. The oracle had already been given and then canonized for the general circumstances of injustice and oppression. Yahweh's revelation of divine mysteries, however, enabled the Essenes to reinterpret Habakkuk's prejudices, traditions, and fusions of horizons for a new relevance to the apocalyptic ideology of the Qumran community in the late Second Temple period. Since the original oracles were no longer accessible, having been forever effaced by Habakkuk's interpretation and later editorial redaction, the Essenes relied on the revelation of divine mysteries to reinterpret Habakkuk's interpretation for a new tradition, the apocalyptic end of days, expecting that the pesher method would reapply universal oracular truths to a new historical context.

Prejudices: Written Prophecy and Apocalyptic Circumstances in the *Habakkuk Pesher*

In terms of hermeneutics/rhetoric, the Essenes developed prejudices that were unique to their own time and place and were thus different from the exigent prejudices experienced by Habakkuk. Nevertheless, while Habakkuk's prejudices were historically situated, the divine oracles received and interpreted by Habakkuk were universal, applicable for all time and in any situation. Unfortunately, the Essenes only had access to Habakkuk's situated interpretation of those original oracles, not the oracles themselves. Thus, these original oracles could only be revealed by the Essenes through a double process of interpretation, or a late Second Temple, Qumran interpretation of Habakkuk's First Temple interpretation of Yahweh's oracle. This double hermeneutic process, unique to Qumran at the time, was called pesher. Pesher interpretation was enabled by the Second Temple written canonization of First Temple oral prophecies, like Habakkuk's, since all sectarians read the same text (instead of hearing it in situ) and assign meaning ideologically. The prejudices of the Essenes emerged in their experience of events that signaled the impending apocalyptic end of days, a context Habakkuk did not know; however, the oracles Habakkuk heard and reported were clearly relevant, since they were universal.

Written Prophecy
Scholars generally agree that true prophecy in ancient Israel ended shortly after the return from exile in Babylon, and Josephus suggests, more

specifically, that prophecy ends with Ezra. For John Barton (1986), prophecy, as the inspired reception of oracles from Yahweh, belonged to a time that long preceded the late Second Temple period, in which the *Habakkuk Pesher* was composed. Yet this shift (from oracular prophecy to none) was not gradual or transitional. Barton argues that there was a sharp break between the oracular prophecy of the biblical period and interpretive prophecy, which began soon after oracular prophecy faded into the past. Barton writes, "There is not a smooth development from classical prophecy to its interpretation by such groups as the Qumran community or the early Church; rather, there is a sharp break, a dislocation, which seems to coincide with the point at which prophetic utterances cease to be the spring from which a living and continuous tradition flows and become instead a closed container in which the unalterable words of the prophet are preserved. All the indications seem to be that this point should be located some time early in the post-exilic age: in what we may call, with deliberate vagueness, 'the age of Ezra'" (1986, 270), and this end of classical prophecy "is marked by the coming into existence of a fixed corpus of prophetic scriptures" (270).

The end of classical prophecy did not signify the end of prophecy altogether. Thomas W. Overholt explains that in the Hebrew Bible, "one type of prophecy ('classical') has been transformed, sometimes in ways which (by the standard of pre-exilic forms) look somewhat strange. But this does not necessarily require us to believe that the phenomenon of prophecy itself came to an end" (1988, 108). Overholt continues, "Though *we* tend to understand certain texts from the Hebrew Bible to say that prophecy had ceased, the Essenes, Christians, and Rabbis obviously did not read them that way" (108). In fact, Jonathan Stökl confirms, "scriptural interpretation at Qumran was understood as prophetic activity" (2015, 287). Thus, the demise of *oracular* prophecy did not cause prophetic inspiration to disappear, though it did alter the nature of prophetic activity in the Second Temple period. Prophecy changed, according to Biddle, from the reception of oracles and their interpretation in writing to the textual interpretation of written prophecy and its application in new contexts (2007, 154–55).

This shift in the character of prophecy may also account for the emergence of sects: older First Temple (preexilic) prophets received oracular communication straight from God and interpreted these divine words in order to clarify them, which resulted in a canonized body of ideas; later Second Temple (postexilic) prophets interpreted written, canonical prophecies, eventually generating ideologies that resulted in identifiable types of interpretation that could be attributed to certain groups and not others. Barton explains that "in Qumran it was the accepted teachings of the community which determined the meaning that was found in Scripture" (1986, 186). Without direct access to new divine oracles, Second Temple prophetic activity took a distinctly interpretive turn, working with the oracles that had already been written and canonized in the books of the biblical prophets. Written prophecies, redacted for canonization, contained oracles that could be reinterpreted in the context of new circumstances, even if these oracles were concealed in the literary language that accompanied their earlier composition and redaction processes. Among the Dead Sea Scrolls, the *Habakkuk Pesher* illustrates that the reinterpretation of biblical prophecies was viewed as a form of prophecy itself, revealing new applications of divine oracles to apocalyptic circumstances not experienced by the original prophets themselves.

The written status of biblical prophecy transformed oral and historically situated oracles into literary works whose admonitions and projections were susceptible to multiple meanings and multiple fulfillments, especially in the apocalyptic worldview of late Second Temple Judaism. Writing does not always record oral events, but when it does, one effect is the extraction of the oral message from its original situational specificity and the transferal of the message into a more generalized context or a more varied array of different contexts. According to Clements, "The loss of the original context in which a prophetic saying had been spoken was replaced, once it was written down, by a new context of a literary nature. One type of context gave way to another with important consequences for the way in which the message was then to be understood. More strikingly still, prophecies could be regarded as held in suspense, so that the time of their fulfillment could be regarded as not finally determined, or they could be regarded as susceptible of more than one fulfillment" (1996, 215). More than in situated oral prophecy, "metaphors and verbal imagery of many kinds came to be recast and reinterpreted away from their original contexts to convey many meanings. Instead of the plain declarations of prophetic utterance, rooted in known events and related to known personalities, greater interest came to be attached to themes and imagery that could readily be applied and adapted to a variety of contexts" (216).

The literary nature of written prophecy, then, makes it applicable to more contexts than just its original oral setting. Barton (1986) points out that this process is visible in the *Habakkuk Pesher*. He writes, "Almost any passage in the Habakkuk commentary from Qumran will illustrate the community's conviction that ancient prophecies referred to events of the recent past or the immediate future with a direct bearing on the community and its relation to the rest of Judaism" (1986, 182). Nissinen agrees, suggesting that literary prophecy "is scribal divination where the text itself serves as the source of revelation and exegesis becomes a revelatory act. While beginnings of the development of prophecy in this direction can be observed already in the Hebrew Bible (esp. in Ezekiel), the pesharim of Qumran present themselves as a full-blown representative of scribal divination" (2009, 60). In pesher, then, scribal divination was the interpretation of biblical prophecies, such as the book of Habakkuk, based on immediate (that is, uniquely late Second Temple) prejudices.

Apocalyptic Circumstances
Generations of scribes, who had redacted prophetic writings for inclusion in what would become the Hebrew Bible, interpreted and reinterpreted written prophecies, introducing ancient oracles into new contexts and understanding them according to emerging apocalyptic traditions. Since original prophetic language referred only to the historical situation in which the oracles had first been delivered, part of the scribal task in redaction was to make prophetic language more literary, more metaphorical, so that its referents could be contemporized through interpretation. According to Clements, scribal interpretation through writing "emphasized the decisively literary character of apocalyptic, with its predilection for metaphors and unusual imagery, often applied in a coded fashion to situations far removed from those envisaged in its original context" (1996, 183). The metaphors and allusions sought by scribes in prophetic texts highlight the literary character of apocalyptic reinterpretations. Clements writes, "The development of Jewish apocalyptic was, therefore, very markedly a scribal activity, developed with the aid of written texts and dependent upon the ability of the interpreter to recognize specific allusions and to make certain verbal connections that would not be obvious to the nonliterate person" (175–76; see also Nissinen 2004, 30). The Essene community believed that the messages of the ancient prophets also pertained to the apocalyptic end of days, which were upon them, and that these messages were coded in literary language requiring specialized interpretation, or pesher. While, for example, certain

elements of Habakkuk's prophecies were obviously fulfilled by the Babylonian conquest and exile, the Qumran community believed that Habakkuk's prophecy was *primarily* (or at least *additionally*) foretelling the oppressive occupation by the Romans in the end of days, an application of this prophecy that was not revealed to or by Habakkuk.

Traditions: Mysteries and the New Covenant in the *Habakkuk Pesher*

Collins points out that "the authors of the pesharim clearly had traditions available to them, whether oral or written, that we do not now have in textual form" (2011, 314). While this is certainly true, we also do have traditions in textual form that clearly influenced the composition of the pesharim, such as divinely revealed mysteries, which are associated with Mesopotamian dream interpretation and the book of Daniel, and the new covenant, a metaphysical reformulation of the material Mosaic covenant that had been violated and was void.

Mysteries
Whereas Habakkuk was influenced by the classical prophetic tradition of interpreting oracles, the Essenes were influenced by the Danielic tradition of interpreting mysteries (*rāz*), which is both prophetic and apocalyptic. By choosing to use the Danielic term for interpretation (*pesher*) instead of the Torahic synonym (*pathar*), the Essenes consciously identified their work with Second Temple Mesopotamian dream interpretation rather than biblical oracle interpretation.[16] This influence should come as no surprise, since, as Klaus Koch points out, "Daniel was regarded by [the Qumran community] as belonging among the prophets" (1985, 122). Maurya P. Horgan explains that "the interpretations in the book of Daniel seek to illuminate the meaning of past and present events, to predict the future, and to press toward the eschatological cataclysm and deliverance," and there are "significant similarities between the type of interpretation found in the book of Daniel and that observed in the pesharim" (1979, 255, 256; see also Jokiranta 2005, 26). Thus, Daniel serves as an appropriate grounding for the interpretive work of the Essenes in the *Habakkuk Pesher* (Fröhlich 1992).

In this newer (Second Temple, Danielic) tradition of pesher interpretation, oracles are no longer accessible, so interpreters, such as the Essenes, must rely on alternative forms of divine revelation, such as mysteries (or *rāz*). According to Devorah Dimant, "Since Habakkuk's mysterious utterances embody a divine message, their hidden meaning may be divulged only with the help of another divine disclosure" (2009, 376). Thus, since the biblical oracles have all been delivered and canonized, and since many were either not fulfilled or were assumed to be subject to multiple fulfillments until the end of days, new disclosures were required in order to understand original oracles and their application to a future that the first prophets could not possibly have understood. These new disclosures came in the form of mysteries. Horgan writes, "The mystery of the dreams in Daniel, the *rāz*, is illuminated in some of the same ways that the Qumran commentators drew out of the *rāz* of the prophetic words" (1979, 255), and this *rāz* "signifies the revelation of heavenly knowledge in late second temple texts" (Goff 2003, 165). This Danielic shift, then, from prophetic interpretation of spoken biblical oracles to the late Second Temple pesher interpretation of written mysteries signifies a new orientation toward communication between Yahweh and the true Israel for the end of days.

The mysteries of Daniel and the Qumran pesharim do not represent new revelations but instead represent revelations that illuminate the continuing relevance of biblical prophecies that may be unfulfilled or may be subject to multiple fulfillments. Thus, in the Second Temple period, the prophetic task was not to seek new oracles, but to reinterpret the continuing relevance of biblical oracles. According to James H. Charlesworth, during the late Second Temple period, "*the prophet* was perceived no longer primarily as God's spokesman but *as the interpreter of God's Word*," and "when we examine Qumran's *Pesharim*, we see the prophet ... portrayed as one who can perform exegesis because of special revelation and the guidance of the Holy Spirit" (2011a, 163). Thus, according to the Qumran community, the Essene leader "was the only one who could interpret Scripture with wisdom, since God had revealed to him all the mysteries in God's Word"; he "alone had been given the key to unlocking the mysteries of Scripture" (163–64, 167).

Some ancient prophecies were never fulfilled, perhaps because Yahweh intended them as warnings, and the warnings were heeded, nullifying the threat of Yahweh's curses. These prophecies, though unfulfilled at the time of delivery (or shortly after), still articulated abstract messages that would be relevant in times to come. Also, even prophecies that had clearly been fulfilled at one time (like Habakkuk's prophecy of destruction at the hands of the Chaldeans) were still general statements that could be reapplied to later circumstances. These reapplications, however, could not simply be the opinions of human interpreters. They needed to be interpretations inspired by Yahweh in order to receive credibility from an oppressed community. Michael H. Floyd writes, "The report [in Habakkuk] would have been read and interpreted to see whether the same pattern of divine activity, identified by the oracle in the context of the Babylonian crisis, might be identified in other contexts as well. This type of interpretation would constitute a kind of prophetic activity in its own right. Readers of the text would attempt to gain, from the record of what Habakkuk had perceived about Yahweh's involvement in one situation, some understanding of how Yahweh might also be involved in another situation" (1993, 477). Since pesher is an interpretation of ancient prophecies, as later fulfillments of earlier oracles, pesher interpretation was considered supplemental to the oracles of ancient prophecy.

The New Covenant
Since the Qumran community believed that ancient prophecies were subject to future and multiple fulfillments, and since only the Essenes were endowed with the ability to interpret the mysteries that explained these later fulfillments, this reclusive community felt the need to exclude some impure Israelites from Yahweh's blessings. Thus, the leaders of the Qumran community established a new covenant to replace the Mosaic covenant that had already been violated. In order for the Yahad to be protected by a divine covenant, which was still the goal, since the material world was treacherous, it would have to establish a brand new covenant, one with new promises and conditions, new blessings and curses. This new covenant calls for the law to be written in the hearts of the Qumran community, requiring a metaphysical commitment to the law rather than just the material completion of its procedures. This new covenant replaces the national inheritance of the Mosaic covenant with a personal commitment and annual recommitment to a strict obedience to the law, and it replaces the future orientation of the Mosaic covenant with an apocalyptic orientation.

The new covenant is described in several Qumran scrolls, including the *Rule of the Community*, the *Damascus Document*, and the *Hodayot*, but it is also mentioned in the *Habakkuk Pesher*. Regarding Habakkuk 1:5, the author of the *Habakkuk Pesher* writes:

[The interpretation of the word concerns] the traitors with the Man of Lies, since they do not [believe in the words of the] Teacher of Righteousness from the mouth of God; (and it concerns) the traito[rs of the] new [covenant] since they did not believe in the covenant of God [and dishonoured] his holy name. Likewise: The interpretation of the word [concerns the trai]tors in the last days. They shall be violators of [the coven]ant who will not believe when they hear all that is going [to happen to] the final generation, from the mouth of the Priest whom God has placed wi[thin the Community,] to foretell the fulfillment of all the words of his servants, the prophets, [by] means of whom God has declared all that is going to happen to his people [Israel]. (column II, lines 1–10)

Here we find concrete references to new traditions that have replaced the traditions of the biblical period that grounded oracular interpretation. These new traditions relate to the Teacher of Righteousness as the new prophet, the new covenant he and the rest of the Essenes have established with God, and the traitors in the end of days who will incur the curses of the new covenant. The Qumran community believed that their new covenant would make them worthy of God's favor during the final battle between the Sons of Light and the Sons of Darkness.

Fusions of Horizons: Pesher Method in the *Habakkuk Pesher*

Pesher is a specialized method of interpretation and an associated genre of interpretive texts found only at Qumran. Since its purpose is to reinterpret the relevance of biblical oracles for the impending end of days, pesher (both the method and the genre) focuses primarily on canonized prophetic texts. Daniel A. Machiela writes, "Pesher methods are applied almost exclusively to texts considered by the interpreter to be prophetic, containing a cryptic message that applies to the present situation of the interpreter and his community, and which is often attuned to the eschatological future. This message is encrypted in the written words and can be decrypted only by an interpreter endowed, as the prophets of old, with God's spirit and inspired through his wisdom—that is, through divine revelation" (2012, 325). The Essenes experienced a conflict between their own prejudices and traditions, and they used the pesher method of interpretation as a way to fuse those horizons, resolving the conflict of their experience into new interpretations of old prophetic texts.

While the genre of texts called pesher is unique to Qumran, the word itself is not. Horgan explains that "the root *pšr*, from which the Hebrew *pēšer* is derived, is a common Semitic root attested in Akkadian, Aramaic, Hebrew, and Arabic, meaning 'loosen,' 'dissolve'" (1979, 231; see also Jassen 2012, 386–89; Brooke 2013, 101–7 for extended discussions of this etymology). Neither the word itself nor its etymology, however, indicates any particular methodology. The method of pesher interpretation is often called atomistic. Alex P. Jassen writes, "The selective nature of pesher exposition is often referred to as 'atomization,' whereby individual words or elements in the scriptural passage are isolated in the pesher interpretation (2012, 378). Thus, "through a variety of exegetical techniques applied to the scriptural text, the ancient prophetic words are recontextualized to apply to these new historical settings" (364).

The method of pesher interpretation is not random, scholars have discovered. In fact, Horgan identifies definite categories into which pesher interpretations fall:

> I observe four categories of interpretation. These categories are not mutually exclusive, and many of the pesher sections could fit into more than one of these groups: (1) The pesher may follow the action, ideas, and words of the lemma closely, developing a similar description in a different context. (2) The pesher may grow out of one or two key words, roots, or ideas, developing the interpretation from these isolated elements apart from the action or description of the lemma. (3) The pesher may consist of metaphorical identifications of figures or things named in the lemma, with or without a description or elaboration of action. (4) There are instances in which the pesher seems to be only loosely related to the lemma. Within these general forms, the pesher is often drawn out or developed by means of one or more of the following techniques: use of synonyms for words in the lemma; use of the same roots as in the lemma, appearing in the same or different grammatical forms; plays on words in the lemma, changing the order of letters of words in the lemma; use of a different textual tradition; and referring back to an earlier lemma or anticipating a following lemma. (1979, 244–45)

While these methods of pesher interpretation may seem creative to modern readers, they were considered the result of divine mysteries revealed to the Essenes in which the revelation was the key to unlocking the meaning of the original prophetic oracle.

But this new divine revelation in no way invalidated the relevance of the original oracle. Timothy H. Lim writes that biblical "prophetic revelation was only partial, since the Qumran community also believed in a form of continuous revelation. While members of the community maintained that God had revealed himself to Habakkuk, the seventh-century prophet saw, as it were, only in part. What the pesherist believed was that Habakkuk did not understand and could not have understood that the words of his own prophecy prefigured events that were to be fulfilled some six centuries later" (2002, 24). Lim continues, "According to the Qumran sectarian, God did reveal to Habakkuk that which would happen in the final generation. What was withheld from him was the precise moment of the end-time and the specific historical references of his prophecy. By interpreting the biblical text in relation to his own situation, the pesherist was asserting that he knew what Habakkuk did not know, that the prophecies were beginning to be fulfilled in his lifetime, and that the end-time was drawing nigh" (26).

The atomistic interpretation characteristic of pesher among the Essenes looked to the biblical prophets for clues to new contexts in which those ancient oracles might be relevant. Maren R. Niehoff agrees, explaining that "this technique of interpretation assumes that the biblical text is a coded prophecy, which requires a symbolic reading in order to uncover the future events foreshadowed by it. The author of 1QpHab decodes the details of the biblical prophecy by applying each of them to a contemporary event, such as the coming of the 'Kittim' or the pursuit of the Teacher of Righteousness from Qumran by the 'Wicked Priest.' In the exegete's view, Habakkuk alluded to these contemporary events pertaining to his own community" (2012, 455). This kind of atomistic interpretation traverses time by recontextualizing the original oracle without challenging its historical validity, and it accomplishes this recontextualization through alternating lemmas (quotations or paraphrases of short passages from prophecy) and peshers (interpretations of those passages), following the continuous structure of the original prophetic book.

The most effective way to convey the structure and rhetoric of pesher interpretation is to analyze representative examples. In the next several paragraphs, I examine some of the most complete lemma/pesher passages from the *Habakkuk Pesher*.

The first lemma/pesher passage that appears in the *Habakkuk Pesher* establishes the purpose of reinterpreting the content of the book of Habakkuk for the end of days in which the Essenes were living.

> Lemma (Habakkuk 1:1–2): "[. . . For how long, YHWH] will I ask for help without [you hearing me; shout: Violence! to you without you saving me?" (column I, lines 1–2)
> Pesher: "[. . . The interpretation of this concerns the beg]inning of the [final] generation." (column I, lines 2–3)

This first pesher reinterpreting Habakkuk's opening gambit assures the reader that Habakkuk's prophecy is still relevant. Violence was rife in Habakkuk's time, but it is rife in the Essenes' time also, so cited prophecies and their reinterpretations were relevant then and are relevant again.

Another lemma/pesher passage, from later in the book of Habakkuk, confirms that God communicated to Habakkuk a message about the end of days, but that God did not tell Habakkuk when the end of days would come.

> Lemma (Habakkuk 2:2): "YHWH answered me and said: Write the vision; inscribe it on tablets so that [he who reads it] takes it on the run." (column VI, lines 15–16)
> Pesher: "And God told Habakkuk to write what was going to happen to the last generation, but he did not let him know the end of the age. . . . Its interpretation concerns the Teacher of Righteousness, to whom God has disclosed all the mysteries of the words of his servants, the prophets." (column VII, line 1–5)

In the end of days, the Teacher of Righteousness received mysteries from God regarding the final timing of the prophecy. While the biblical prophets spoke the truth, revealing what God had communicated, they did not fully understand the timing of these truths. Thus, the abstract meaning of prophecy takes on more specific contextual meaning as a result of the mysteries communicated by God to the Teacher of Righteousness.

Another lemma/pesher passage confirms that the time of the prophecies received during the First Temple period remains in the future, so perhaps the biblical prophecies were more like warnings than predictions.

> Lemma (Habakkuk 2:3): "For the vision has an appointed time, it will have an end and not fail." (column VII, line 6)
> Pesher: "Its interpretation: the final age will be extended and go beyond all that the prophets say, because the mysteries of God are wonderful." (column VII, lines 7–8)

Unfortunately for the Essenes, God's mysteries revealed that the biblical warnings have now become predictions, inevitabilities.

Another lemma/pesher passage exemplifies what I (and others) have called atomistic interpretation, wherein the Essene author substitutes terms (in this case names) relevant to the time of Habakkuk with terms relevant to the time of the Essenes.

> Lemma (Habakkuk 1:4): "[And justice does not emerge as the winner, for the evildoer acc]osts the upright man." (column I, line 12)
> Pesher: "[Its interpretation: the evildoer is the Wicked Priest and the upright man] is the Teacher of Righteousness." (column I, line 13)

It is not clear in the Habakkuk lemma who the upright man is (maybe high priest Azariah), but the evildoer is surely Jehoiakim, the Israelite king who ignored Josiah's cultic reforms. In the Essene pesher, the same terms, evildoer and upright man, have correlative referents in the end of days, the Wicked Priest (probably the Hasmonean Jonathan) and the Teacher of Righteousness (the founder of the Essene community, who had died before the *Habakkuk Pesher* was composed). This lemma/pesher passage is a good example of the kind of prophetic language that is relevant in an abstract way to many circumstances, not only in the late First Temple period, but also—and equally so—in the late Second Temple period.

Essene hatred of the Wicked Priest is no grand surprise, since the Wicked Priest tried to kill the Teacher of Righteousness on the Day of Atonement.

> Lemma (Habakkuk 2:15): "Woe to anyone making his companion drunk, spilling out his anger! He even makes him drunk to look at their festivals!" (column XI, lines 2–3)
>
> Pesher: "Its interpretation concerns the Wicked Priest who pursued the Teacher of Righteousness to consume him with the ferocity of his anger in the place of his banishment, in festival time, during the rest of the day of atonement. He paraded in front of them to consume them and make them fall on the day of fasting, the sabbath of their rest." (column XI, lines 4–8)

Again, Jehoiakim is likely the angry drunk in the lemma, and Jonathan is probably the Wicked Priest in the pesher. The Essenes favored a solar calendar in which festivals fell on the same day of the week each year, but the Hasmonean high priests had replaced it with a lunar calendar that was easier to integrate with pagan rites and rituals, which were also based mostly on lunar calendars. In the pesher above, the Wicked Priest pursued and threatened the Teacher of Righteousness on the Essenes' Day of Atonement, but this day was probably not the Day of Atonement for the Wicked Priest.

Such an affront could not go unnoticed by God, and the punishment of the Wicked Priest is the theme of another lemma/pesher passage.

> Lemma (Habakkuk 2:8): "For the human blood [spilt] and the violence done to the country, the city and all its /occupants/." (column IX, line 8)
>
> Pesher: "Its interpretation concerns the Wicked Priest, since for the wickedness against the Teacher of Righteousness and the members of his council God delivered him into the hands of his enemies to disgrace him with a punishment, to destroy him with bitterness of soul for having acted wickedly against his elect." (column IX, lines 9–12)

The Wicked Priest, who at this point in the *Habakkuk Pesher* may represent all of the Hasmonean high priests, whose sins were consistent from person to person, shed Israelite blood (like Habakkuk's internal strife). Thus, God delivered him (them) to the swords and spears of the Roman legions as punishment for the threat of violence.

It was not only the Wicked Priest who was culpable in the Essenes' eyes; there was also a community of religious leaders who stood by as the Wicked Priest threatened the Teacher of Righteousness.

> Lemma (Habakkuk 1:13): "Why are you staring, traitors, and you maintain your silence when a wicked person consumes someone more upright than himself?" (column V, lines 8–9)
> Pesher: "Its interpretation concerns the House of Absalom and the members of his council, who kept silent at the time of the reproach of the Teacher of Righteousness, and did not help him against the Man of Lies, who rejected the Law in the midst of their whole Comm[unity]." (column V, lines 9–12)

Habakkuk dealt with faithless onlookers, choosing loyalty to the wicked person over someone more upright, and the Essenes dealt with the House of Absalom (probably a sobriquet for a competing religious sect), choosing loyalty to the Man of Lies over loyalty to the Teacher of Righteousness.

Turning from the specific crime of threatening the Teacher of Righteousness on the Day of Atonement, the Essene peshers explore more general sins of the Wicked Priests and other historical priests as well. The three nets of Belial from the *Damascus Document* are clearly invoked in the next few lemma/pesher passages.

> Lemma (Habakkuk 2:5–6): "Surely wealth will corrupt the boaster and one who distends his jaws like the abyss and is as greedy as death will not be restrained.... They shall say: Ah, one who amasses the wealth of others! How long will he load himself with debts?" (column VIII, lines 3–8)
> Pesher: "Its interpretation concerns the Wicked Priest, who is called by the name of loyalty at the start of his office. However, when he ruled over Israel his heart became conceited, he deserted God and betrayed the laws for the sake of riches. And he stole and hoarded wealth from the brutal men who had rebelled against God. And he seized public money, incurring additional serious sins. And he performed repulsive acts of every type of filthy licentiousness." (column VIII, lines 8–13)

In the lemma above, wealth and greed (the first net of Belial) corrupt Israelite leaders, just as they corrupted the Hasmonean high priests and kings. Perhaps the Wicked Priest has shifted here from Jonathan to John Hyrcanus or even Alexander Jannaeus, who expanded Israelite territories and enriched the nation of Israel at the direct expense of cultic purity.

Another lemma/pesher passage seems to refer more directly to John Hyrcanus and Alexander Jannaeus, who built a Hasmonean state palace in the cursed city of Jericho, displaying their wealth and power at the expense of the people they were supposed to serve.

> Lemma (Habakkuk 2:12–13): "Woe to him who builds a city with blood and founds a town on a misdeed! Does this not stem from YHWH of hosts? The peoples wear themselves out for fire and the nations are exhausted for nothing." (column X, lines 5–8)
>
> Pesher: "The interpretation of the word concerns the Spreader of Deceit, who has misdirected many, building a useless city with blood and erecting a community by subterfuge for his own renown, wearing out many by useless work and by making them conceive acts of deceit, so that their labours are for nothing; so that those who derided and insulted God's chosen will go to the punishment of fire." (column X, lines 9–13)

The Essene pesher turns to a different sobriquet, so a different referent (from the Wicked Priest) is likely. John Hyrcanus and Alexander Jannaeus became rich through conquest and built their palace in the cursed city of Jericho with what the Essenes considered blood money.

Greed and licentiousness had marked the reigns of the Hasmonean high priests and kings, and these qualities, as qualities of the high priests especially, defiled the sanctuary because they entered the Holy of Holies in an impure condition.

> Lemma (Habakkuk 2:17): "Owing to the blood of the city and the violence (against) the country." (column XII, lines 6–7)
>
> Pesher: "Its interpretation: the city is Jerusalem since in it the /Wicked/ Priest performed repulsive acts and defiled the Sanctuary of God. The violence against the country are the cities of

Judah which he plundered of the possessions of the poor." (column XII, lines 7–10)

Although the Essenes do not mention the three nets of Belial in the *Habakkuk Pesher*, it is clear that these themes (wealth, fornication, and defilement of the Temple) are problems the Essenes had been concerned about for a long time.

Another lemma/pesher passage is particularly interesting from the perspective of the new metaphysical covenant established by the Essenes at Qumran.

> Lemma (Habakkuk 2:16): "You are more glutted with insults than with awards. Drink up also and stagger! The cup of YHWH's right hand will turn against you and disgrace come upon your glory." (column XI, lines 8–11)
> Pesher: "Its interpretation concerns the Priest whose name has exceeded his glory because he did not circumcise the foreskin of his heart and has walked on paths of drunkenness to slake his thirst; but the cup of God's anger will engulf him, heaping up [shame upon him]." (column XI, lines 12–15)

Circumcision was a physical symbol of God's covenant with Abraham, and was an actual procedure performed (ritually, of course) on male Israelite children. However, there is a tendency among the Essenes to view the biblical covenants as no longer materially based, requiring a metaphysical commitment in the end of days. Here circumcision is taken not just as a medical procedure but also as an act of commitment to the law and to one God. Thus, while the priest in the pesher is physically circumcised, he lacks the metaphysical commitment in his heart that the new Essene covenants now require.

The end for Habakkuk and the Judeans came at the hands of the Babylonians (though at the time Habakkuk received the oracle, it looked more likely that the Chaldeans would be their conquerors). Another lemma/pesher passage not only makes an atomistic substitution of names, but also attributes the qualities associated with the First Temple name to the Second Temple name as well.

> Lemma (Habakkuk 1:6): "For see, I will mobilize the Chaldeans, a cru[el and determined] people." (column I, lines 10–11)
> Pesher: "Its interpretation concerns the Kittim, who are swift and powerful in battle, to slay many [with the edge of the sword]." (column II, lines 12–13)

The Chaldeans are described as cruel and determined, just like the Kittim (a sobriquet for the Romans). The Romans at the end of the first century BCE were cruel and powerful, with well-trained armies that could destroy any foe at the time. Again, the pesher does not invalidate the claim of the lemma; the pesher recognizes in the lemma a more universal truth than Habakkuk was able to recognize.

Rhetorics most often emerge out of institutional contexts in which uses of language become regularized through practice. In First Temple Israel, prophetic rhetorics emerged out of the institutional context of the Jerusalem Temple and its authoritative foundation in the Torah, Prophets, and Writings, which were becoming increasingly settled in an ongoing process of canon formation. The interpretation of prophetic texts dominated rhetorics in Second Temple Israel, since sacred texts contained absolute truths, but interpretations of these texts varied widely from sect to sect. These variations resulted from different prejudices interpreted in the context of different traditions, resulting in different fusions of horizons. Thus, pesher method is the fusion of horizons (prejudices and traditions) in the process of interpretation. The Qumran community viewed themselves as living at the end of a historical process, the end of days in which God would return from heaven to live in glory with the Essenes, destroying all evil. Communities that believe they understand history as a complete process with a beginning and an end always have to account for the nature of that end, and that end, in the case of the Essenes, is apocalypse in the end of days.

CONCLUSION

For the most part, this book is an extended case study of rhetoric in certain sectarian texts among the Dead Sea Scrolls emplaced within the contexts of their rhetorical ecologies. In the introduction, I noted that "case study" is one kind of scholarly work Edelman (2003) calls for in his appeal to increase our understanding of Israelite and Jewish rhetorics broadly conceived. But Edelman also calls for "careful scholarly studies of the diachronic movement of Jewish rhetoric" (2003, 114). While a careful analysis of how the Dead Sea Scrolls inform the transition from biblical rhetoric to talmudic rhetoric is beyond the scope of this book, I will conclude with at least some notes pointing in that direction. The diachronic movement across ancient Israelite and Jewish rhetorics, especially from the biblical period to the talmudic period, cannot be studied in any complete sense without a thorough treatment of the Dead Sea Scrolls, since those Essene texts represent the only significant documentary evidence from that formative and transitional time. However, most of the efforts to historicize Israelite and Jewish rhetorics move too quickly from Bible to Talmud.

In "Ancient Traditions, Modern Needs: An Introduction to Jewish Rhetoric," Edelman's periodization of Jewish rhetorics moves from the Assyrian and Babylonian exiles to the talmudic period with only one sentence on the six hundred years between: "This period [between exiles and Talmud] represents a growing separation in Jewish life between assimilationists and religious trends as illustrated in the conflict between the Maccabees and the

Greek speaking Jews" (2003, 116). Edelman is right, of course, but there is so much more to those six hundred years than one sentence can describe. And in 2014, Michael Bernard-Donals and Janice W. Fernheimer, in the introduction to their edited collection, *Jewish Rhetorics: History, Theory, Practice*, explain that "there are a number of Jewish rhetorics, all of which have at their core a significant body of rhetorical precedent for their modes of writing and argumentation, precedents that reside in biblical texts, the Talmud, Midrash, rabbinical responses (*responsa*) to contemporary questions about religious practice and social ethics, secular engagements with and petitions to local and national government bodies, and historical writing" (ix; see also xv). The Dead Sea Scrolls are absent from this list of influences on Jewish rhetorical traditions, and only one author in the collection, Richard Hidary, mentions the Dead Sea Scrolls, though only in passing (2014, 17 and 31).[1]

The impression one gets from these histories is that the Roman destruction of the Second Temple was *the* watershed event that transformed Judaism, with nearly immediate effect. However, what we learn from the Dead Sea Scrolls is that some of the characteristics of rhetoric we believed emerged in talmudic contexts had actually existed for nearly two hundred years before the destruction of the Second Temple. In other words, where we once perceived a sea change in Jewish rhetorics and their contexts at 70 CE, the Dead Sea Scrolls demonstrate that there was, in fact, a gradual transition over the course of centuries.

If the late Second Temple period and its documentary texts, the Dead Sea Scrolls, are largely absent from our understanding of the diachronic movement of Jewish rhetorics, then what exactly are we missing? Or, in other words, what do the Dead Sea Scrolls add to our understanding of the transition from Israelite rhetorics of the biblical period to rabbinic rhetorics of the talmudic period and after? In order to illustrate the contribution of the Dead Sea Scrolls to a more robust understanding of the diachronic movement of Israelite and Jewish rhetorics, I will examine three salient transitions: from Temple to synagogues, from priests to rabbis, and from sacrifice to prayer.

FROM TEMPLE TO SYNAGOGUES

Following the exodus from Egypt and the conquest of the promised land, early Israelites represented a collection of twelve tribes affiliated by their common covenant with Yahweh and joined by their common reverence for the portable shrine that housed the ark of the covenant. Shortly before 1000 BCE, the militaristic Philistines conquered Israel because the twelve tribes were only loosely affiliated and did not function effectively as a single unit. In order to unify their interests, the twelve tribes of Israel shifted their social structure to a more unified monarchy (though the tribes themselves did not dissolve), with Saul elected the first king. David, who succeeded Saul as king of Israel, pushed the Philistines back out of the promised land. Seeking a more permanent institutionalized means to unify Israelite social identity and religious practice, David declared Jerusalem the capital of Israel and moved the ark of the covenant there, appointing Abiathar and Zadok as head priests. Toward the end of his life, David's succession was fraught with conflict, but Solomon eventually won the support of David and the Israelites, and he was anointed king by Zadok. Among *many* other things, Solomon used the proceeds from his tremendous economic success to build the First Temple, which became the central and authoritative location for both the rule of the monarchy and the worship of Yahweh (Bright 2000, 224). In Solomon's Temple, under the direction of Zadok (now the first sole high priest), Israelites worshipped Yahweh, and only Yahweh, through annual festivals and regular sacrifices and offerings, all as required in the evolving texts that would become the Torah.

Soon after Solomon's death, the finally unified kingdom split into two, with Israel to the north and Judah (which included Jerusalem) to the south. Following the fall of the Northern Kingdom of Israel to the Assyrians, Judah became a vassal of Assyria, and, under King Menasseh, the Temple became a site for pagan rituals, sacred prostitution, divination, magic, and even human sacrifice (Bright 2000, 312). The material Temple stood strong, but its ideological function was in ruins. Despite purifying reforms executed by Menasseh's successor, Josiah, subsequent monarchs, including Jehoahaz and Jehoiakim, were unable to resist the military and ideological forces of Egypt, Assyria, and Babylon, thus returning the Temple to an impure state.

The prophets had been warning all along of impending doom. Viewing instability in the region as an opportunity, King Nebuchadnezzar of Babylon swept in to conquer Judah, and in 587 BCE he destroyed Jerusalem, exiled the Israelites from the promised land, and disconnected them from the Temple and its cultic functions. Although the Temple had been razed to the ground, it remained a sacred site for displaced Israelites and a sacrificial location for the few who remained in the region (Bright 2000,

344–45). John Bright writes, "As for the Temple, though burned to the ground, it remained a holy spot to which pilgrims continued to journey... to offer sacrifice among the blackened ruins. A cult of some sort was probably carried on there, if sporadically, through the exile period" (344–45).

Nearly fifty years after the fall of Jerusalem to Nebuchadnezzar, Cyrus conquered Babylon and became its king, formally ending the exile in 538 BCE and allowing the Israelites to return to Palestine. Cyrus ordered the rebuilding of the Temple in Jerusalem and returned all of the Israelites' sacred treasures that Nebuchadnezzar had stolen. During the Second Temple period, the reinstallation of the ark of the covenant in the Temple's inner sanctum insured God's renewed presence among the Israelites, and the sacrificial cult was again performed by Zadokite priests at the Temple in honor of their God in residence. The evolving canonization of the Torah after the Babylonian exile increasingly embodied (or entitled) the Temple itself with vital significance as the only sanctioned location for the ritual cult of the Mosaic covenant.

The Second Temple in Jerusalem was destroyed in 70 CE by Roman generals Vespasian and Titus, putting an end to the primary institutional context of Israelite religion. With Roman occupation and oppression, many Israelites fled the region, settling in small groups throughout Europe, Africa, and Asia Minor. Without a functioning central institution, Israelites in the diaspora would adapt to their new circumstances, establishing alternative institutions for the context of permanent (they thought) exile. These alternative institutions were the synagogues, local community centers, and places of worship that replaced the centrality of the Jerusalem Temple. Synagogues themselves predate the destruction of the Second Temple by several centuries, but their function in the Second Temple period was primarily social. After the destruction of the Second Temple, however, diasporic synagogues adopted many of the religious functions once performed only in the centralized Temple. Lee I. Levine writes, "For all the controversy surrounding the Temple in the late Second Temple period... it remained down to its very end, in 70 CE, the most central, preeminent, and sacred religious framework in Jewish life. Thus, it is no wonder that, with its destruction, there was an urgent need to fill the vacuum, at least in part, by appropriating certain Temple practices for the synagogue" (2005, 535). These appropriations became so salient in the post-70 CE synagogue that the institution itself, in terms of both architecture and ideology, "began to emulate the Temple" (202).

So far, the history I have told about the transition from Temple to synagogue around 70 CE is entirely accurate. However, the Dead Sea Scrolls complicate the history of these institutional transformations. While it is true that the Temple was destroyed in 70 CE, it is also true that the community of Essenes had abandoned the Temple as a context for cultic worship and the rhetoric it entailed nearly two hundred years before its destruction, establishing their settlement at Qumran as an alternative site for religious, not just social, activities. Thus, while synagogues had taken on more and more religious functions after the material destruction of the Temple in 70 CE, the Essenes at Qumran had already begun that process after the ideological destruction of the Temple by wicked priests during the second century BCE.

4QMMT was composed around 150 BCE, during the earliest phase of Essene sectarian formation, and its primary concern is the defilement of the Temple as a result of improper ritual observance by the newly installed Hasmonean high priest (probably Jonathan). This scroll engages in rhetorical identification, citing canonized scriptures as common ideological ground, yet it also offers different interpretations of certain sacrificial regulations from those practiced by Jonathan and the attending priests in the Temple. According to the *Habakkuk Pesher*, the high priest, now called the "Wicked Priest," was incensed by this Essene epistle and tried to have the leader of the Essenes, the Teacher of Righteousness, killed on the Day of Atonement. Since the Temple was impure and the high priest (and subsequent Hasmonean high priests) had no intention of adopting a more strict orthodoxy, the Essenes believed that the primary material and rhetorical functions of the Temple (purification and atonement) were ineffectual, and that the Jerusalem Temple, as the legitimating institution of Israelite religion, was hopelessly lost. So the Essenes retreated into the desert to establish an alternative institution that would fulfill the religious functions of purification and atonement and also serve the social functions that were characteristic of Second Temple synagogues.

In the *Rule of the Community*, the Essenes recognized that the religious functions of the Jerusalem Temple were forever lost to their community of the new covenant, so they established themselves (the Yahad) as a new "holy house" for pure worship:

> In the Community council (there shall be) twelve men and three priests, perfect in everything that has been revealed about all the

law to implement truth, justice, judgment, compassionate love and unassuming behavior of each person to his fellow to preserve faithfulness on the earth with firm purpose and repentant spirit in order to atone for sin, doing justice and undergoing trials in order to walk with everyone in the measure of truth and the regulation of time. When these things exist in Israel the Community council shall be founded on truth, like an everlasting plantation, a holy house for Israel and the foundation of the holy of holies for Aaron, true witnesses for the judgment and chosen by the will (of God) to atone for the earth and to render the wicked their retribution. It (the Community) will be a tested rampart, the precious cornerstone that does not [...] whose foundations do not shake or tremble in their place. It will be the most holy dwelling for Aaron with total knowledge of the covenant of justice and in order to offer a pleasant aroma; and it will be a house of perfection and truth in Israel [...] in order to establish a covenant in compliance with the everlasting decrees. (column VIII, lines 1–10)

And, later, "the men of the community shall set themselves apart (like) a holy house for Aaron, in order to enter the holy of holies, and (like) a house of the Community for Israel, (for) those who walk in perfection" (1QS, column IX, lines 5–6). Here the Community Council and the Essenes themselves become the conceptual architecture of a new Temple, the ideological (no longer material) foundation of the Holy of Holies in which God appears to the high priest once a year. This holy house of the Essene community was only a temporary replacement, however, until a pure eschatological Temple could be constructed according to the ideal architecture described in the *Temple Scroll*. Thus, by at least 100 BCE, the Essene community had abandoned the Temple institution and established Qumran as an alternative context for the worship of Yahweh.

FROM PRIESTS TO RABBIS

Lester L. Grabbe explains that "the priesthood in general, and the High Priest in particular, dominated the Jewish state during the Second Temple period" (2010, 42). High priests, and the Temple's staff of other attending priests, were descended from Aaron (the high priests, by way of Zadok), acquiring ethos from lineage. Priests wielded tremendous political and religious power throughout the land of Israel, reaching their peak with the Hasmonean family of high priests, who usurped the Zadokite line and declared themselves kings. With Roman occupation beginning in 63 BCE, however, the Temple priests were entirely stripped of political power, and their religious power was limited to the Temple cult. Nevertheless, even under the Roman yoke, Grabbe writes, priests "maintained control of the temple and were still the most important figures of the religious establishment" (42). At the Jerusalem Temple, the high priest and attending priests presided over the annual calendar of sacrificial feasts and festivals; performed blood sacrifices, grain and fruit offerings, and libations; interpreted the increasingly canonical scriptures; and educated Israelites in Torah law. The priests (including the high priest) continued to perform these religious rites and rituals, Grabbe explains, "until the Temple was finally destroyed in 70 CE" (43), at which time all cultic functions performed by priests ceased. Thus, Levine explains, "the destruction of the Jerusalem Temple in 70 brought an end to a millennium of priestly political and religious hegemony. For an elite that had been accorded the highest status in Jewish society and that had shouldered the bulk of the ritual, cultural, judicial, and political responsibilities for many centuries, the sudden absence of its base of power was undoubtedly traumatic" (2005, 519; see also Hidary 2014, 16).

Following 70 CE, Levine explains, the newly emerging rabbis, leaders of the postdestruction synagogues, "were not restricted to a single caste or socioreligious group. In principle, anyone could head the institution" (2005, 2). Rabbis of the Second Temple period were nonpriestly teachers and social functionaries. However, rabbis of postdestruction synagogues became prominent *religious* functionaries. In fact, Levine explains, "increased rabbinic involvement was connected to the gradual transformation of the synagogue in the first centuries CE from a multipurpose communal institution into one with a more prominent religious profile" (497). However, it is not the case that, after 70 CE, priests disappeared; they were simply absorbed into a less hierarchical political and religious system that still valued former priests' knowledge and piety. Levine writes, "Priests were amply represented among the sages throughout much of the Talmudic period" (520). Thus, although priests required the institution of the Temple to perform their roles as priests, former priests were still valued members of synagogues, sometimes taking on secondary leadership roles in this new legitimating institution.

So far, the history I have told about the transition from priests to rabbis around 70 CE is entirely accurate. However, as above, the Dead Sea Scrolls complicate the history of these leadership transformations. Certainly Zadokite priests established the Essene community, but it is not clear to what extent priestly heritage continued to provide ethos in what the Essenes believed were the end of days. In the Temple, the highest offices would have been the high priest, attending priests, and Levites. For a community that rejected the Temple as a legitimate institution, it makes sense that they would also reject its administration, consequently creating a new system of leadership. Since the sacrificial cult was administered by wicked priests who had violated the sanctity of the Temple and invalidated the priesthood, the Essenes chose a form of administration that would emphasize teaching and instruction and deemphasize the technical performance of rituals in the Temple apparatus.

The founder and early leader of the Essene community was called the Teacher of Righteousness, though he was almost certainly also a priest of the Zadokite line. Successors to the Teacher of Righteousness may have been called the Instructor, and they may or may not have been priests. The Teacher of Righteousness was, according to the *Damascus Document*, raised up specifically to direct the Essenes in the path of Yahweh's heart (column I, line 11; see also 4QPsalms Pesher[a] [4Q171, 4QpPs[a]], column 3, lines 13–17). The *Habakkuk Pesher* explains that God revealed to the Teacher of Righteousness "all the mysteries of the words of his servants, the prophets" (1QpHab, column VII, line 4). These mysteries formed the basis of knowledge the Teacher of Righteousness would convey to the Essenes, and access to these mysteries shifted the Essene leader's identity from procedural priest to divine prophet. The Teacher of Righteousness had abandoned the role of priest with its cultic responsibilities and accepted the role of instructor, leading the Essenes forward toward redemption not through ritual obligations but through knowledge. 1QMicah Pesher (1Q14, 1QpMic) explains, "[... The interpretation of this co]ncerns the Teacher of Righteousness who [teaches the law to his council] of the Community, those who will be saved on the day of [judgment]" (fragment 10, lines 6–9). Thus, this Teacher of Righteousness is not a general educator; his role is to educate only the Essenes (and, in particular, the Community Council) in God's mysteries, ensuring their survival as a remnant in the end of days.

The *Damascus Document* describes the communal leadership of the Essenes as the Holy Council (column XX, lines 24–25), and the *Micah Pesher* and the *Rule of the Community* describe this leadership as the Community Council (1QpMic, fragment 10, line 7; 1QS, column VIII, lines 1 and 5, among other places). In a crucial passage, quoted above, the *Rule of the Community* defines the Community Council as a group of twelve men and three priests, and it attributes only the highest virtues to these elite community members (column VIII, line 1, and passim). In other words, 80 percent of the Community Council that leads and guides the Essene community are *not* priests. On the one hand, this is remarkable for an Israelite community that identifies itself as the "sons of Zadok," the first high priest who was appointed by Solomon. On the other hand, it should not seem so remarkable, since, according to the Essenes, the priesthood in general was thoroughly corrupt and thus invalid. Although the Essenes obviously did not devalue the ethos of the Zadokite priests, it is clear that they did make institutional space for nonpriestly leadership over a century before the destruction of the Jerusalem Temple.

FROM SACRIFICE TO PRAYER

As the Torah became settled and formalized, the rituals it prescribed also became normative, and the primary function of the priests in the Second Temple period was to perform the sacrificial cult, thus fulfilling covenantal obligations, ensuring purity, and guaranteeing redemption and atonement for the nation of Israel. In other words, sacrifices and offerings were the mechanism through which purity, redemption, and atonement could be achieved. Performance of this sacrificial cult was the primary function of the priests (especially the high priest), and its only legitimate location was the Temple. According to Grabbe, "The main activity of the Temple was blood sacrifice. There were required sacrifices on a daily, weekly, and monthly basis and also at the major religious festivals. If an individual committed a trespass of the law, a sacrifice was required. If one wanted to thank God for blessings, particular sacrifices could be given" (2010, 40). More specifically, as Phillip Sigal explains,

> the cultic roster included the *olah*, a burnt offering, all of which "ascended" (the verb *alah* means "to go up") to God in smoke; *shelamim*, conciliatory offerings denoting renewed communication with God; *todah*, a thanksgiving offering; *nedabah*, a freewill offering denoting pious devotion; *neder*, a vow offering; *hatat* and *asham*, expiatory and guilt or reparation offerings; *minhah*, a vegetable offering; *lehem hapanim*, the Bread of the Presence arranged upon the table in the sanctuary; and *qetoret*, incense (from the verb *qatar*, "to go up in smoke"). In addition, blood and fat were offered, both of which were considered life-giving. There were also various sacrifices accompanying ablutions after childbirth, disease, sexual emissions, and the like, and those expressing gratitude, expiation, and reconciliation. Furthermore, there was an array of Sabbath and holy day offerings, celebrated in processions with accompanying singers and musical instruments, aside from the twice-daily *tamid* (perpetual burnt offerings). (1988, 17–18)

On any given day, the Temple would be teeming with Israelites and priests performing sacrificial rites and rituals.

Following the destruction of the Second Temple and the dissolution of its official priesthood in 70 CE, rabbis sought to replace the sacrificial cult with another form of ritual observance that would nevertheless fulfill covenantal obligations, ensure purity, and guarantee redemption and atonement for Jewish communities in the diaspora. These rabbis replaced sacrifice with prayer, among other things. According to David L. Weddle, "The disastrous loss of the Temple in Jerusalem brought an end to a millennium of sacrifices, displaced the hereditary priesthood, and stripped political authority from Jewish leaders. Jewish teachers (known as Pharisees, who were precursors of the rabbis) translated the anachronistic laws of animal sacrifice into moral and religious requirements of prayer, fasting, charity, good works, and Torah study" (2017, 69; see also Levine 2005, 241; Delia Marx 2013, 66–68). Levine agrees, explaining that after 70 CE, "prayer served as a substitute for sacrifices" (2005, 546). This transition from sacrifice to prayer must not be underestimated, since post-70 CE Jewish communities still believed the Torah represented the infallible word of God, and God mandated animal sacrifice in the Torah. Weddle writes, "In the process of appropriating Jewish scriptures in which sacrifice is a central theme, rabbinic interpreters faced the problem of retaining the significance of sacrifice in its absence. Animal sacrifice could not be performed as prescribed by Torah without temple, priesthood, or victims. So either large sections of Torah must be regarded as rendered irrelevant by the destruction of the Temple or they must be assigned a religious meaning beyond their literal enactment" (2017, 69). The validity of the Torah was retained in rabbinic Judaism through the meticulous reinterpretation of sacrificial rites as rites of prayer and devotion.

So far, the history I have told about the transition from sacrifice to prayer around 70 CE is entirely accurate. However, as above (again), the Dead Sea Scrolls complicate the history of these ritual transformations. According to James VanderKam, by the middle of the second century BCE, the Essenes had already stopped offering animal sacrifices: "One can interpret the animal bones found at Qumran as the remains of meals, not of sacrificial animals. Instead, the members sent up prayer and praise as sacrifices of the lips to the creating, sustaining, and saving God" (1994, 116). Schiffman agrees, explaining that "the Qumran sect, who refused to participate in the Temple rituals, and others who were too distant from the Temple to do so, had already instituted prayers to substitute for the daily sacrifices. The rise of the synagogue as a house of prayer in the first century coincided with the loss of the Temple. By the time the Temple was destroyed, its replacement had already been created" (2003, 37).

Since the Essenes never lost the hope of returning to a pure Temple (at first the material one, and later the eschatological one) as its legitimate priestly administrators, they also never lost interest in the sacrificial cult, which was the primary function of the Temple in Israelite worship. However, the existing Temple was hopelessly impure, an unfit venue for repentance, purification, and atonement. The old nationalist Mosaic covenant with material blessings and curses required animal sacrifice. The new voluntary Essene covenant with metaphysical blessings and curses required an alternative form of sacrifice that would replace the Temple apparatus and yet still fulfill the requirements of Torah law until the Essenes could return to a pure Temple. The replacement form of sacrifice for the new Essene covenant was prayer.

But the Essenes could not challenge the mandates of the Torah with interpretations originating in the minds of sectarians. Their justification for transitioning from sacrifice to prayer must be grounded in sacred scriptures in order to be valid. For this purpose of legitimation, the Essenes cite Proverbs 15.8: "The sacrifice of the wicked is an abomination, but the prayer of the just is like an agreeable offering" (CD, column XI, lines 20–21). This theme is reinforced in the *Rule of the Community*, which states, "In order to atone for the fault of the transgression and for the guilt of sin and for approval for the earth, without the flesh of burnt offerings and without the fats of sacrifice—the offering of the lips in compliance with the decree will be like the pleasant aroma of justice and the correctness of behavior will be acceptable like a freewill offering" (1QS, column IX, lines 4–5). At Qumran, prayer had replaced sacrifice as early as the middle of the second century BCE, more than two hundred years before the destruction of the Temple in 70 CE.

In the preceding chapters, I have described various central rhetorical strategies employed throughout the Dead Sea Scrolls: identification, distinction, speech acts, dissociation, embodiment, entitlement, erasure, and interpretation, to name only a few. These strategies comprise rhetorics that are persuasive, epistemic, and material. Further, the Dead Sea Scrolls complicate the traditional histories of Israelite and Jewish rhetorics from the biblical period to the talmudic period. For all of these reasons, the texts from Qumran are worth the attention of rhetoric scholars.

As I reflect on the process that has led me to these final few sentences, I can't help wishing I had listened in Sunday school when my father taught lessons about the Dead Sea Scrolls. He believed they were important, just as I do now, but our beliefs are grounded in very different systems of value. For my father, the Dead Sea Scrolls confirmed what he had understood all his life, that the Bible he read was the Bible everyone read, the true word of God, from its canonization till today. For me, the Dead Sea Scrolls are examples of rhetorical texts from a historical period that, until 1947, had very little documentary evidence available for study, and these texts teach us some surprising things about the transition of rhetoric from the biblical period to the talmudic period. Different systems of value. My father read the *Great Isaiah Scroll* to confirm that his understanding of Isaiah was theologically sound. I read the *Rule of the Community* to see how the Yahad used material rhetoric as a strategy for communal formation. Different systems of value. Yet we both found reasons to read the Dead Sea Scrolls, and we both found things we wanted to say about them. I hope this book will encourage others to read the Dead Sea Scrolls and find things they want to say.

NOTES

INTRODUCTION

1. During the time of the divided kingdom in the First Temple period (1200–586 BCE), the territory to the north was called Israel and the territory to the south, which included Jerusalem, was called Judah. During this time, only the northern tribes were called Israelites. However, in the Second Temple period (516 BCE–70 CE), following the return from Babylonian exile, this north/south tribal division dissipated, and Jerusalem became the capital city of a more unified nation called Israel. Although the Zadokite priests had remained in Judah throughout the divided kingdom, responsible for performing required rites and rituals in the Jerusalem Temple, the Dead Sea Scrolls do not refer to their descendants, the Essenes, as Judahites. In fact, the *Damascus Document* makes it clear that the new covenant of the Essenes was formed in Damascus, not Judah, where the old covenants were formed and then violated. As John S. Bergsma makes clear, the Essenes preferred the names "Israel" and "Israelites" over "Judah" and "Judahites" (2008, 172). Also, according to Steven Weitzman, "the word 'Judaism,' appearing for the first time in the second century BCE, is an example of [the] fusion of Judean and Greek culture" (2017, 211), which likely would have been distasteful to the Essenes. Thus, although the adjective "Jewish" does apply to at least some of the Israelite communities of the late Second Temple period, throughout this book I refer to the Essenes and most of their contemporaries as "Israelites" because this is the term the Essenes themselves used and preferred. I do not, however, alter any quotations that refer to the Essenes and their contemporaries as Jewish or Jews or their religion as Judaism. I also refer to the community that copied or wrote most of the Dead Sea Scrolls as "Essenes." While it is true that the word "Essene" never appears in the Dead Sea Scrolls, the general scholarly consensus (though not unanimous) is that the Essene community described by Josephus in the first century of the Common Era (CE) is the same community that occupied Qumran and called themselves the Yahad.

2. The Second Temple period begins in the late sixth century BCE (circa 516) with the reconstruction of the Jerusalem Temple following the Babylonian exile, and it ends with the destruction of the Temple (again) by Roman forces in 70 CE (Hodge 2003, x). It is widely accepted that most of the Dead Sea Scrolls were copied or composed between 170 BCE and 68 CE (Hodge, 31). While it is anachronistic to suggest that there was a settled canon in the Second Temple period, it is not anachronistic to refer to the process of canonization, which was well underway at the time. Although there was no unified Bible in the Second Temple period, scholars generally refer to scrolls that would later appear in the Bible as "biblical."

3. The Dead Sea Scrolls include over 850 documents broken into over 55,000 individual fragments. For various reasons, most of these 850 documents are extremely fragmentary and only around ten are "in

any sense intact" (Shanks 1998, xiiv). In this book, I describe and analyze the rhetorical situations and rhetorical ecologies of six nearly complete documents among the Dead Sea Scrolls: *Miqṣat Maʿaśeh ha-Torah* (4QMMT), the *Rule of the Community* (1QS), the *Damascus Document* (CD), the *Purification Rules* (4QTohorot A and B), the *Temple Scroll* (11QT), and the *Habakkuk Pesher* (1QpHab). I focus primarily on the sectarian scrolls that define the community of Essenes and elaborate their primary concerns throughout the last 150 years before the Common Era (BCE). Other documents, such as the *War Scroll* and the *Hodayot*, are crucial for a complete understanding of the Dead Sea Scrolls, but they lend themselves less well to the kind of rhetorical analysis I undertake throughout this book. Thus, I reserve those scrolls, and dozens more, for differently focused future work.

4. The notion of *rhetorical ecology* has been extended into more specific but obviously related concepts like ambience (Thomas Rickert 2013), new materialism (Laurie E. Gries 2015), trophics (Caroline Gottschalk Druschke 2019), noosphere (Robert Inkster 2000), and ecocomposition (Sidney I. Dobrin and Christian R. Weisser 2002). All of these extensions are useful in their own ways (in fact, I discuss Gries's understanding of new materialism in a later chapter). My own use of the term "rhetorical ecologies" in relation to the Dead Sea Scrolls is most heavily influenced by Marilyn M. Cooper (1986), Jenny Edbauer (2005), Michael Weiler and W. Barnett Pearce (2006), and Nathaniel A. Rivers and Ryan P. Weber (2011).

5. I use the phrase "Essene priests and leaders" because the *Rule of the Community* describes Essene leadership as a "community council" made up of three "priests" and twelve "men" (column VIII, line 1). In other words, not all (or not many) Essene community leaders were necessarily priests. Although I refer to manuscript 1QS (the most complete text of the *Rule of the Community*) throughout this book, it is important to recognize that at least ten additional copies of this scroll were discovered in Cave 4 (4Q255–64). There are some differences between 1QS and the Cave 4 copies, so while 1QS is the most useful scroll for analysis, it is probably not the only version of the text studied at Qumran.

6. The year 31 BCE, a few years into Herod's reign in Judea, would prove difficult, a sure sign to an apocalyptic sect like the Essenes that the end of the world was nigh. Eshel writes, "In this year Herod defeated the Nabateans in a battle near Philadelphia (Amman), a severe earthquake destroyed many settlements in the Land of Israel (including Qumran), Octavianus defeated Mark Antony in the battle of Actium and following this victory adopted the name Augustus, Mark Antony and Cleopatra VII committed suicide, and Herod executed Hyrcanus II, the son of Alexander Jannaeus" (2008, 178). Since most of the peshers among the Dead Sea Scrolls refer to people and events after the fall of Jerusalem to Pompey and before the watershed events of 31 BCE, it is relatively certain that these prophetic commentaries, including the *Habakkuk Pesher*, were composed at Qumran between 63 and 31 BCE, during Roman occupation.

7. The story of the discovery and publication of the Dead Sea Scrolls has been told hundreds of times, often with competing details. My own version of this story relies heavily on published accounts by other scholars, including Michael Baigent and Richard Leigh (1991), Edward M. Cook (1994), Harry Thomas Frank (1992), Jason Kalman (2012), Lawrence H. Schiffman (1995b), and especially Hershel Shanks (1998).

8. Although Edelman (2003) does not provide dates for these periods, most

scholars agree that the classical biblical period extends from the construction of the First Temple in Jerusalem in the late tenth century BCE to the conquest of Palestine by Alexander the Great in 322 BCE; the Hellenistic period runs from 322 BCE until around 70 CE, when the Romans destroyed the Second Temple; and the talmudic period extends from the destruction of the Second Temple by Rome in 70 CE to 500 CE, when the Babylonian Talmud was compiled and recorded. It is also useful to break the Hellenistic period down even further into three subperiods: the Hellenistic period proper, from 322 BCE until the Hasmonean revolt and purification of the Jerusalem Temple in 164 BCE; the Hasmonean period, from 164 BCE until the Roman conquest of Palestine in 63 BCE; and the Roman period, from 63 BCE until the destruction of the Second Temple in 70 CE. Throughout the Hasmonean and Roman periods, common Israelites remained largely Hellenized, even as some of their leaders resisted Hellenization.

9. These sources include Evans 2018; Fraade 2000, 2003; Høgenhaven 2003; McComiskey 2010, 2015a, 2015b; Newsom 2010; and Sharp 1997.

CHAPTER 1

1. Frank Moore Cross defines "priestly orthopraxy" as "correct orthodox practice and observance" (1993, 25). 4QMMT is sometimes called the "Halakhic Letter" because of its concern with regulations governing priestly orthopraxy, and the term *halakhah* (plural *halakhot*) appears throughout scholarship on 4QMMT. However, this appellation is misleading. First, *halakhah* is a *post*-Second Temple rabbinic term, appearing first in the Mishnah circa 200 CE; in other words, the Essene community did not call their laws *halakhot*. In the rabbinic tradition, the term *halakhot* refers to all of the laws and their related regulations and practices (of which there may be thousands), both those in the Torah and others derived from exegetical interpretation. However, in 4QMMT, what later rabbis would have generally called *halakhot* are actually divided into two distinct groups: laws that are beyond the vagaries of theological dispute, and works or practices of the law that require interpretation and exposition. Since I discuss these two categories of statements in 4QMMT (that is, laws and works of the law) separately and wish to keep their characteristics distinct, I intentionally avoid using the more general (and anachronistic) term *halakhah*.

2. See Kampen and Bernstein 1996, 1; Qimron 1996a, 9; and Qimron and Strugnell 1994, 1. Since all the repeated lines in each overlapping copy are nearly identical, and since some copies extend beyond the cutoff points of other copies, it is possible, with a certain degree of confidence, to create a composite text, giving readers a more authentic sense of what the Essene community might have written and read during the Second Temple period. The first editors of the manuscript for the Discoveries in the Judean Desert series (volume 10), Qimron and Strugnell, compiled just such a composite text of 4QMMT.

3. Moshe J. Bernstein (1996, 30), Hanan Eshel (1996, 64), and Daniel R. Schwartz (1996, 79) agree with this early date of composition, and Schiffman confirms that "with MMT we have clearly returned to the early days of sectarian law" (1996, 98). Miguel Pérez Fernández suggests 50 BCE to 50 CE as dates for the copies but agrees that the original epistle was probably composed around 150 BCE (1997, 193).

Paleographic dating uses records of gradual shifts in the conventions of script writing (the shapes of letters, for example) to date texts. Texts with Hebrew letters showing certain characteristic shapes can be dated quite accurately, often to within a dozen years. However, in the case of 4QMMT, the date we arrive at through paleographic analysis is only the date designating when the text was *copied*. Linguistic analysis tracks historical changes in vocabulary and usage and can be used to date the *original* text of which only copies survive.

4. The term "nonbiblical" is misleading, since the texts that would become the Hebrew Bible are very much present throughout all of the scrolls found near Qumran. Here "nonbiblical" simply means they are not books found in the canonical Hebrew Bible. Bernstein points out that "one of the few universally agreed upon characteristics of Qumran literature," including the so-called sectarian (or nonbiblical) texts, "is its bibliocentricity, the crucial role which Hebrew Scripture plays as source and model for the themes, language, and subject matter of the various kinds of documents from the Dead Sea caves" (1996, 29). See also Frölich 1998.

5. Although most scholars believe that 4QMMT was written (and, presumably, sent) to an external audience, there are some who reject this argument (for example, Fraade 2000, 2003; Abegg 1999), suggesting that it was intended only for intracommunal study. I agree with the majority who believe that 4QMMT was originally written as a letter and probably delivered, most likely with negative results; however, I also believe that the repeated copying of this text demonstrates its importance for internal use later in the sect's history.

6. Since very small fragments of the solar calendar are preserved in only one copy of 4QMMT (4Q394), and since we are able to read only copies of the original epistle sent to Jerusalem, it is possible that the calendar was added later by a copyist as an aid to studying the disputes that led to the formation of the sect (Fernández 1997, 192; Schiffman 1996, 82–86). Nevertheless, this possibility should not diminish our understanding of the important place the solar calendar held in the ritual practices of the Essene community. According to Kamm, the Essenes "disregarded the Jewish lunar calendar of 354 days in favor of one based on the sun, whereby the year was divided into fifty-two weeks exactly, in four seasons each of thirteen weeks. Thus the year began, and every festival fell, on precisely the same day of the week on each occasion, [so never on the Sabbath,] and the community did not necessarily celebrate the special days at the same time as their fellow Jews" (1999, 163).

7. Qimron and Strugnell (1994) translate the Hebrew phrase *ma'aseh ha-torah* "precepts of the law," which does not preserve well enough (like the term *halakhah*) 4QMMT's distinction between laws and works of the law. Florentino García Martínez (1996a) translates *ma'aseh ha-torah* "works of the law," which more accurately preserves the sense of deeds and activities associated with legal regulations (see also Martinez 1996b, 23–27; Abegg 1999, 2001).

8. Although scholars tend to agree that the audience (the singular "you") of 4QMMT's third section (C) is the non-Zadokite Hasmonean high priest Jonathan (Eshel 1996, 61), there are, of course, dissenters, and their dissent is usually based on alternative dates of composition for 4QMMT. Stanislaw Medala (1999), for example, dates 4QMMT to the first half of the second century BCE, making the audience Alcimus, a Hellenizing non-Zadokite who was high priest from 162 to 159 BCE. However, Alcimus was a brutal dictator who administered the Jerusalem Temple about a decade before the Essene

community even began forming as a breakaway sect, making Alcimus an unlikely audience of the conciliatory 4QMMT. Jonathan's younger brother Simon was high priest from 142 to 135 BCE. Simon is also unlikely as the audience of 4QMMT, since he crushed all opposition in order to consolidate his power, and he arranged for a decree stating that all future high priests would come not from the line of Zadok but from the Hasmonean dynasty. So a conciliatory letter stating legal opposition would have failed in its intent and insured the death of its authors. Jonathan spent some years purifying the Temple and gaining the trust of the Israelites before he was appointed high priest in 152, and then held the position tenuously for a decade (Cross 1993, 30). Since Jonathan was interested (certainly more than Alcimus or Simon) in gaining favor among the Israelite populations, and since it is generally recognized that the group that eventually settled at Qumran withdrew from the Temple cult around 152 (Medala, 11), Jonathan is by far the most likely candidate for the audience of 4QMMT.

There is also some controversy over the authorship of 4QMMT. Most scholars (too many to cite here, since it is almost all of them) believe that the community at Qumran was formed by deposed Zadokite priests who were later identified as Essenes. This interpretation is derived from the evidence of Josephus's descriptions of this sect in the *Antiquities of the Jews* and the *Wars of the Jews*, which were written during the first century CE. Although common, this view is not universal. Lester L. Grabbe (1997) and Lawrence H. Schiffman (1995b) believe that the legal regulations described in 4QMMT resemble Sadducean laws in the Mishnah (circa 200 CE), so they claim Sadducean authorship for the text. Medala (1999) finds resemblances between the legal regulations described in 4QMMT and Pharisaic *halakhah* in the Mishnah, so he claims Pharisaic authorship for the text. I take the most common position that Josephus's detailed descriptions of Essene doctrines quite closely match the core doctrines represented in the sectarian scrolls, including 4QMMT. Although I reject any connection between the Essenes and the Pharisees, there may be some connection between the Essenes and the Sadducees, whose name derives from Zadok. The Essenes may have originated as a conservative group among the Sadducees before breaking away entirely and moving to Qumran. However, since the Essenes would have evolved into a distinct sect in opposition to the Sadducees, it would be inaccurate to equate the two sects.

9. For more on the early history of the Israelites and Judaism, see John Bright's (2000) *A History of Israel*, Michael D. Coogan's (1998) edited volume *The Oxford History of the Biblical World*, and Antony Kamm's (1999) *The Israelites: And Introduction*. I draw much from these sources in my discussion of 4QMMT's rhetorical ecology.

10. Cross explains that the very origin of the Essene community emerged from intrigue surrounding priestly succession:

> In the days of Antiochus IV Epiphanes (175–63 BCE), the orderly succession of Zadokite high priests failed. The high priestly office became a prize dispensed by the Seleucid overlord Antiochus, to be purchased by the highest bidder. The strife between rivals for the theocratic office soon developed into civil war, and in the resulting chaos Antiochus found opportunity to carry out his fearful massacres, terminating in the notorious desecration of the Temple and the Hellenization of Holy Jerusalem. The stage was set for the

rise of the Maccabees, whose destiny it was to lead the Jews in a heroic war of independence, and who, having won popularity by freeing Judah from foreign suzerains, themselves usurped the high priestly office. In this way, the ancient Zadokite house gave way to the lusty, if illegitimate, Hasmonean dynasty. (1993, 28)

It is important to remember, though, that although Jonathan was not a Zadokite when he became high priest in 152 BCE, neither were any of the high priests since 171 BCE, when Menelaus bribed his way into the position.

11. Although Schiffman has been vigorously engaged in debates about the sectarian identity of the Qumran community, even he agrees that "the vast majority of legal rulings regarding the observances of sacrificial law, Sabbath, purity laws, and other *halakhic* practices were common to Second Temple period Jews. This common Judaism was practiced by the masses . . . who had little to do with the detailed disputes of the various elites who had enrolled in the sectarian groups. The debates and differences of opinion we observe are often blown out of proportion. It must be remembered that our sources tend to emphasize disagreements over commonalities" (2000, 138).

12. Although I find Brooke's (1997) argument irrefutable, there is scholarship preceding Brooke's that argues for a less direct connection to scripture for the laws of 4QMMT: Qimron and Strugnell argue that the citation formula "it is written" does not introduce direct quotations of scripture, which, they believe, indicates that the authors of 4QMMT are presenting laws of their own interpretation (1994, 140). This view, however, is generally no longer accepted. Bernstein, taking a position between Brooke and Qimron and Strugnell, believes that "it is written" introduces mostly paraphrases and indirect references to scripture, with only a few explicit citations: "It is immediately clear that [*katub*, "it is written"] in MMT need not precede a quotation, but that paraphrase is to be considered [*katub*] as well" (1996, 39).

13. Wherever possible, I use Martin G. Abegg Jr., Peter Flint, and Eugene Ulrich's translations of biblical texts in *The Dead Sea Scrolls Bible*, since these are translations of the very Hebrew documents that were read and studied by the Essene community. These and all subsequent references to the sectarian texts of the Dead Sea Scrolls come from Florentino García Martínez's (1996a) translations in *The Dead Sea Scrolls Translated: The Qumran Texts in English*, 2nd ed.

14. Whereas the citation formula "it is written" appears throughout sections B and C of 4QMMT, all of the formulae for introducing interpretations of the law appear only in section B.

15. Archaeological evidence shows that the Essenes first occupied Qumran around 100 BCE (Magness 2002, 65), but the date of 4QMMT is likely around 150 BCE. Thus, there may have been as much as a fifty-year period when those who would become the Qumran community were dispersed throughout the general population. 4QMMT represents this community's desire to return to the Temple cult, if the Temple priests abide by the strict works of the law described in 4QMMT. But later texts among the Dead Sea Scrolls, composed after the group's settlement at Qumran, represent a more solidified anti-templar ideology. See Magness 2002 for a detailed discussion of the archaeology of the Qumran site and its relation to the Dead Sea Scrolls.

16. For arguments that the authors of 4QMMT employ a polemical, combative, or confrontational tone, see Kampen and Bernstein 1996, 5 and 6; Qimron and Strugnell 1994, 110; Schiffman 1995a; Shemesh and Werman 2003, 122. Scholars who find the tone polemical and oppositional are often (though not always) the

same scholars who search for parallels between 4QMMT and the sectarian legal debates described in the Mishnah. In other words, working anachronistically from the conflictual tone of the Mishnah, these scholars also find opposition and polemics (where others do not) in 4QMMT.

17. As Regev notes, "A positive response from the addressee should lead to the end of the [Essene] authors' self-imposed withdrawal and their renewed participation in the Temple cult" (2003, 254). However, as we see from later Qumran documents, no such identification was achieved, and the Qumran community remained in exile until the Roman legions sacked Judea during the middle decades of the first century CE. In fact, the high priest to whom 4QMMT was addressed becomes, in later Qumran documents, the "Wicked Priest" (Eshel 2008, 2 and elsewhere). In the *Psalms Pesher* (4Q171), the author relates that the Wicked Priest spied on the "just man" (probably the community's leader, also called the Teacher of Righteousness) because of the works and laws that the Essene leader had sent to him; and the *Habakkuk Pesher* (1QpHab) says that the Wicked Priest tried to have the Teacher of Righteousness killed (column XI, lines 4–8). Ultimately, the Essene authors' attempt at identification failed, as did their sincere effort to persuade the high priest to purify the Temple and align his (and his staff's) priestly orthopraxy more closely with Mosaic law (Regev 2003, 256). 4QMMT, then, represents the Essene community's final effort to reestablish ties with the Jerusalem Temple, yet their effort was rejected and met only with suspicion and violence.

CHAPTER 2

1. A covenant is a mutual (divine-human) promise with certain conditions attached, usually imposed by God on the human recipients of the blessings associated with the promise. The Torah describes a number of covenants (between God and Adam, Abraham, Noah, Isaac, and Jacob, for example), each with its own different emphasis. The Mosaic covenant is a conditional promise God made to provide blessings to the Israelite nation in exchange for strict obedience to the law, and it is most fully described in Deuteronomy 26:18–19: "[And the LORD has promised today that you are his people, his treasured possession, as he promised yo]u, and that you are to keep [all his commandments.] And he shall set you h[igh above all the nations tha]t he has made, [for fame and] for praise and for ho[nor; and for you to be a holy people to the LOR]D your God, just as [he] has sp[oken] to you" (Abegg, Flint, and Ulrich 1999, 181). The blessings and curses associated with the old Mosaic covenant are distinctly material: if the Israelites obey God's commandments, then God's people will be blessed with numerous children, productive crops, and healthy livestock (Deuteronomy 28:1–13; Abegg, Flint, and Ulrich 1999, 182–83); if the Israelites violate God's commandments, then they will be cursed with infertility, drought, blight, and plague (Deuteronomy 28:1–13; Abegg, Flint, and Ulrich 1999, 182–83). According to Ellen Juhl Christiansen, the new covenant reformulated at Qumran is substantially different from the one delivered by God to Moses on Mount Sinai. Christiansen writes, "The emphasis has *shifted* from concrete blessings of place and collective existence to an individualized reward, which is expressed in future categories, as eschatological hope. The concern is with covenantal blessings of peace and long life, building on the dualistic principle of goodness and truth and applying the divine promise individually, not collectively" (1998, 88–89).

2. The name Essene does not appear anywhere in the Dead Sea Scrolls. In the *Rule of the Community* and elsewhere (the *Damascus Document*, the *Habakkuk Pesher*, the *Micah Pesher*, the *Rule of the*

Congregation, the *Rule of the Blessings*, the *Hymns Scroll*, the *Baptismal Liturgy*, the *Decrees*, the *Songs of the Sage*, and the *Ritual of Purification*), the group refers to itself as the Yahad, a term that appears over forty times throughout 1QS.

3. Over the past sixty-five years, literally hundreds of articles and books have been written, in whole or part, about issues related to the *Rule of the Community*. Some of the most recent, since 2000, include the following. On the relationship of the *Rule of the Community* to the Hebrew Bible (or Old Testament), see Klein 2009; Lucas 2010; Nitzan 2010; Shemesh 2008; and Timmer 2008. On the relationship of the *Rule of the Community* to the New Testament, see Cirafesi 2011–12; Timmer 2009; and Tukasi 2008. On the identity of the community associated with the *Rule of the Community*, see Berg 2007; Hempel 2011. On the requirement of purity and punishments for impurity in the *Rule of the Community*, see Ginsburskaya 2010; Himmelfarb 2001; and Toews 2003. On the nature of the Hebrew language used in the *Rule of the Community*, see Isaksson 2008; Rendsburg 2010.

4. For a more detailed analysis of the dualistic spirit in the *Rule of the Community*, especially in relation to the themes of light and dark, see Leaney 1966, 37–56; Xervatis 2010.

5. There are several passages in the *Rule of the Community* that describe the dualist nature of the human spirit. The following is representative:

> He [God] created man to rule the world and placed within him two spirits so that he would walk with them until the moment of his visitation: they are the spirits of truth and of deceit. In the hand of the Prince of Lights is dominion over all the sons of justice; they walk on paths of light. And in the hand of the Angel of Darkness is total dominion over the sons of deceit; they walk on paths of darkness. Due to the Angel of Darkness all the sons of justice stray, and their sins, their iniquities, their failings and their mutinous deeds are under his dominion in compliance with the mysteries of God, until his moment, and all their punishments and their periods of grief are caused by the dominion of his enmity; and all the spirits of their lot cause the sons of light to fall. However, the God of Israel and the angel of his truth assist all the sons of light. (column III, lines 17–25)

Here the term "visitation" refers to the eschatological end of days foretold by the prophets in the Hebrew Bible. The end of days will see the redemption of obedient Israelites and the utter destruction of disobedient others.

6. The *Rule of the Community* goes into some detail regarding the qualities of the Sons of Light:

> These are their [that is, the Sons of Light's] paths in the world: to enlighten the heart of man, straighten out in front of him all the paths of justice and truth, establish in his heart respect for the precepts of God; it is a spirit of meekness, of patience, generous compassion, eternal goodness, intelligence, understanding, potent wisdom which trusts in all the deeds of God and depends on his abundant mercy; a spirit of knowledge in all the plans of action, of enthusiasm for the decrees of justice, of holy plans with firm purpose, of generous compassion with all the sons of truth, of magnificent purity which detests all unclean idols, of unpretentious behavior with moderation in everything, of prudence in respect of

truth concerning the mysteries of knowledge. These are the counsels of the spirit for the sons of truth in the world. (column IV, lines 2–6)

7. The description of the Sons of Darkness in the *Rule of the Community* employs the kind of harsh language one would expect in a dualist ideology: "However, to the spirit of deceit belong greed, frailty of hands in the service of justice, irreverence, deceit, pride and haughtiness of heart, dishonesty, trickery, cruelty, much insincerity, impatience, much insanity, impudent enthusiasm, appalling acts performed in a lustful passion, filthy paths for indecent purposes, blasphemous tongue, blindness of eyes, hardness of hearing, stiffness of neck, hardness of heart in order to walk in all the paths of darkness and evil cunning" (column IV, lines 9–11).

8. Notable examples of this early effort to link speech act theory and rhetoric include Benjamin 1976, Campbell 1973, Gaines 1979, Kolenda 1971, McGuire 1977, Sanders 1976, and Wallace 1970. In 1987, Reed Way Dasenbrock linked speech act theory specifically with the development of the New Rhetoric. Later scholars would continue this movement, appropriating pragmatic strategies from speech act theory as a means to operationalize theories and practices of rhetoric and argumentation. For example, Walter H. Beale's (1987) pragmatic theory of rhetoric, Jürgen Habermas's (1984) theory of communicative action, and Frans H. van Eemeren and Rob Grootendorst's (2004) pragma-dialectical approach to argumentation all draw extensively from speech act theory as a pragmatic foundation for their respective treatments of rhetoric and argumentation.

9. Toward the end of *How to Do Things with Words*, Austin ([1962] 1975) points out that all utterances are performative, since all utterances are *at least* locutionary acts, eliminating the need for a constative category. James Bohman (1988) and Jeff Mason (1994) argue that perlocutionary acts are more relevant to rhetoric than illocutionary acts because perlocution is oriented toward real effects, a primary concern of rhetoric. However, in my view, rhetoric is also concerned with intent and action, making all of speech act theory, including illocution, relevant to the study and practice of rhetoric.

10. According to Frank Moore Cross, the Dead Sea Scrolls in general "reflect a historical struggle for power between high priestly families. The [Essene community] withdrew in defeat and formed their community in exile, which was organized as a counter-Israel led by a counter-priesthood, or, viewed with [Essene] eyes, as the true Israel of God led by the legitimate priesthood" (1993, 26). Christiansen agrees, suggesting "that the community has a function that is equivalent to priestly service, and that God's presence is to be found within the community behind 1QS, rather than in the Jerusalem Temple" (1998, 89).

CHAPTER 3

1. For arguments that the *Rule of the Community* and the *Damascus Document* were directed toward two different audiences within the same sect, see Baumgarten and Schwartz 1995, 5, 7; Collins 2006; Knibb 1987, 14–15; Metso 2000, 86; 2006, 222–23; VanderKam 1994, 57, 91; and Vermes 2004, 26–48. For alternative views, see Davies 1982, 1994, 2000; Regev 2010; and Wassen 2005. The *Damascus Document* was a living text that was revised frequently throughout the life of the Essene sect. However, most scholars believe that it reached its final form, represented in CD, around 100 BCE (Wassen 2005, 24).

2. One notable exception to the dearth of scholarship on the *Damascus Document*

between the discovery of the Cairo manuscripts and the discovery of the Dead Sea copies is Louis Ginzberg's (1976) *An Unknown Jewish Sect*, first published in German in 1922.

3. For detailed discussions of the reconstruction and meaning of the Cave 4 fragments of the *Damascus Document*, see Baumgarten 1999; Stegemann 2000; and Wassen 2005.

4. According to Hartmut Stegemann (2000), the extremely fragmentary Cave 4, 5, and 6 copies generally duplicate complete text from CD, and most of the sections in the Cave 4, 5, and 6 fragments that either precede or follow CD are so fragmentary that they are not useful for detailed analysis.

5. Perelman also discusses dissociation in his 1982 solo effort, *The Realm of Rhetoric*, but this later discussion is inferior to the one that appears in *The New Rhetoric*, coauthored with Olbrechts-Tyteca. Other sources, not directly relevant to the present discussion, treat dissociation as a rhetorical strategy, applying it to different rhetorical texts: Cloud 2014; Fernheimer 2008; Grootendorst 1999; Gross and Dearing 2010; Lynch 2006; Maddux 2013; Schiappa 1985; Stahl 2002; Vorster 1992; Waisanen 2011.

6. M. A. Van Rees states the matter a little more succinctly: "A notion that originally was considered by the audience as a conceptual unity is split up into two new notions, each of which contains only part of the original one, one notion containing the aspects of the original notion that belong to the realm of the merely apparent, the other containing the aspects of the original notion that belong to the realm of the real" (2009, xi). Van Rees's (2009) *Dissociation in Argumentative Discussions* is by far the most detailed treatment of dissociation as a rhetorical strategy thus far. However, Van Rees approaches dissociation specifically from a pragma-dialectical perspective, limiting her treatment to its use in critical discussions.

7. According to Angela Kim Harkins (2015), the *Damascus Document*'s Admonition (and, I would add, each dissociation that is enacted in it) takes a hortatory tone in order to prepare the emotional state of its audience for increased obedience to the strict legal requirements that follow. Harkins writes, "By experientially placing themselves within narratives of repeated failure to uphold the obligations of the Law, Second Temple readers of the Admonition could have cultivated a predisposition for cooperative living and obedience to the Law" (2015, 306). Hempel agrees, suggesting that the "Admonition introduces us to the Laws of the Damascus Document and is, therefore, vital in determining how those laws were intended to be read" (1998, 316).

8. Richard M. Weaver (1985) describes three categories of ultimate terms: god terms, devil terms, and charismatic terms. According to Weaver, "By 'god term' we mean that expression about which all other expressions are ranked as subordinate and serving dominations and powers. Its force imparts to others their lesser degree of force, and fixes the scale by which degrees of comparison are understood" (212). These terms are so salient that they not only guide action but demand sacrifice. Weaver writes, "This capacity to demand sacrifice is probably the surest indicator of the 'god term,' for when a term is so sacrosanct that the material goods of this life must be mysteriously rendered up for it, then we feel justified in saying that it is in some sense ultimate" (214). Later, Weaver writes, "The counterpart of the 'god term' is the 'devil term'" (222). Devil terms personify an enemy and help to define communities, if only in negative terms. Weaver writes:

> There seems indeed to be some psychic law which compels every nation to have in its national imagination an enemy. Perhaps this is but a version of the tribal need for a

scapegoat, or for something which will personify "the adversary." If a nation did not have an enemy, an enemy would have to be invented to take care of those expressions of scorn and hatred to which peoples must give vent. When another political state is not available to receive the discharge of such emotions, then a class will be chosen, or a race, or a type, or a political faction, and this will be held up to a particularly standardized form of repudiation. Perhaps the truth is that we need the enemy in order to define ourselves. (222)

The meanings of god terms and devil terms can generally be accounted for through historical development and social context. However, the meanings of charismatic terms are less directly identifiable. According to Weaver, charismatic terms are "terms of considerable potency whose referents it is virtually impossible to discover or to construct through imagination" (227). Weaver writes, "It is the nature of the charismatic term to have a power which is not derived, but which is in some mysterious way given. . . . In effect, they are rhetorical by common consent, or by 'charisma'" (227). Weaver continues, "The charismatic term is given its load of impulsion without reference, and it functions by convention. The number of such terms is small in any one period, but they are perhaps the most efficacious terms of all" (228).

9. Timothy H. Lim (2013) points out that the prohibition against polygamous marriages is actually a more stringent interpretation of similar laws in Leviticus 18, which do account for the possibility of multiple wives in a lifetime.

10. Catherine M. Murphy concludes:

> Wealth is an issue for the *Damascus Document* community. It is present in all the redactional stages of the document. It is mentioned in almost every generic category, from the admonition to the various legal subgenres. The discussion of wealth reveals that financial practices, particularly commercial and sacrificial exchanges, played a role in the spawning of the community and in shaping later stages of its identity. The document stipulates that wealth be used to build up the community rather than to elevate the individual, and does so in explicit contradistinction to the practice of outsiders. Wealth is a boundary marker for the community as well as a proper domain for its scrutiny and judgment. Private property is made public domain within the limited bounds of the association. . . . In choosing to live a different lifestyle, the Damascus covenanters step into the end time they anticipate, and give economic witness to the eschatological justice for which they hope. (1991, 128–29)

11. Ben Zion Wacholder explains the third net (defilement of the Temple) a little bit differently, suggesting that the passage "deals with three prohibitions: 1) having sexual intercourse in the Temple (probably in Jerusalem); 2) lying with a woman during her flux; and 3) marrying the daughter of one's brother or sister" (2007, 201).

12. David Instone Brewer points out that "the section concerning the Nets of Belial in the *Damascus Document* may be directed against the Pharisees, but it criticizes practices which were condoned also by Sadducees and presumably by other groups, so it may be addressed to the opponents of Qumran generally" (1998, 565). Jonathan Klawans explains that the three nets of Belial cause not just ritual impurity but more serious moral impurity (1998, 409–15).

13. The Torah is the foundation of all Judaism, including the Qumran Essenes.

However, in the process of canonization, the Torah was opened up to sectarian interpretations, and each sect believed its interpretations would lead to salvation and the blessings of the covenants. Collins explains that "the movement of the New Covenant had its origin in disputes over the correct interpretation of the Torah" (2011, 303; see also Wacholder 2007, 216–17). For the Qumran Essenes, the Torah remains as central as it was for any sect of the time; however, their stringent interpretations of Torah law, almost as important as the Torah itself, appear throughout the sectarian texts like the *Damascus Document*. According to Davies, "The Israel of CD is constituted by scrupulous obedience to the *torah* as revealed in its own covenant. This new *torah* is created by exegetical development of the scriptural *torah* rather than by a new text, though the new *torah* may be expressed in texts such as CD itself" (2000, 33). Davies continues, "The laws governing the life of this group, then, are regarded as Mosaic *torah*, and a distinction is made between the written scriptural text which the New Covenanters share with historical Israel and its fuller explication in the laws of the group" (33; see also Davies 1982, 54).

14. For an extended discussion of this passage in relation to the historical origins of the Qumran community, see Vander-Kam 2011 and Collins 2011. Grossman (2002) argues that it is possible to read for history in the *Damascus Document* as long as textual interpretation is contextualized through discourse.

15. It is likely that the Scoffer, according to VanderKam, "is the leader/founder of the group we know as the Pharisees" (2011, 60; see also VanderKam 2003).

16. Although Damascus is referred to as a real location in the *Damascus Document*, most scholars agree that its primary reference is symbolic, "a place defined by its holiness" (Christiansen 1988, 78). Chaim Milkowski disagrees, suggesting that an early vestige of the Qumran community was actually exiled to Damascus, where they encounter the "Expounder of the Torah" (1982, 103–6). Although I am interested in Milkowski's speculation, I do not find enough evidence in the *Damascus Document* itself to grant his conclusion.

17. Christiansen recognizes that "in CD there is a tension between ethnic identity with a strong awareness of the past and a particularistic self-understanding which limits membership to those who belong by choice and subscribe to voluntaristic group conditions" (1998, 72). Thus, Christiansen continues, "while CD is conscious of past tradition, values, and beliefs, it is also aware of a broken covenant" (85).

18. Bergsma is careful to point out, however, that this desire to dissociate Judah from the ideal Essene community "does not mean that the community is anti-Judahite. On the contrary, the tribe of Judah has an honored place with the *Yahad*; but the *Yahad* aspires to be all of 'Israel,' not just 'Judah'" (2008, 187).

19. For an alternative interpretation of the relationship between the Essenes of the *Damascus Document* and the "princes of Judah," see Hultgren 2004.

CHAPTER 4

1. Unlike the *Purification Rules*, the *Temple Scroll* actually covers a wide-ranging scope of subjects. For book-length treatments of the *Temple Scroll* in general, see Charlesworth 2011b, Crawford 2000, Maier 2009, Qimron 1996b, Schiffman and Martinez 2008, Wise 1990a, and Yadin 1985. For book-length treatments of the relationship between the *Temple Scroll* and the Bible, see Levinson 2013, Riska 2001, and Swanson 1995. Searches for "Temple Scroll" in ATLA and JSTOR result in thousands of hits, so I will leave interested

scholars to play around with additional key words that interest them. Some of the articles, not cited in the body of this chapter, that have deeply influenced my own understanding of the *Temple Scroll* include Callaway 1988; Gilders 2006; Schiffman 1994a, 1994b; and Wise 1990b.

2. Schiffman dates the *Purification Rules* to "the early first century BCE" (1995b, 299) and the *Temple Scroll* to "sometime after 120 BCE" (257).

3. In 1841, Marx received a PhD in Classical Greek Philosophy from Berlin University, and, interestingly, we know from an 1837 letter to his father that Marx (then only nineteen years old) had both read and translated parts of Aristotle's *Rhetoric*. But nowhere (in the letter or in anything else that Marx subsequently wrote) is there any further discussion of this text or of rhetoric in general. It is important to note, too, that during his late teens and early twenties, Marx was still heavily involved in idealist philosophies and had not yet been bitten by the materialism bug.

4. *Pragma* is the Greek term for "things," "matter"; it is similar in meaning to the Latin term *res*.

5. Obvious exceptions to the general applicability of new material rhetorics in the context of the Dead Sea Scrolls include the viral distribution of visual memes (Gries 2015, 86–87) and chronotopic lamination (42–45). These phenomena require a context of networked technologies that did not exist in the Second Temple period.

6. Jameson's (1972) *The Prison-House of Language* precedes Bourdieu's ([1980] 1990) description of habitus, and Bourdieu does not invoke Jameson in his work, but the functional similarities between prison-house and habitus are evident in comparison. One difference, not to be ignored, is that Jameson's prison-house is the thought-model that produces and constrains structuralist and Russian formalist literary criticism, and Bourdieu's habitus is a system of structured dispositions that produces and constrains related cultural practices.

7. 4QPurification Rules B^c explains further aspects of the creation and use of *me niddah*:

[. . . the cedar,] the hyssop, and the [scarlet . . .] [. . .] pure from every impurity of [. . .] the priest who atones with the heifer's blood and all the [. . .] [. . .] and the sewn tunic with which atonement was made for the precept [. . .] [. . .] in water [and it will be im]pure till the evening. Whoever carries the vase of the water of purification will be im[pure . . .] [. . . No-one should sprinkle] the water of purification upon the impure, [ex]cept a pu[re] priest [. . .] [. . . upon] them, since he atones for the impure. And a wicked man should not sprinkle over the impure. [. . .] [. . .] the water of purification. And they shall enter the water and shall be pure of the impurity of the corpse [. . .] [. . .] other. The prie[st] shall scatter over them the water of purification to purify [. . .] rather, they will be purified and their flesh [will be pu]re. (4Q277, fragment 1, lines 1–10)

8. The *Temple Scroll* also, of course, discusses ritual impurities. For discussions of ritual impurities in the *Temple Scroll*, see Anderson 1992; Callaway 1986; Milgrom 1991, 1993a, 1993b; and Werrett 2007, 107–79.

9. Klawans points out that the *Temple Scroll* includes lesser violations in its list of sins resulting in moral defilement that the Bible does not list, including bribery (2000, 51).

10. Fitzmyer lists these festivals and sacrifices in order: "The Tamid-Offering,

Offerings at the Beginning of the Months, Offering for the Consecration, Passover and Unleavened Bread, Feast of Sheafwaving, Feast of Weeks: First Fruits of Grain, First Fruits of Wine, First Fruits of Oil, Burnt Offerings of the Tribes, The Day of Atonement, and The Feast of Tabernacles" (2007, 206).

CHAPTER 5

1. Texts among the Dead Sea Scrolls are included in the pesher genre if they use the term *pesher* to introduce interpretive language and also engage in the passage-by-passage interpretive method that is characteristic of pesher texts. Two kinds of peshers have been discovered near Qumran, thematic and continuous. Thematic peshers collect topically related quotations from several prophetic books and interpret their meaning passage by passage. These scrolls include *Words of Moses* (1Q22), *Liturgical Text* (1Q30), *Ordinances* (4Q159), *Florilegium* (4Q174), *Catena* (4Q177), *Ages of Creation* (4Q180), *Exposition on the Patriarchs* (4Q464), *Melchizedec* (11Q13), and some sections of the *Damascus Document* (CD and certain Cave 4 fragments). Continuous peshers interpet quotations from a single prophetic book in sequential order from beginning to end. These scrolls include *Isaiah Pesher* (4Q161–65), *Hosea Pesher* (4Q166–67), *Micah Pesher* (1Q14), *Nahum Pesher* (4Q169), *Habakkuk Pesher* (1QpHab), *Zephaniah Pesher* (1Q15 and 4Q170), *Malachi Pesher* (5Q10), and *Psalms Pesher* (1Q16, 4Q171, and 4Q173). With the exception of the *Habakkuk Pesher*, these other pesher texts, whether thematic or continuous, are extremely fragmentary and/or emphasize textual summary rather than interpretation. Thus, among the Qumran scrolls, only the *Habakkuk Pesher* fully illustrates the pesher genre and method, which is why I have chosen to focus on it in this chapter. See Lim 2002 for further discussion of the categories and dates of the peshers.

2. The MT version of the book of Habakkuk includes three chapters. However, the *Habakkuk Pesher* interprets only the first two, and there is a blank space after chapter 2 in the scroll, indicating that the pesher is complete, that is, it is neither a damaged scroll nor a work that was interrupted before a final section was completed (Horgan 1979, 11). There are a couple of possible reasons for this discrepancy. First, some scholars argue that chapter 3 was a later addition to Habakkuk (see Dangl 2001, 145–46, for a summary), so it is possible that the Qumran community knew it as a two-chapter book. However, it is unlikely that chapter 3 would have been added that late to the redacted and canonized text of Habakkuk. Second, and more likely, the pesher method is intended to interpret only prophetic discourse (Dimant 2009; Horgan 1979; Jassen 2012; Lange and Pleše 2012; Niehoff 1992, 2012), and chapter 3 of the book of Habakkuk was viewed by the Essenes as a liturgical (not prophetic) addition to the first two prophetic chapters. Thus, chapter 3 was not viewed as requiring or prompting pesher interpretation, even though it was likely known as part of the complete text of Habakkuk in the Second Temple period. Either way, throughout this chapter, I consider only the first two chapters of Habakkuk, since these are the only chapters subjected to interpretation in the *Habakkuk Pesher*.

3. The complex evolution of hermeneutics as a practice and a discipline is recounted in numerous sources, but I find Stanley E. Porter and Jason C. Robinson's (2011) *Hermeneutics: An Introduction to Interpretive Theory* to be the most comprehensive in scope.

4. Gadamer's 1997 essay, "Rhetoric and Hermeneutics," is a case in point. Here he traces the historical intersections of romantic hermeneutics and Renaissance rhetoric in terms of reading (hermeneutics) and speaking (rhetoric), but he never discusses his own concepts from philosophical hermeneutics as aspects of rhetoric.

5. My analysis of hermeneutics/rhetoric in the *Habakkuk Pesher* is preceded by an analysis of hermeneutics/rhetoric in the prophecy of the book of Habakkuk because the pesher relies significantly on this prophecy. Brooke points out that "when considering the continuous pesharim in particular, the controlling influence of the scriptural text must be the starting point. To begin with, it is apparent that the interpreter is aware of the structure and purpose of the original context from which he is working" (1994, 340); and Horgan explains that "the pesher grows out of the biblical text" (1979, 244). See also Lange and Pleše (2012) and Jassen (2012) for similar arguments about the close relationship between the biblical text and the pesher.

6. While complaints are a common genre in the biblical psalms, and oracles are a common genre in the biblical prophets, Michael H. Floyd explains that only Jeremiah and Habakkuk join these two genres (complaint and oracle) into a unified form (1991, 397). Jeremiah and Habakkuk were historical contemporaries, speaking and writing prophecies at the end of the First Temple period.

7. There is little agreement about how to translate the Hebrew word *tôkaḥat* in the book of Habakkuk, partly because the word has two different deictic or directional senses. A "complaint" would originate with Habakkuk and be directed toward Yahweh, similar to the word's outgoing directional sense in Job. A "reproof" would originate with Yahweh and be directed toward Habakkuk and the Judeans, similar to the word's incoming directional sense in Isaiah and Proverbs. Both senses (complaint and reproof) are relevant to the context of the book of Habakkuk, since Habakkuk certainly complains to Yahweh and Yahweh certainly rebukes Habakkuk and the Judeans. Thus, in a general sense, it may not be necessary to choose just one meaning, since both meanings are present to the word and both are relevant to the context. However, for my interpretive purposes here, I will emphasize the sense of complaint because it allows me to more clearly situate the book of Habakkuk within the biblical tradition. For a brief discussion of these translations, see Robertson 1983, 54.

8. Michael E. W. Thompson explains why Jehoiakim must be the cause of Judean strife described in Habakkuk's first complaint:

> As a result of their victory at Carchemish in 605 BC the Babylonians gained possession of Syria-Palestine. In 604 or 603 BC Jehoiakim, who reigned in Jerusalem from 609 to 598 BC, became the "servant" (2 Ki. 24:1) of Nebuchadnezzar. This further allows us to understand that the internal Judean social ills spoken of in 1:2-4 were those perpetrated in Jehoiakim's reign. We read of Jehoiakim shedding much innocent blood (2 Ki. 24:4), while Jeremiah's words about him were caustic in the extreme (Je. 22:13-19; 26:1-23). Such would have given more than adequate grounds for the complaint in 1:2-4. (1993, 36)

For additional explanations of the historical context of the book of Habakkuk, see also Bakon 2011, 25-28; Holladay 2001; Hunn 2009; Janzen 1982; O'Connell 1979, 227-30; and Pinker 2008.

9. Robert I. Vasholz (1992) suggests that Habakkuk's first complaint is about

external oppression and that the second complaint is an expansion of the first, but this view does not account for why external oppressors would care about the paralysis of the law.

10. Ancient Judean oracles are also oral in their original form. Mowinckel recognizes the oral origin of these prophetic utterances, explaining that "the prophets were oral preachers, and that their sayings have been transmitted (at least partially) by word of mouth for some time before they were written down" (2002, 3); these sayings thus represent "an *originally oral tradition*" (11). The power accorded to oracles was, according to Ronald E. Clements, "exemplary of the great power that was believed to exist in the spoken word. Oracles were not mere words, but forceful weapons which could secure the attainment of the blessing or curse which they contained" (1965, 31). Visual oracles (Habakkuk saw his oracles as visions) were reported in speech directly to an audience of Judean monarchs, Temple priests, and common citizens, and they were only written down later, if ever. In the case of the book of Habakkuk, however, they were written down immediately, at least according to the prophecy itself.

11. Emerton (1977), Floyd (1993), Janzen (1980), Pinker (2007), Robertson (1983), Scott (1985), and Wendland (1999) all offer finely detailed explanations and interpretations of Habakkuk's second oracle (2.4). E. Ray Clendenen (2014) focuses especially on the last word of the oracle, "fidelity" or "faith." Chris Heard (1997) offers an ethical deconstruction (in the technical, Derridean sense) of unjust violence in the book of Habakkuk; however, he does not place these acts of injustice in the context of the Mosaic covenant, which specifies curses for infidelity, choosing instead to play with language and invoke contexts that are entirely his own.

12. It is important to note that these blessings and curses are material in nature (Freedman and Miano 2003, 11). If the Israelites obey Yahweh's laws in keeping with the Mosaic covenant, they will be blessed in their land, children, livestock, and grain; and their enemies will advance, but then flee in fear. If the Israelites disobey Yahweh's law in violation of the covenant, they will be cursed in their land, children, livestock, and grain; and their enemies will advance and conquer the Israelites.

13. The great eighth-century prophets (Amos, Elijah, Hosea, Micah, Isaiah) deeply affected biblical tradition by altering, through their preaching and prophecies, the nature of Yahweh's relationship to the people of Israel as it was signified in the Mosaic covenant. Ernest W. Nichols (1995) argues that before the rise in prominence of the eighth-century prophets, Yahweh's covenant with His people, delivered to Moses on Mount Sinai, was understood to be permanent and indissoluble, despite occasional legal infidelities (polytheism, idolatry, intermarriage, etc.). Nichols writes, "When offences were committed or when there was any other sign that Yahweh's favor had been lost, the organs of the cult (lament, sacrifice, etc.) were there to restore it. Thus Israel's well-being (*šālōm*) was believed to be permanently guaranteed by Yahweh" (347). Through the covenant, the structure of kingship was legitimated and the process of redemption was ensured. However, the eighth-century prophets disrupted this notion of permanent and unconditional devotion of Yahweh to his people and, instead, "turned Yahweh's righteousness against Israel, . . . vehemently denying that his will and Israel's well-being were simply identical" (348). The preaching and prophecies of the eighth-century prophets resulted in the transformation of the Mosaic covenant from an unconditional promise, legitimating the institutional structure of the kingship, to a conditional

agreement, delegitimating the monarchy if it did not support righteous behavior in the eyes of Yahweh. The notion that Yahweh might reject his very own people represents an ideological shift that favored the religious power of priests and prophets over the political power of kings. This specifically prophetic tradition, which shifted Israelite religion from election to choice, is the tradition inherited by subsequent preexilic prophets, including Habakkuk.

14. The literary (or metaphorical) character of prophetic texts may have been added by the prophet as a means to explain oracular messages, or it may have been added later in the process of canonical redaction. Favoring the former view, Benjamin L. Merkle writes, "The prophets often communicated a divine message in earthly language" (2002, 17). Favoring the latter view, Matthijs J. de Jong writes, "Whereas the prophetic legacy lies at the root of the prophetic books, the basic literary layer of the books can be understood as a scribal reinterpretation of the prophetic legacy in the light of later circumstances" (2011, 45).

15. It is likely that Habakkuk played a role in Temple administration, "perhaps as a priest or Levite" (Sweeney 1991, 70; see also Wilson 1980, 260, 278), and his written oracles may have been used in complaint or lamentation liturgies. Mowinckel explains, "The prophecies of Habakkuk have been arranged according to a cultic-liturgical scheme, for instance. And they are also probably meant as the connected parts in a cultic festival of humiliation and prayer" (2002, 52; see also Floyd 1993, 476; Rast 1983, 170; Wolff 1978, 21). Wilson agrees, suggesting that "if the prophets participated in temple rituals, then their words and deeds were presumably governed to a certain extent by the requirements of the liturgy" (1980, 260). As Habakkuk's oracles became increasingly associated with recurring liturgical contexts, and the prophet himself became disassociated from Yahweh's messages, Habakkuk may have revised or scribes redacted (*further* interpreted) Habakkuk's original written oracles and interpretations into the prophecy now canonized as the book of Habakkuk.

16. Although Daniel is included in the canonical Tanakh (among the Writings), its date of composition is very late and may even overlap with the lifetime of the Essenes' Teacher of Righteousness, and some have even claimed that the Teacher of Righteousness actually penned Daniel, or parts of it (Brooke 2009, 8; Trever 1985, 1987). George J. Brooke further points out the overlap of terminology between the book of Daniel and the *Habakkuk Pesher*: "The interpretation, *pešar*, sought by Nebuchadnezzar is of a mystery, *rāz*" (2009, 8).

CONCLUSION

1. I do not mean to criticize Edelman or Bernard-Donals and Fernheimer for not including the Dead Sea Scrolls in their histories of Jewish rhetorics, since their excellent and exhaustive work has been formative in my own scholarship. Critique based on "lack" is always weak, and it would be impossible for these scholars to list all of the events and texts that might represent every moment throughout a three-thousand-year history. I only mean to point out that the Dead Sea Scrolls and the period they represent do not seem to be on the radar for scholars studying the diachronic movement of Israelite and Jewish rhetorics.

In an insightful passage, Bernard-Donals and Fernheimer do mention the Second Temple, but not the Dead Sea Scrolls:

> In the thousand years between the rise of Athens as a hub of literacy

and philosophy and the partition of the Roman Empire, Jewish culture underwent a drastic shift as Jews went from the Babylonian exile, to the culture that emerged around the second Temple, to a longer (and, some might argue, more permanent) exile that led to the diasporas throughout Europe and Western and Central Asia, and to the formation of the rabbinical tradition that gave birth to the Talmud. These cultural shifts were inevitably buffeted by the cultures (and the peoples) with which (and with whom) Jews, particularly Jewish thinkers and scholars, interacted. (2014, xvi)

BIBLIOGRAPHY

Abegg, Martin G., Jr. 1999. "4QMMT C 27, 31 and 'Works of Righteousness.'" *Dead Sea Discoveries* 6, no. 2: 139–47.
———. 2001. "4QMMT, Paul, and 'Works of the Law.'" In *The Bible at Qumran: Text, Shape, and Interpretation*, edited by Peter W. Flint, 203–16. Grand Rapids, MI: Eerdmans.
Abegg, Martin G., Jr., Peter Flint, and Eugene Ulrich, trans. 1999. *The Dead Sea Scrolls Bible*. New York: HarperCollins.
Althusser, Louis, and Etienne Balibar. 1979. *Reading Capital*. Translated by Ben Brewster. London: Verso.
Altieri, Charles. 1997. "Toward a Hermeneutics Responsive to Rhetorical Theory." In *Rhetoric and Hermeneutics in Our Time: A Reader*, edited by Walter Jost and Michael J. Hyde, 90–107. New Haven: Yale University Press.
Anderson, Gary A. 1992. "The Interpretation of the Purification Offering in the *Temple Scroll* (11QTemple) and Rabbinic Literature." *Journal of Biblical Literature* 111, no. 1: 17–35.
Anderson, Jeff S. 2014. *The Blessing and the Curse: Trajectories in the Theology of the Old Testament*. Eugene, OR: Cascade.
Aune, James Arnt. 1994. *Rhetoric and Marxism*. Boulder, CO: Westview Press.
Austin, J. L. (1962) 1975. *How to Do Things with Words*. 2nd ed. Edited by J. O. Urmson and Marina Sbisà. Cambridge, MA: Harvard University Press.

Baigent, Michael, and Richard Leigh. 1991. *The Dead Sea Scrolls Deception*. New York: Touchstone.
Bakon, Shimon. 2011. "Habakkuk: From Perplexity to Faith." *Jewish Bible Quarterly* 39, no. 1: 25–30.
Barton, John. 1986. *Oracles of God: Perceptions of Ancient Prophecy in Israel After the Exile*. London: Darton, Longman, and Todd.
Baumgarten, Albert I. 1998. "Ancient Jewish Sectarianism." *Judaism* 47, no. 4: 387–403.
———. 2000. "The Perception of the Past in the *Damascus Document*." In *The Damascus Document: A Centennial of Discovery*, edited by Joseph M. Baumgarten, Esther G. Chazon, and Avital Pinnick, 1–26. Leiden: Brill.
Baumgarten, Joseph M. 1999. "Corrigenda to the 4Q Mss of the *Damascus Document*." *Revue de Qumran* 19, no. 2: 217–25. http://www.jstor.org/stable/24608803.
———. 2000. "The Use of *me niddah* for General Purification." In *The Dead Sea Scrolls: Fifty Years After Their Discovery; Proceedings of the Jerusalem Congress, July 20–25, 1997*, edited by Lawrence H. Schiffman, Emanuel Tov, and James C. VanderKam, 481–85. Jerusalem: Israel Exploration Society.
Baumgarten, Joseph M., and Daniel R. Schwartz. 1995. "*Damascus Document* (CD)." In *The Dead Sea Scrolls: Hebrew, Aramaic, and Greek Texts with English Translations*, vol. 2, *Damascus Document, War Scroll,*

and Related Documents, edited by James H. Charlesworth, 4–9. Louisville: Westminster John Knox Press.

Bautch, Richard J. 2012. "The Formulary of Atonement (Lev 16:21) in Penitential Prayers of the Second Temple Period." In *The Day of Atonement in Early Jewish and Christian Traditions*, edited by Thomas Hieke and Tobias Nicklas, 33–45. Leiden: Brill.

Beale, Walter H. 1987. *A Pragmatic Theory of Rhetoric*. Carbondale: Southern Illinois University Press.

Benjamin, James. 1976. "Performatives as a Rhetorical Construct." *Journal of Philosophy and Rhetoric* 9, no. 2: 84–95.

Berg, Shane E. 2007. "An Elite Group Within the *Yahad*: Revisiting 1QS 8–9." In *Qumran Studies: New Approaches, New Questions*, edited by Michael Thomas Davis and Brent A. Stawn, 161–77. Grand Rapids, MI: Eerdmans.

Bergsma, John S. 2008. "Qumran Self-Identity: 'Israel' of 'Judah'?" *Dead Sea Discoveries* 15, no. 1: 172–89. http://www.jstor.org/stable/40387605.

Bernard-Donals, Michael, and Janice W. Fernheimer. 2014. Introduction to *Jewish Rhetorics: History, Theory, Practice*, edited by Michael Bernard-Donals and Janice W. Fernheimer, vii–xxx. Waltham: Brandeis University Press.

Bernstein, Moshe J. 1996. "The Employment and Interpretation of Scripture in 4QMMT: Preliminary Observations." In *Reading 4QMMT: New Perspectives on Qumran Law and History*, edited by John Kampen and Moshe J. Bernstein, 29–51. Atlanta: Scholars Press.

Biddle, Mark E. 2007. "Obadiah-Jonah-Micah in Canonical Context: The Nature of Prophetic Literature and Hermeneutics." *Interpretation* 61, no. 2: 154–66.

Biesecker, Barbara A. 1989. "Rethinking the Rhetorical Situation from Within the Thematic of 'Difference.'" *Philosophy and Rhetoric* 22, no. 2: 110–30.

Bineham, Jeffery L. 1995. "The Hermeneutic Medium." *Philosophy and Rhetoric* 28, no. 1: 1–16.

Blair, Carole. 1999. "Contemporary U.S. Memorial Sites as Exemplars of Rhetoric's Materiality." In *Rhetorical Bodies*, edited by Jack Selzer and Sharon Crowley, 16–57. Madison: University of Wisconsin Press.

Bohman, James. 1988. "Emancipation and Rhetoric: The Perlocutions and Illocutions of the Social Critic." *Journal of Philosophy and Rhetoric* 21, no. 3: 185–204.

Bourdieu, Pierre. (1980) 1990. *The Logic of Practice*. Translated by Richard Nice. Cambridge: Polity.

Bourgel, Jonathan. 2016. "The Destruction of the Samaritan Temple by John Hyrcanus: A Reconsideration." *Journal of Biblical Literature* 135, no. 3: 505–23.

Brewer, David Instone. 1998. "Nomological Exegesis in Qumran 'Divorce' Texts." *Revue de Qumran* 18, no. 4: 561–79. http://www.jstor.org/stable/24609112.

Bright, John. 2000. *A History of Israel*. 4th ed. Louisville: Westminster John Knox Press.

Brooke, George J. 1994. "The Pesharim and the Origins of the Dead Sea Scrolls." In *Methods of Investigation of the Dead Sea Scrolls and the Khirbet Qumran Site: Present Realities and Future Prospects*, edited by Michael O. Wise, Norman Golb, John J. Collins, and Dennis G. Pardee, 339–52. New York: New York Academy of Sciences.

———. 1997. "The Explicit Presentation of Scripture in 4QMMT." In *Legal*

Texts and Legal Issues, edited by Moshe Bernstein, Florentino García Martínez, and John Kampen, 67–88. Leiden: Brill.

———. 2009. "From Bible to Midrash: Approaches to Biblical Interpretation in the Dead Sea Scrolls by Modern Interpreters." In Northern Lights on the Dead Sea Scrolls, edited by Anders Klostergaard Petersen, Torleif Elgvin, Cecilia Wassen, Hanne von Weissenberg, and Mikael Winninge, 2–19. Leiden: Brill.

———. 2013. Reading the Dead Sea Scrolls: Essays in Method. Atlanta: Society of Biblical Literature.

Büchner, Dirk. 1997. "Inside and Outside the Camp: The Halakhic Background to Changes in the Septuagint Leviticus, with Reference to Two Qumran Manuscripts." Journal of Northwest Semitic Languages 23:151–62.

Burke, Kenneth. (1941) 1973. The Philosophy of Literary Form. 3rd ed. Berkeley: University of California Press.

———. (1961) 1970. The Rhetoric of Religion: Studies in Logology. Berkeley: University of California Press.

———. 1966. "What Are Signs of What? (A Theory of 'Entitlement')." In Language as Symbolic Action: Essays on Life, Literature, and Method, 359–79. Berkeley: University of California Press.

———. 1969. The Rhetoric of Motives. Berkeley: University of California Press.

Callaway, Phillip. 1986. "Source Criticism of the Temple Scroll: The Purity Laws." Revue de Qumran 12, no. 2: 213–22.

———. 1988. "The Temple Scroll and the Canonization of Jewish Law." Revue de Qumran 13, no. 1: 239–50. http://www.jstor.org/stable/24608850.

Campbell, Edward F., Jr. 1998. "A Land Divided: Judah and Israel from the Death of Solomon to the Fall of Samaria." In The Oxford History of the Biblical World, edited by Michael D. Coogan, 206–41. New York: Oxford University Press.

Campbell, Jonathan G. 2000. "4QMMT^d and the Tripartite Canon." Journal of Jewish Studies 51:181–90.

Campbell, Paul Newell. 1973. "A Rhetorical View of Locutionary, Illocutionary, and Perlocutionary Acts." Quarterly Journal of Speech 59, no. 3: 284–96.

Charlesworth, James H. 2011a. "Revelation and Perspicacity in Qumran Hermeneutics?" In The Dead Sea Scrolls and Contemporary Culture, edited by Adolfo D. Roitman, Lawrence H. Schiffman, and Shani Tzoref, 161–80. Leiden: Brill.

———. 2011b. The Temple Scroll and Related Documents. Louisville: Westminster John Knox Press.

Christiansen, Ellen Juhl. 1998. "The Consciousness of Belonging to God's Covenant and What It Entails According to the Damascus Document and the Community Rule." In Qumran Between the Old and New Testaments, edited by Frederick H. Cryer and Thomas L. Thompson, 69–97. Sheffield, UK: Sheffield Academic Press.

Cirafesi, Wally V. 2011–12. "The Priestly Portrait of Jesus in the Gospel of John in the Light of 1QS, 1QSa, and 1QSb." Journal of Greco-Roman Christianity and Judaism 8:83–105.

Clements, Ronald E. 1965. Prophecy and Covenant. Naperville, IL: Alec R. Allenson.

———. 1996. Old Testament Prophecy: From Oracles to Canon. Louisville: Westminster John Knox Press.

Clendenen, E. Ray. 2014. "Salvation by Faith or by Faithfulness in the Book of Habakkuk." Bulletin for Biblical Research 24, no. 4: 505–13.

Cloud, Dana L. 1994. "The Materiality of Discourse as Oxymoron: A

Challenge to Critical Rhetoric." *Western Journal of Communication* 58:141–63.

Cloud, Doug. 2014. "The Social Consequences of Dissociation: Lessons from the Same-Sex Marriage Debate." *Argumentation and Advocacy* 50, no. 3: 157–67.

Cogan, Mordechai. 1998. "Into Exile: From the Assyrian Conquest of Israel to the Fall of Babylon." In *The Oxford History of the Biblical World*, edited by Michael D. Coogan, 242–75. New York: Oxford University Press.

Collins, John J. 2006. "The Yahad and 'the Qumran Community.'" In *Biblical Traditions in Transmission*, edited by Charlotte Hempel and Judith M. Lieu, 81–95. Leiden: Brill.

———. 2011. "Reading for History in the Dead Sea Scrolls." *Dead Sea Discoveries* 18, no. 3: 295–315. https://doi.org/10.1163/1568851711 X602403.

———. 2014. *Scriptures and Sectarianism: Essays on the Dead Sea Scrolls*. Grand Rapids, MI: Eerdmans.

Coogan, Michael D., ed. 1998. *The Oxford History of the Biblical World*. New York: Oxford University Press.

Cook, Edward M. 1994. *Solving the Mysteries of the Dead Sea Scrolls: New Light on the Bible*. Grand Rapids, MI: Zondervan.

Cooper, Marilyn M. 1986. "The Ecology of Writing." *College English* 48, no. 4: 364–75.

Coward, Rosalind, and John Ellis. 1977. *Language and Materialism: Developments in Semiology and the Theory of the Subject*. Boston: Routledge.

Crawford, Sidnie White. 2000. *The Temple Scroll and Related Texts*. Sheffield, UK: Sheffield Academic Press.

Cross, Frank Moore. 1993. "The Historical Context of the Scrolls." In *Understanding the Dead Sea Scrolls*, edited by Hershel Shanks, 20–32. New York: Vintage.

Czajkowski, Kimberley. 2016. "Lost and Stolen Property at Qumran: The 'Oath of Adjuration.'" *Journal for the Study of Judaism* 47:88–103. https://doi.org/10.1163/15700631 -12340447.

Dangl, Oskar. 2001. "Habakkuk in Recent Research." *Currents in Research: Biblical Studies* 9:131–68.

Dasenbrock, Reed Way. 1987. "J. L. Austin and the Articulation of a New Rhetoric." *College Composition and Communication* 38, no. 3: 291–305.

Davies, Philip R. 1982. *The Damascus Covenant*. Sheffield, UK: Sheffield Academic Press.

———. 1994. "The 'Damascus' Sect and Judaism." In *Pursuing the Text*, edited by John C. Reeves and John Kampen, 70–84. Sheffield, UK: Sheffield Academic Press.

———. 2000. "The Judaism(s) of the Damascus Document." In *The Damascus Document: A Centennial of Discovery*, edited by Joseph M. Baumgarten, Esther G. Chazon, and Avital Pinnick, 27–43. Leiden: Brill.

Dimant, Devorah. 2009. "Exegesis and Time in the Pesharim from Qumran." *Revue des études juives* 168, nos. 3–4: 373–93. https://doi .org/10.2143/REJ.168.3.2044660.

Dobrin, Sidney I., and Christian R. Weisser. 2002. *Natural Discourse: Toward Ecocomposition*. Albany: State University of New York Press.

Druschke, Caroline Gottschalk. 2019. "The Trophic Future of Rhetorical Ecologies." *Enculturation: A Journal of Rhetoric, Writing, and Culture* 28. http://enculturation .net/a-trophic-future.

Edbauer, Jenny. 2005. "Unframing Models of Public Distribution: From

Rhetorical Situation to Rhetorical Ecologies." *Rhetoric Society Quarterly* 35, no. 4: 5–24.
Edelman, Samuel M. 2003. "Ancient Traditions, Modern Needs: An Introduction to Jewish Rhetoric." *Journal of Communication and Religion* 26, no. 2: 113–25.
Eemeren, Frans H. van, and Rob Grootendorst. 2004. *A Systematic Theory of Argumentation: The Pragma-Dialectical Approach*. Cambridge: Cambridge University Press.
Elman, Yaakov. 1996. "Some Remarks on 4QMMT and the Rabbinic Tradition: or, When Is a Parallel Not a Parallel." In *Reading 4QMMT: New Perspectives on Qumran Law and History*, edited by John Kampen and Moshe J. Bernstein, 99–128. Atlanta: Scholars Press.
Emerton, J. A. 1977. "The Textual and Linguistic Problems of Habakkuk II.4–5." *Journal of Theological Studies* 28, no. 1: 1–18.
Eshel, Hanan. 1996. "4QMMT and the History of the Hasmonean Period." In *Reading 4QMMT: New Perspectives on Qumran Law and History*, edited by John Kampen and Moshe J. Bernstein, 53–65. Atlanta: Scholars Press.
———. 2008. *The Dead Sea Scrolls and the Hasmonean State*. Grand Rapids, MI: Eerdmans.
Evans, Annette. 2018. "Almsgiving as a Rhetorical Device in 4QTobit?" *Hervormde Teologiese Studies* 74, no. 3: 1–6.
Evans, Craig. 2003. "Covenant in the Qumran Literature." In *The Concept of the Covenant in the Second Temple Period*, edited by Stanley E. Porter and Jacqueline C. R. de Roo, 55–80. Leiden: Brill.
Fabry, Heinz-Josef. 2003. "The Reception of Nahum and Habakkuk in the Septuagint and Qumran." In *Emanuel: Studies in Hebrew Bible, Septuagint, and Dead Sea Scrolls in Honor of Emanuel Tov*, edited by Shalom M. Paul, Robert A. Kraft, Lawrence H. Schiffman, and Weston W. Fields, 241–56. Leiden: Brill.
Falk, D. K. 2007. "Scriptural Inspiration for Penitential Prayer in the Dead Sea Scrolls." In *Seeking the Favor of God*, vol. 1, *The Origins of Penitential Prayer in Second Temple Judaism*, edited by M. J. Boda, D. K. Falk, and R. A. Werline, 127–57. Atlanta: Society of Biblical Literature.
Fernández, Miguel Pérez. 1997. "4QMMT: Redactional Study." *Revue de Qumran* 18, no. 2: 191–205.
Fernheimer, Janice W. 2008. "From Jew to Israelite: Making 'Uncomfortable Communions' and *The New Rhetoric*'s Tools for Invention." *Argumentation and Advocacy* 44, no. 4: 198–212.
Fitzmyer, Joseph A. 2007. *A Guide to the Dead Sea Scrolls and Related Literature*. Grand Rapids, MI: Eerdmans.
Floyd, Michael H. 1991. "Prophetic Complaints About the Fulfillment of Oracles in Habakkuk 1:2–17 and Jeremiah 15:10–18." *Journal of Biblical Literature* 110, no. 3: 397–418.
———. 1993. "Prophecy and Writing in Habakkuk 2,1–5." *Zeitschrift für die Alttestamentliche Wissenschaft* 105, no. 3: 462–81.
Fraade, Steven D. 2000. "To Whom It May Concern: 4QMMT and Its Addressee(s)." *Revue de Qumran* 19, no. 76: 507–26.
———. 2003. "Rhetoric and Hermeneutics in *Miqṣat Ma'aśeh ha-Torah* (4QMMT): The Case of the Blessings and the Curses." *Dead Sea Discoveries* 10, no. 1: 150–61.

Frank, Harry Thomas. 1992. "Discovering the Scrolls." In *Understanding the Dead Sea Scrolls*, edited by Hershel Shanks, 3–19. New York: Biblical Archaeology Society.

Freedman, David Noel, and David Miano. 2003. "People of the New Covenant." In *The Concept of the Covenant in the Second Temple Period*, edited by Stanley E. Porter and Jacqueline C. R. de Roo, 7–26. Atlanta: Society of Biblical Literature.

Fröhlich, Ida. 1992. "Pesher, Apocalyptic Literature, and Qumran." In *The Madrid Qumran Congress*, edited by Julio Trebolle Barrera and Luis Vegas Montaner, 1:295–305. Leiden: Brill.

———. 1998. "'Narrative Exegesis' in the Dead Sea Scrolls." In *Biblical Perspectives: Early Use and Interpretation of the Bible in Light of the Dead Sea Scrolls*, edited by Michael E. Stone and Esther G. Chazon, 81–99. Leiden: Brill.

Gadamer, Hans-Georg. 1975. *Truth and Method*. Translated by Joel Weinsheimer and Donald G. Marshall. New York: Continuum.

———. 1976. *Philosophical Hermeneutics*. Translated and edited by David E. Linge. Berkeley: University of California Press.

———. 1997. "Rhetoric and Hermeneutics." Translated by Joel Weinsheimer. In *Rhetoric and Hermeneutics in Our Time: A Reader*, edited by Walter Jost and Michael J. Hyde, 45–59. New Haven: Yale University Press.

Gaines, Robert N. 1979. "Doing by Saying: Toward a Theory of Perlocution." *Quarterly Journal of Speech* 65, no. 3: 207–17.

Gilders, William K. 2006. "Blood Manipulation Ritual in the 'Temple Scroll.'" *Revue de Qumran* 22, no. 4: 519–45. http://www.jstor.org/stable/24640826.

———. 2012. "The Day of Atonement in the Dead Sea Scrolls." In *The Day of Atonement in Early Jewish and Christian Traditions*, edited by Thomas Hieke and Tobias Nicklas, 63–73. Leiden: Brill.

Ginsburskaya, Mila. 2010. "The Right of Counsel and the Idea of Purity in the *Rule of the Community* (1QS) and the *Rule of the Congregation* (1QSa)." In *Qumran Cave 1 Revisited*, edited by Daniel K. Falk, Sarianna Metso, Donald W. Parry, and Eibert J. C. Tigchelaar, 77–90. Leiden: Brill.

Ginzberg, Louis. (1922) 1976. *An Unknown Jewish Sect*. Edited and translated by Ralph Marcus et al. New York: Jewish Theological Seminary of America.

Goff, Matthew J. 2003. "The Mystery of Creation in 4QInstruction." *Dead Sea Discoveries* 10, no. 2: 163–86.

Goldsmith, Galen L. 2011. "The Cutting Edge of Prophetic Imagery." *Journal of Biblical and Pneumatological Research* 3:3–18.

Grabbe, Lester L. 1997. "4QMMT and Second Temple Jewish Society." In *Legal Texts and Legal Issues*, edited by Moshe Bernstein, Florentino García Martínez, and John Kampen, 89–108. Leiden: Brill.

———. 2010. *An Introduction to Second Temple Judaism: History and Religion of the Jews in the Time of Nehemiah, the Maccabees, Hillel and Jesus*. New York: Bloomsbury.

Greene, Ronald Walter. 1998. "Another Materialist Rhetoric." *Critical Studies in Mass Communication* 15:21–41.

Greenspoon, Leonard J. 1998. "Between Alexandria and Antioch: Jews and Judaism in the Hellenistic Period." In *The Oxford History of the Biblical World*, edited by Michael D. Coogan, 317–51. New York: Oxford University Press.

Gries, Laurie E. 2015. *Still Life with Rhetoric: A New Materialist Approach for Visual Rhetorics*. Logan: Utah State University Press.

Grootendorst, Rob. 1999. "Innocence by Dissociation: A Pragma-Dialectical Analysis of Incorrect Dissociation in the Vatican Document 'We Remember: A Reflection on the Shoah.'" In *Proceedings of the Fourth International Conference of the International Society for the Study of Argumentation*, edited by Frans H. van Eemeren, Rob Grootendorst, J. Anthony Blair, and Charles A. Willard, 286–89. Amsterdam: Stichting Internationaal Centrum voor de Studie van Argumentatie en Taalbeheersing.

Gross, Alan G., and Ray D. Dearing. 2010. *Chaim Perelman*. Carbondale: Southern Illinois University Press.

Grossman, Maxine L. 2002. *Reading for History in the Damascus Document: A Methodological Study*. Leiden: Brill.

———. 2008. "Cultivating Identity: Textual Virtuosity and 'Insider' Status." In *Defining Identities: We, You, and the Other in the Dead Sea Scrolls*, edited by Florentino García Martínez and Mladen Popović, 1–11. Leiden: Brill.

Gruen, Erich S. 1998. *Heritage and Hellenism: The Reinvention of Jewish Tradition*. Berkeley: University of California Press.

Habermas, Jürgen. 1984. *The Theory of Communicative Action*. Translated by Thomas McCarthy. 2 vols. Boston: Beacon.

Hagedorn, Anselm C., and Shani Tzoref. 2013. "Attitudes to Gentiles in the Minor Prophets and in Corresponding Pesharim." *Dead Sea Discoveries* 20, no. 3: 472–509. https://doi.org/10.1163/15685179-2341287.

Harkins, Angela Kim. 2015. "The Emotional Re-experiencing of the Hortatory Narratives Found in the Admonition of the *Damascus Document*." *Dead Sea Discoveries* 22, no. 3: 285–307. https://doi.org/10.1163/15685179-2341363.

Harrington, Hannah K. 1997. "Holiness in the Laws of 4QMMT." In *Legal Texts and Legal Issues*, edited by Moshe Bernstein, Florentino García Martínez, and John Kampen, 109–28. Leiden: Brill.

———. 2001. "Holiness and Law in the Dead Sea Scrolls." *Dead Sea Discoveries* 8, no. 2: 124–35.

———. 2004. *The Purity Texts*. New York: Clark.

———. 2011. "Ritual Purity." In *The Dead Sea Scrolls and Contemporary Culture*, edited by Adolfo D. Roitman, Lawrence H. Schiffman, and Shani Tzoref, 329–47. Leiden: Brill.

Heard, Chris. 1997. "Hearing the Children's Cries: Commentary, Deconstruction, and the Book of Habakkuk." *Semeia* 77:75–89.

Hempel, Charlotte. 1998. *The Laws of the Damascus Document: Sources, Tradition, and Redaction*. Leiden: Brill.

———. 2000. "The Laws of the Damascus Document and 4QMMT." In *The Damascus Document: A Centennial of Discovery*, edited by Joseph M. Baumgarten, Esther G. Chazon, and Avital Pinnick, 69–84. Leiden: Brill.

———. 2011. "1QS 6:2c–4a: Satellites or Precursors of the Yahad?" In *The Dead Sea Scrolls and Contemporary Culture*, edited by Adolfo D. Roitman, Lawrence H. Schiffman, and Shani Tzoref, 31–40. Leiden: Brill.

Hidary, Richard. 2014. "The Rhetoric of Rabbinic Authority: Making the Transition from Priest to Sage." In *Jewish Rhetorics: History, Theory,*

Practice, edited by Michael Bernard-Donals and Janice W. Fernheimer, 16–45. Waltham: Brandeis University Press.

Himmelfarb, Martha. 2001. "Impurity and Sin in 4QD, 1QS, and 4Q512." *Dead Sea Discoveries* 8, no. 1: 9–37.

Hodge, Stephen. 2003. *The Dead Sea Scrolls Rediscovered*. Berkeley: Seastone.

Høgenhaven, Jesper. 2003. "Rhetorical Devices in 4QMMT." *Dead Sea Discoveries* 10, no. 2: 187–204.

Holladay, William L. 2001. "Plausible Circumstances for the Prophecy of Habakkuk." *Journal of Biblical Literature* 120, no. 1: 123–42.

Horgan, Maurya P. 1979. *Pesharim: Qumran Interpretations of Biblical Books*. Washington, DC: Catholic Biblical Association of America.

Hultgren, Stephen. 2004. "A New Literary Analysis of 'CD' XIX–XX, Part I: 'CD' XIX:1–32a (with 'CD' VII:4b–VIII:18b): The Midrashim and the 'Princes of Judah.'" *Revue de Qumran* 21, no. 4: 549–78. http://www.jstor.org/stable/24640903.

Hunn, Debbie. 2009. "Habakkuk 2.4b in Its Context: How Far Off Was Paul?" *Journal for the Study of the Old Testament* 34, no. 2: 219–39. https://doi.org/10.1177/0309089209356413.

Hyde, Michael J., and Craig R. Smith. 1979. "Hermeneutics and Rhetoric: A Seen but Unobserved Relationship." *Quarterly Journal of Speech* 65, no. 4: 347–63.

Inkster, Robert. 2000. "Rhetoric and the Ecology of the Noosphere." In *Inventing a Discipline: Rhetoric Scholarship in Honor of Richard E. Young*, edited by Maureen Daly Gogan, 109–22. Urbana, IL: National Council of Teachers of English.

Isaksson, Bo. 2008. "Circumstantial Qualifiers in Qumran Hebrew: Reflections on Adjunct Expressions in the Manual of Discipline (1QS)." In *Conservatism and Innovation in the Hebrew Language of the Hellenistic Period*, edited by Jan Joosten and Jean-Sebastien Rey, 79–91. Leiden: Brill.

Jameson, Fredric. 1972. *The Prison-House of Language: A Critical Account of Structuralism and Russian Formalism*. Princeton: Princeton University Press.

Janzen, J. Gerald. 1980. "Habakkuk 2:2–4 in the Light of Recent Philological Advances." *Harvard Theological Review* 73, nos. 1–2: 53–78.

———. 1982. "Eschatological Symbol and Existence in Habakkuk." *Catholic Bible Quarterly* 44, no. 3: 394–414.

Jassen, Alex P. 2012. "The Pesharim and the Rise of Commentary in Early Jewish Scriptural Interpretation." *Dead Sea Discoveries* 19, no. 3: 363–98. https://doi.org/10.1163/15685179-2341237.

Johnson, Marshall D. 1985. "The Paralysis of Torah in Habakkuk I.4." *Vetus Testamentum* 35, no. 3: 257–66.

Jokiranta, Jutta. 2005. "Pesharim: A Mirror of Self-Understanding." In *Reading the Present in the Qumran Library: The Perception of the Contemporary by Means of Scriptural Interpretations*, edited by Kristin De Troyer and Armin Lange, 23–34. Atlanta: Society of Biblical Literature.

Jong, Matthijs J. de. 2011. "Biblical Prophecy—A Scribal Enterprise: The Old Testament Prophecy of Unconditional Judgment Considered as a Literary Phenomenon." *Vetus Testamentum* 61, no. 1: 39–70. https://doi.org/10.1163/156853311X551493.

Josephus. 1987. *The Antiquities of the Jews*. In *The Works of Josephus: Complete and Unabridged*, trans. William Whiston, 27–542. New York: Hendrickson.

Kalman, Jason. 2012. *Hebrew Union College and the Dead Sea Scrolls*. Cincinnati: Hebrew Union College—Jewish Institute of Religion.

Kamm, Antony. 1999. *The Israelites: An Introduction*. London: Routledge.

Kampen, John, and Moshe J. Bernstein. 1996. Introduction to *Reading 4QMMT: New Perspectives on Qumran Law and History*, edited by John Kampen and Moshe J. Bernstein, 1–7. Atlanta: Scholars Press.

Kim, Jintae. 2010. "The Concept of Atonement in the Qumran Literature and the New Covenant." *Journal of Greco-Roman Christianity and Judaism* 7:98–111.

Klawans, Jonathan. 1998. "Idolatry, Incest, and Impurity: Moral Defilement in Ancient Judaism." *Journal for the Study of Judaism* 29, no. 4: 391–415.

———. 2000. *Impurity and Sin in Ancient Judaism*. New York: Oxford University Press.

Klein, Anja. 2009. "From the 'Right Spirit' to the 'Spirit of Truth': Observations on Psalm 51 and 1QS." In *The Dynamics of Language and Exegesis at Qumran*, edited by Devorah Dimant and Reinhard G. Kratz, 42–72. Tübingen: Mohr Siebeck.

Knib, Michael A. 1987. *The Qumran Community*. Cambridge: Cambridge University Press.

Koch, Klaus. 1985. "Is Daniel Also Among the Prophets? *Interpretation* 39, no. 2: 117–30.

Kolenda, Konstantin. 1971. "Speech Acts and Truth." *Journal of Philosophy and Rhetoric* 4, no. 4: 230–41.

Konishi, Takuzo. 2003. "Dissociation and Its Relation to the Theory of Argument." In *Proceedings of the Fifth Conference of the International Society for the Study of Argumentation*, edited by Frans H. van Eemeren, J. Anthony Blair, Charles A. Willard, and A. Francisca Snoeck Henkemans, 637–40. Amsterdam: Stichting Internationaal Centrum voor de Studie van Argumentatie en Taalbeheersing.

Kvalvaag, Robert W. 1998. "The Spirit in Human Beings in Some Qumran Non-biblical Texts." In *Qumran Between the Old and New Testaments*, edited by Frederick H. Cryer and Thomas L. Thompson, 159–80. Sheffield, UK: Sheffield Academic Press.

Lange, Armin, and Zlatko Pleše. 2012. "Transpositional Hermeneutics: A Hermeneutical Comparison of the Derveni Papyrus, Aristobulus of Alexandria, and the Qumran Pesharim." *Journal of Ancient Judaism* 3:15–67.

Leaney, A. R. C. 1966. *The Rule of Qumran and Its Meaning: Introduction, Translation, and Commentary*. Philadelphia: Westminster Press.

Leff, Michael. 1997. "Hermeneutical Rhetoric." In *Rhetoric and Hermeneutics in Our Time: A Reader*, edited by Walter Jost and Michael J. Hyde, 196–214. New Haven: Yale University Press.

Levine, Lee I. 2002. *Jerusalem: Portrait of the City in the Second Temple Period*. Philadelphia: Jewish Publication Society.

———. 2005. *The Ancient Synagogue: The First Thousand Years*. New Haven: Yale University Press.

Levinson, Bernard M. 2013. *A More Perfect Torah: At the Intersection of Philology and Hermeneutics in Deuteronomy and the Temple Scroll*. Warsaw, IN: Eisenbrauns.

Lim, Timothy H. 2002. *Pesharim*. Sheffield, UK: Sheffield Academic Press.

———. 2013. "A New Solution to an Exegetical Crux (CD IV.20–21)."

Revue de Qumran 26, no. 2: 275–84. http://www.jstor.org/stable/24663186.

Lucas, Alec J. 2010. "Scripture Citations as an Internal Redactional Control: 1QS 5:1–20a and Its 4Q Parallels." *Dead Sea Discoveries* 17, no. 1: 30–52.

Lynch, John. 2006. "Making Room for Stem Cells: Dissociation and Establishing New Research Objects." *Argumentation and Advocacy* 42, no. 3: 143–56.

Machiela, Daniel A. 2012. "The Qumran Pesharim as Biblical Commentaries: Historical Context and Lines of Development." *Dead Sea Discoveries* 19, no. 3: 313–62. https://doi.org/10.1163.15685179-2341236.

Maddux, Kristy. 2013. "Religious Dissociation in 2012 Campaign Discourse." *Rhetoric and Public Affairs* 16, no. 2: 355–68.

Magness, Jodi. 2002. *The Archaeology of Qumran and the Dead Sea Scrolls*. Grand Rapids, MI: Eerdmans.

Maier, Johann, ed. 2009. *Temple Scroll: An Introduction, Translation, and Commentary*. Sheffield, UK: Sheffield Academic Press.

Mailloux, Steven. 1985. "Rhetorical Hermeneutics." *Critical Inquiry* 11, no. 1: 620–41. http://www.jstor.org/stable/1343420.

———. 2006. *Disciplinary Identities: Rhetorical Paths of English, Speech, and Composition*. New York: Modern Language Association.

Martínez, Florentino García, trans. 1996a. *The Dead Sea Scrolls Translated: The Qumran Texts in English*. 2nd ed. Leiden: Brill.

———. 1996b. "4QMMT in a Qumran Context." In *Reading 4QMMT: New Perspectives on Qumran Law and History*, edited by John Kampen and Moshe J. Bernstein, 15–27. Atlanta: Scholars Press.

Marx, Delia. 2013. "The Missing Temple: The Status of the Temple in Jewish Culture Following Its Destruction." *European Judaism: A Journal for the New Europe* 46, no. 2: 61–78.

Marx, Karl. 1979. "To (Father) Heinrich Marx." November 10, 1837. Letter 1 in *The Letters of Karl Marx*, edited and translated by Saul K. Padover, 4–12. Englewood Cliffs, NJ: Prentice-Hall.

Marx, Karl, and Frederick Engels. (1846) 1976. *The German Ideology*. Translated by Clemens Dutt, W. Lough, and C. P. Magill. In *Karl Marx, Frederick Engels: Collected Works*, 5:19–584. New York: International.

Mason, Jeff. 1994. "Rhetoric and the Perlocutionary Field." *Journal of Philosophy and Rhetoric* 27, no. 4: 410–14.

McComiskey, Bruce. 2010. "Laws, Works, and the End of Days: Rhetorics of Identification, Distinction, and Persuasion in *Miqṣat Maʿaśeh ha-Torah* (Dead Sea Scroll 4QMMT)." *Rhetoric Review* 29, no. 3: 221–38.

———. 2015a. "Material Rhetoric and the Ritual Transfiguration of Impure Flesh in the *Purification Rules* (Dead Sea Scrolls 4QTohorot A and 4QTohorot B)." In *Rhetoric Across Borders*, edited by Anne Teresa Demo, 13–22. Anderson, SC: Parlor.

———. 2015b. "Performative Rhetorical Strategies in the Rule of the Community (Dead Sea Scroll 1QS)." *Journal of Communication and Religion* 38, no. 3: 89–106.

McGee, Michael Calvin. 1982. "A Materialist's Conception of Rhetoric." In *Explorations in Rhetoric: Studies in Honor of Douglas Ehninger*, edited by Ray E. McKerrow, 23–48. Glenview, IL: Scott, Foresman.

McGuire, R. R. 1977. "Speech Acts, Communicative Competence, and the Paradox of Authoring." *Journal

of Philosophy and Rhetoric 10, no. 1: 30–45.
Medala, Stanislaw. 1999. "The Character and Historical Setting of 4QMMT." *Qumran Chronicle* 4:1–27.
Merkle, Benjamin L. 2010. "Old Testament Restoration Prophecies Regarding the Nation of Israel: Literal or Symbolic?" *Southern Baptist Journal of Theology* 14, no. 1: 14–25.
Metso, Sarianna. 2000. "The Relationship Between the *Damascus Document* and the Community Rule." In *The Damascus Document: A Centennial of Discovery*, edited by Joseph M. Baumgarten, Esther G. Chazon, and Avital Pinnick, 85–93. Leiden: Brill.
———. 2006. "Whom Does the Term Yahad Identify?" In *Biblical Traditions in Transmission*, edited by Charlotte Hempel and Judith M. Lieu, 213–35. Leiden: Brill.
Meyers, Eric M., and Mark A. Chancey. 2012. *Alexander to Constantine: Archaeology of the Land of the Bible*. Vol. 3. New Haven: Yale University Press.
Milgrom, Jacob. 1976. *Cult and Conscience: The Asham and the Priestly Doctrine of Repentance*. Leiden: Brill.
———. 1991. "Deviations from Scripture in the Purity Laws of the *Temple Scroll*." In *Jewish Civilization in the Hellenistic-Roman Period*, edited by Shemaryahu Talmon, 159–67. Salem, OR: Trinity Press International.
———. 1993a. "The Concept of Impurity in 'Jubilees' and the 'Temple Scroll.'" *Revue de Qumran* 16, no. 2: 277–84.
———. 1993b. "On the Purification Offering in the *Temple Scroll*." *Revue de Qumran* 16, no. 1: 99–101.
Milkowski, Chaim. 1982. "Again: 'Damascus' in Damascus Document and in Rabbinic Literature." *Revue de Qumran* 11, no. 1: 97–106. http://www.jstor.org/stable/24606831.

Mowinckel, Sigmund. 2002. *The Spirit and the Word: Prophecy and Tradition in Ancient Israel*. Minneapolis: Fortress Press.
Murphy, Catherine M. 1991. "The Disposition of Wealth in the Damascus Document Tradition." *Revue de Qumran* 19, no. 1: 83–129. http://www.jstor.org/stable/24609052.
Newsom, Carol A. 1990. "Kenneth Burke Meets the Teacher of Righteousness: Rhetorical Strategies in the *Hodayot* and the *Serek Ha-Yahad*." In *Of Scribes and Scrolls: Studies in the Hebrew Bible, Intertestamental Judaism, and Christian Origins*, edited by Harold W. Attridge, John J. Collins, and Thomas H. Tobin, SJ, 121–31. Lanham: University Press of America.
———. 2010. "Rhetorical Criticism and the Dead Sea Scrolls." In *Rediscovering the Dead Sea Scrolls: An Assessment of Old and New Approaches and Methods*, edited by Maxine L. Grossman, 198–214. Grand Rapids, MI: Eerdmans.
Nichols, Ernest W. 1995. "Prophecy and Covenant." In *"This Place Is Too Small for Us": The Israelite Prophets in Recent Scholarship*, edited by Robert P. Gordon, 345–53. Warsaw, IN: Eisenbrauns.
Niehoff, Maren R. 1992. "A Dream Which Is Not Interpreted Is Like a Letter Which Is Not Read." *Journal of Jewish Studies* 43, no. 1: 58–84.
———. 2012. "Commentary Culture in the Land of Israel from an Alexandrian Perspective." *Dead Sea Discoveries* 19, no. 3: 442–63. https://doi.org/10.1163/15685179-2341239.
Nissinen, Martti. 2004. "What Is Prophecy? An Ancient Near Eastern Perspective." In *Inspired Speech: Prophecy in the Ancient Near East*, edited by

John Kaltner and Louis Stulman, 17–37. London: T&T Clark.
———. 2009. "Pesharim as Divination: Qumran Exegesis, Omen Interpretation, and Literary Prophecy." In *Prophecy After the Prophets?* edited by Kristin De Troyer and Armin Lange, 43–60. Leuven: Peeters.
Nitzan, Bilha. 2010. "The Decalogue Pattern in the Qumran *Rule of the Community*." In *Dualism in Qumran*, edited by Géza G. Xeravits, 166–87. New York: T&T Clark.
O'Connell, Kevin G. 1979. "Habakkuk—Spokesman to God." *Currents in Theology and Mission* 6, no. 4: 227–31.
Overholt, Thomas W. 1988. "The End of Prophecy: No Players Without a Program." *Journal for the Study of the Old Testament* 42:103–15.
Palmer, Richard E. 1997. "What Hermeneutics Can Offer Rhetoric." In *Rhetoric and Hermeneutics in Our Time: A Reader*, edited by Walter Jost and Michael J. Hyde, 108–31. New Haven: Yale University Press.
Perelman, Chaim. 1982. *The Realm of Rhetoric*. Translated by William Kluback. Notre Dame: University of Notre Dame Press.
Perelman, Chaim, and Lucie Olbrechts-Tyteca. 1969. *The New Rhetoric: A Treatise on Argumentation*. Translated by John Wilkinson and Purcell Weaver. Notre Dame: University of Notre Dame Press.
Pinker, Aron. 2007. "Habakkuk 2.4: An Ethical Paradigm or a Political Observation?" *Journal for the Study of the Old Testament* 32, no. 1: 91–112. https://doi.org/10.1177/0309083767.
———. 2008. "Historical Allusions in the Book of Habakkuk." *Jewish Bible Quarterly* 36, no. 3: 143–52.

Porter, Stanley E., and Jason C. Robinson. 2011. *Hermeneutics: An Introduction to Interpretive Theory*. Grand Rapids, MI: Eerdmans.
Price, Randall. 2005. *The Temple and Bible Prophecy*. Eugene, OR: Harvest House.
Qimron, Elisha. 1996a. "The Nature of the Reconstructed Composite Text of 4QMMT." In *Reading 4QMMT: New Perspectives on Qumran Law and History*, edited by John Kampen and Moshe J. Bernstein, 9–13. Atlanta: Scholars Press.
———. 1996b. *The Temple Scroll: A Critical Edition*. Jerusalem: Israel Exploration Society.
Qimron, Elisha, and John Strugnell, eds., in consultation with Y. Sussmann and with contributions by Y. Sussmann and A. Yardeni. 1994. *Qumran Cave 4, V: Miqṣat Maʿaśeh Ha-Torah*. Discoveries in the Judean Desert 10. Oxford: Clarendon.
Rast, Walter E. 1983. "Habakkuk and Justification by Faith." *Currents in Theology and Mission* 10, no. 3: 169–75.
Regev, Eyal. 2003. "Abominated Temple and a Holy Community: The Formation of the Notions of Purity and Impurity in Qumran." *Dead Sea Discoveries* 10:243–78.
———. 2004. "Moral Impurity and the Temple in Early Christianity in Light of Ancient Greek Practice and Qumranic Ideology." *Harvard Theological Review* 94, no. 4: 383–411.
———. 2010. "Between Two Sects: Differentiating the Yahad and the Damascus Covenant." In *The Dead Sea Scrolls: Texts and Context*, edited by Charlotte Hempel, 431–49. Leiden: Brill.
Rendsburg, Gary A. 2010. "Qumran Hebrew (with a Trial Cut [1QS])." In *The Dead Sea Scrolls at 60*, edited by

Lawrence H. Schiffman and Shani Tzoref, 217–46. Leiden: Brill.
Rickert, Thomas. 2013. *Ambient Rhetoric: The Attunements of Rhetorical Being*. Pittsburgh: University of Pittsburgh Press.
Ricoeur, Paul. 1997. "Rhetoric—Poetics—Hermeneutics." In *Rhetoric and Hermeneutics in Our Time: A Reader*, edited by Walter Jost and Michael J. Hyde, 60–72. New Haven: Yale University Press.
Riska, Magnus. 2001. *The Temple Scroll and the Biblical Tradition: A Study of Columns 2–13:9*. Helsinki: Finnish Exegetical Society.
Rivers, Nathaniel A., and Ryan P. Weber. 2011. "Ecological, Pedagogical, Public Rhetoric." *College Composition and Communication* 63, no. 2: 187–218.
Robertson, O. Palmer. 1983. "'The Justified (by Faith) Shall Live by His Steadfast Trust'—Habakkuk 2:4." *Covenant Seminary Review* 9, nos. 1–2: 52–71.
Roo, Jacqueline C. R. de. 2000. "Was the Goat for Azazel Destined for the Wrath of God?" *Biblica* 81, no. 2: 233–42. http://www.jstor.org/stable/42614263.
Sanders, E. P. 2000. "The Dead Sea Sect and Other Jews: Commonalities, Overlaps, and Differences." In *The Dead Sea Scrolls in Their Historical Context*, edited by Timothy Lim, 7–43. Edinburgh: T&T Clark.
Sanders, Robert E. 1976. "In Defense of Speech Acts." *Journal of Philosophy and Rhetoric* 9, no. 2: 112–15.
Schechter, Solomon S. 1910. *Documents of Jewish Sectaries*. Vol. 1, *Fragments of a Zadokite Work*. Cambridge: Cambridge University Press. https://archive.org/stream/SchechterFragmentsOfAZadokiteWork1910/Schechter-Fragments-of-a-Zadokite-work-1910_djvu.txt.

Schiappa, Edward. 1985. "Dissociation in the Arguments of Rhetorical Theory." *Journal of the American Forensic Association* 22, no. 2: 72–82.
Schiffman, Lawrence H. 1994a. "The Temple Scroll and the Nature of Its Law: The Status of the Question." In *The Community of the Renewed Covenant*, edited by Eugene Ulrich and James VanderKam, 37–55. Notre Dame: University of Notre Dame Press.
———. 1994b. "The Theology of the Temple Scroll." *Jewish Quarterly Review* 85, nos. 1–2: 109–23. http://www.jstor.org/stable/1454954.
———. 1995a. "Origin and Early History of the Qumran Sect." *Biblical Archaeologist* 58, no. 1: 37–48.
———. 1995b. *Reclaiming the Dead Sea Scrolls: Their True Meaning for Judaism and Christianity*. New York: Doubleday.
———. 1996. "The Place of 4QMMT in the Corpus of Qumran Manuscripts." In *Reading 4QMMT: New Perspectives on Qumran Law and History*, edited by John Kampen and Moshe J. Bernstein, 81–98. Atlanta: Scholars Press.
———. 2000. "Halakhah and Sectarianism in the Dead Sea Scrolls." In *The Dead Sea Scrolls in Their Historical Context*, edited by Timothy H. Lim, 132–42. Edinburgh: T&T Clark.
———. 2003. "Jerusalem: Twice Destroyed, Twice Rebuilt." *Classical World* 97, no. 1: 31–40.
Schiffman, Lawrence H., and Florentino Garcia Martinez, eds. 2008. *The Courtyards of the House of the Lord: Studies in the Temple Scroll*. Leiden: Brill.
Schleiermacher, Friedrich D. E. 2006. "General Hermeneutics." In *The Hermeneutics Reader*, edited by

Kurt Mueller-Vollmer, 73–86. New York: Continuum.

Schrag, Calvin O. 1997. "Hermeneutic Circles, Rhetorical Triangles, and Transversal Diagonals." In *Rhetoric and Hermeneutics in Our Time: A Reader*, edited by Walter Jost and Michael J. Hyde, 132–46. New Haven: Yale University Press.

Schwartz, Daniel R. 1996. "MMT, Josephus, and the Pharisees." In *Reading 4QMMT: New Perspectives on Qumran Law and History*, edited by John Kampen and Moshe J. Bernstein, 67–80. Atlanta: Scholars Press.

Scott, James M. 1985. "A New Approach to Habakkuk II.4–5a." *Vetus Testamentum* 35, no. 3: 330–40.

Selzer, Jack. 1999. "Habeas Corpus: An Introduction." In *Rhetorical Bodies*, edited by Jack Selzer and Sharon Crowley, 3–15. Madison: University of Wisconsin Press.

Shanks, Hershel. 1998. *The Mystery and Meaning of the Dead Sea Scrolls*. New York: Vintage.

Sharp, Carolyn J. 1997. "Phinehan Zeal and Rhetorical Strategy in 4QMMT." *Revue de Qumran* 18, no. 70: 207–22.

Shemesh, Aharon. 2008. "The Scriptural Background of the Penal Code in the *Rule of the Community* and the *Damascus Document*." *Dead Sea Discoveries* 15, no. 2: 191–224.

Shemesh, Aharon, and Cana Werman. 2003. "Halakhah at Qumran: Genre and Authority." *Dead Sea Discoveries* 10:104–29.

Sigal, Phillip. 1988. *Judaism: The Evolution of a Faith*. Grand Rapids, MI: Eerdmans.

Stahl, Roger. 2002. "Carving Up Free Exercise: Dissociation and 'Religion' in Supreme Court Jurisprudence." *Rhetoric and Public Affairs* 5, no. 3: 439–58. http://www.jstor.org/stable/41939766.

Stegemann, Hartmut. 2000. "Towards Physical Reconstructions of the Qumran *Damascus Document* Scrolls." In *The Damascus Document: A Centennial of Discovery*, edited by Joseph M. Baumgarten, Esther G. Chazon, and Avital Pinnick, 177–200. Leiden: Brill.

Stökl, Jonathan. 2015. "Prophetic Hermeneutics in the Hebrew Bible and Mesopotamia." *Hebrew Bible and Ancient Israel* 4, no. 3: 267–92. https://doi.org/10.1628/219222715 X14507102280810.

Swanson, Dwight D. 1995. *The Temple Scroll and the Bible: The Methodology of 11QT*. Leiden: Brill.

Sweeney, Marvin A. 1991. "Structure, Genre, and Intent in the Book of Habakkuk." *Vetus Testamentum* 41, no. 1: 63–83.

Tanakh. 1985. Philadelphia: Jewish Publications Society.

Thompson, Michael E. W. 1993. "Prayer, Oracle, and Theophany: The Book of Habakkuk." *Tyndale Bulletin* 44, no. 1: 33–53.

Timmer, Daniel C. 2008. "Sectarianism and Soteriology: The Priestly Blessing (Numbers 6,24–26) in the Qumranite Community Rule (1QS)." *Biblica* 89:389–96.

———. 2009. "Variegated Nomism Indeed: Multiphase Eschatology and Soteriology in the Qumranite Community Rule (1QS) and the New Perspective on Paul." *Journal of the Evangelical Theological Society* 52, no. 4: 341–56.

Toews, Casey. 2003. "Moral Purification in 1QS." *Bulletin for Biblical Research* 13, no. 1: 71–96.

Trever, J. C. 1985. "The Book of Daniel." *Biblical Archaeologist* 48, no. 2: 89–102.

———. 1987. "The Qumran Teacher— Another Candidate?" In *Early Jewish and Christian Exegesis: Studies in*

Memory of William Hugh Brownlee, edited by C. A. Williams and W. F. Stinespring, 101–21. Atlanta: Scholars Press.

Tukasi, Emmanuel O. 2008. *Determinism and Petitionary Prayer in John and the Dead Sea Scrolls: An Ideological Reading of John and the Rule of the Community (1QS)*. London: T&T Clark.

VanderKam, James C. 1994. *The Dead Sea Scrolls Today*. Grand Rapids, MI: Eerdmans.

———. 2003. "Those Who Look for Smooth Things, Pharisees, and Oral Law." In *Emanuel: Studies in Hebrew Bible, Septuagint, and the Dead Sea Scrolls*, edited by Shalmon M. Paul, Robert A. Kraft, Lawrence H. Schiffman, and Weston W. Fields, 465–77. Leiden: Brill.

———. 2011. "The Pre-History of the Qumran Community with a Reassessment of CD 1:5–11." In *The Dead Sea Scrolls and Contemporary Culture*, edited by Adolfo D. Roitman, Lawrence H. Schiffman, and Shani Tzoref, 59–76. Leiden: Brill.

Van Rees, M. A. 2009. *Dissociation in Argumentative Discussions: A Pragma-Dialectical Perspective*. New York: Springer.

Vasholz, Robert I. 1992. "Habakkuk: Complaints or Complaint?" *Presbyterion* 18, no. 1: 50–52.

Vermes, Geza. 1999. *An Introduction to the Complete Dead Sea Scrolls*. Minneapolis: Fortress Press.

———. 2004. *The Complete Dead Sea Scrolls in English*. Rev. ed. New York: Penguin.

Volgger, David. 2006. "The Day of Atonement According to the Temple Scroll." *Biblica* 87, no. 2: 251–60.

Vološinov, V. N. 1973. *Marxism and the Philosophy of Language*. Translated by Ladislav Matejka and I. R. Titunik. Cambridge, MA: Harvard University Press.

Vorster, J. N. 1992. "Dissociation in the Letter to the Galatians." *Neotestamentica* 26, no. 2: 297–310. http://www.jstor.org/stable/43048039.

Wacholder, Ben Zion. 2007. *The New Damascus Document: The Midrash on the Eschatological Torah and the Dead Sea Scrolls; Reconstruction, Translation, and Commentary*. Leiden: Brill.

Waisanen, Don. 2011. "Political Conversion as Intrapersonal Argument: Self-Dissociation in David Brock's *Blinded by the Right*." *Argumentation and Advocacy* 47, no. 4: 228–45.

Wallace, Karl R. 1970. "Speech Act and Unit of Communication." *Journal of Philosophy and Rhetoric* 3, no. 3: 174–81.

Wassen, Cecilia. 2005. *Women in the Damascus Document*. Atlanta: Society of Biblical Literature.

Weaver, Richard M. 1985. *The Ethics of Rhetoric*. Davis, CA: Hermagoras Press.

Weddle, David L. 2017. *Sacrifice in Judaism, Christianity, and Islam*. New York: New York University Press.

Weiler, Michael, and W. Barnett Pearce. 2006. *Reagan and Public Discourse in America*. Tuscaloosa: University of Alabama Press.

Weitzman, Steven. 2017. *The Origin of the Jews: The Quest for Roots in a Rootless Age*. Princeton: Princeton University Press.

Wendland, Ernst. 1999. "'The Righteous Live by Their Faith' in a Holy God: Complementary Compositional Forces and Habakkuk's Dialogue with the Lord." *Journal of the Evangelical Theological Society* 42, no. 4: 591–628.

Werman, Cana. 2000. "The Sons of Zadok." In *The Dead Sea Scrolls: Fifty Years After Their Discovery*, edited by

Lawrence H. Schiffman, Emanuel Tov, and James C. VanderKam, 623–30. Jerusalem: Israel Exploration Society.

Werrett, Ian C. 2007. *Ritual Purity and the Dead Sea Scrolls*. Leiden: Brill.

Whitehead, Philip. 2016. "Habakkuk and the Problem of Suffering: Theodicity Deferred." *Journal of Theological Interpretation* 10, no. 2: 265–81.

Wilson, Robert W. 1980. *Prophecy and Society in Ancient Israel*. Minneapolis: Fortress Press.

Wise, Michael Owen. 1990a. *A Critical Study of the Temple Scroll from Cave 11*. Chicago: Oriental Institute of the University of Chicago, 1990.

———. 1990b. "The Eschatological Vision of the Temple Scroll." *Journal of Near Eastern Studies* 49, no. 2: 155–72. http://www.jstor.org/stable/545739.

Wolff, Hans Walter. 1978. "Prophecy from the Eighth Through the Fifth Century." *Interpretation* 32, no. 1: 17–30.

Xeravits, Géza G., ed. 2010. *Dualism in Qumran*. New York: T&T Clark.

Yadin, Yigael. 1985. *The Temple Scroll: The Hidden Law and the Dead Sea Sect*. New York: Random House.

Zulick, Margaret D. 1998. "The Normative, the Proper, and the Sublime: Notes on the Use of Figure and Emotion in Prophetic Argument." *Argumentation* 12, no. 4: 481–92.

———. 2003. "Prophecy and Providence: The Anxiety over Prophetic Authority." *Journal of Communication and Religion* 26, no. 2: 195–207.

RESOURCES FOR THE STUDY OF THE DEAD SEA SCROLLS

Although I believe the Dead Sea Scrolls are worthy of attention from rhetoric scholars, I would be remiss not to mention that there are significant challenges in the study of the Dead Sea Scrolls. Some of these challenges include the problem of translation, the difficulty of the original languages, the obscurity of certain reference works, and the fragmentary status of many of the scrolls. In order to address some of these challenges, I offer the following resources.

GRAMMARS

Kelley, Page H. 2018. *Biblical Hebrew: An Introductory Grammar*. 2nd ed. Revised by Timothy G. Crawford. Grand Rapids, MI: Eerdmans.

Kutz, Karl V., and Rebekah L. Josberger. 2018. *Learning Biblical Hebrew: Reading for Comprehension; An Introductory Grammar*. Bellingham, WA: Lexham.

Pratico, Gary D., and Miles V. van Pelt. 2014. *Basics of Biblical Hebrew: Grammar*. 2nd ed. Grand Rapids, MI: Zondervan.

Roden, Chet. 2016. *Elementary Biblical Hebrew: An Introduction to the Language and Its History*. San Diego: Congella.

LEXICONS

Brown, Francis, Samuel Rolles Driver, and Charles A. Briggs. 1996. *The Brown-Driver-Briggs Hebrew and English Lexicon*. Peabody, MA: Hendrickson.

Kohler, Ludwig, Walter Baumgarten, and Johann Jakob Stamm. 2002. *The Hebrew and Aramaic Lexicon of the Old Testament*. 2 vols. Leiden: Brill.

CONCORDANCES

Abegg, Martin G., Jr., with James E. Bowley and Edward M. Cook. 2003. *The Dead Sea Scrolls Concordance*. Vol. 1, *The Non-biblical Texts from Qumran*. 2 pts. Leiden: Brill.

———. 2017. *The Dead Sea Scrolls Concordance*. Vol. 2, *The Non-Qumran Documents*. Leiden: Brill.

Charlesworth, James H. 1992. *Graphic Concordance of the Dead Sea Scrolls*. Louisville: Westminster John Knox Press.

MANUSCRIPT EDITIONS

The Dead Sea Scrolls: Hebrew, Aramaic, and Greek Texts with English Translations. 1994–2018. Edited by James H. Charlesworth et al. 8 vols. Tübingen: Mohr Siebeck.

Discoveries in the Judean Desert. 1955–2009. 40 vols. Oxford: Clarendon.

DIGITAL MANUSCRIPTS

Israel Antiquities Authority. *The Leon Levy Dead Sea Scrolls Digital Library.* https://www.deadseascrolls.org.il/home.

The Israel Museum, Jerusalem. *The Digital Dead Sea Scrolls.* http://dss.collections.imj.org.il.

ELECTRONIC LIBRARIES

Parry, Donald W., ed. 2015. *Dead Sea Scrolls Electronic Library: Biblical Texts.* Leiden: Brill.

Tov, Emanuel, ed. 2016. *Dead Sea Scrolls Electronic Library: Non-biblical Texts.* Leiden: Brill.

TRANSLATIONS

Abegg, Martin, Jr., Peter Flint, and Eugene Ulrich, trans. 1999. *The Dead Sea Scrolls Bible.* New York: HarperCollins.

Martínez, Florentino García, trans. 1996. *The Dead Sea Scrolls Translated: The Qumran Texts in English.* Translated by Wilfred G. E. Watson. 2nd ed. Grand Rapids, MI: Eerdmans.

Vermes, Geza, trans. 2012. *The Complete Dead Sea Scrolls in English.* 7th ed. New York: Penguin.

Wise, Michael, Martin Abegg Jr., and Edward Cook, trans. 2005. *The Dead Sea Scrolls: A New Translation.* Rev. ed. New York: HarperCollins.

STUDY EDITION

Martínez, Florentino García, and Eibert J. C. Tigchelaar, trans. 1997–98. *The Dead Sea Scrolls: Study Edition.* 2 vols. Leiden: Brill.

ENCYCLOPEDIA

Schiffman, Lawrence H., and James C. VanderKam, eds. 2000. *Encyclopedia of the Dead Sea Scrolls.* 2 vols. Oxford: Oxford University Press.

INTERNET RESOURCE

The Hebrew University of Jerusalem. *Orion Center for the Study of the Dead Sea Scrolls and Associated Literature.* http://orion.mscc.huji.ac.il/.

JOURNALS DEDICATED TO PUBLISHING SCHOLARSHIP ON THE DEAD SEA SCROLLS

Dead Sea Discoveries. https://brill.com/view/journals/dsd/dsd-overview.xml.

The Qumran Chronicle. http://enigmapress.pl/chronicle.php.

Revue de Qumran. http://revuedequmran.fr/index.php/en.

INDEX

Aaron, 111, 126, 179
abuses, 56–57
adjuration, oath of, 93–94
Ahaz, King, 144
Alcimus, 29–30, 188–89n8
Alexander Jannaeus, 6, 8, 49, 101, 102–3, 104–5, 170
Alexander the Great, 4–5
Althusser, Louis, 106
Altieri, Charles, 135
ambiguous laws, 36–41
Amon, 144
Amos, 200–201n13
Ananelus, 11
Anderson, Jeff S., 54
animal sacrifice, 36–41, 58, 126–28, 181–84
annual renewal ceremony, in *Rule of the Community*, 20, 66–69, 72, 73
Antigonus, 11, 104
Antiochus IV, 28–30, 101, 189n10
apocalypse, 12–13, 159–60
apparent aspect, 74–75
apparent Essenes, and dissociative rhetoric in *Damascus Document*, 21, 91–95
apparent humanity, and dissociative rhetoric in *Damascus Document*, 20, 82–85
apparent Israel, and dissociative rhetoric in *Damascus Document*, 21, 95–98
apparent Israelites, and dissociative rhetoric in *Damascus Document*, 20–21, 85–88
apparent remnants, and dissociative rhetoric in *Damascus Document*, 21, 88–91
appearance, dynamic of real and, in dissociative argumentation, 77–79
argumentation by means of association, 76
arguments based on structure of reality, 76

arguments establishing structure of reality, 76
Aristobulus I, 6, 104
arrogance, 152
Asael (Azazel), 126–28
association, argumentation by means of, 76
Assyria, 144–45, 151, 175
atomistic pesher interpretation, 164–65, 167
atonement, 61, 125–29
Aune, James Arnt, 106
Austin, J. L., 21, 55–57, 62, 66, 70, 109, 119, 193n9
Azazel (Asael), 126–28

Babylon, 145, 146, 156, 175
Balibar, Etienne, 106
Barton, John, 157, 158–59
Baumgarten, Albert I., 80, 88, 91
Baumgarten, Joseph M., 122
Beale, Walter H., 193n8
Belial, nets of, 81–82, 169–71, 195nn11–12
Bergsma, John S., 95, 96, 98, 185n1, 196n18
Bernard-Donals, Michael, 174, 201–2n1
Bernstein, Moshe J., 33, 187n3, 190n12
Bible
  canonization of, 2
  editorial redaction in, 153
Biddle, Mark E., 153–54, 157
Biesecker, Barbara A., 3
Bineham, Jeffery L., 138
Blair, Carole, 105–6
blessing, in new covenant initiation, 63, 64–65
Bohman, James, 193n9
book of Habakkuk, 12, 22, 130, 131–33, 134, 138, 142–54, 198n2, 199n5
boundary creation, 80–81
Bourdieu, Pierre, 110, 197n6
Bourgel, Jonathan, 7, 103

Brewer, David Instone, 195n12
bribery, 125
Bright, John, 110, 145, 146–47, 176
Brooke, George J., 33–34, 199n5, 201n16
Büchner, Dirk, 41
bull, sacrificed by Aaron, 126
Burke, Kenneth, 21, 26, 31, 35, 51, 109, 114–15, 124

calendar
    lunar, 168, 188n6
    solar, 25, 168, 188n6
"camp," 39–41
Campbell, Edward F. Jr., 110
Campbell, Jonathan G., 32
ceremonies. *See* rituals
Chaldea / Chaldeans, 146, 152, 172
Chancey, Mark A., 102
charismatic terms, 114–15, 194–95n8
Charlesworth, James H., 161
Christiansen, Ellen Juhl, 53–54, 191n1, 193n10, 196n17
circumcision, 171
classical biblical period, 17, 186–87n8
classical prophecy, end of, 156–57
Clements, Ronald E., 150, 151, 153, 158, 159, 200n10
Clendenen, E. Ray, 200n11
Cloud, Dana L., 106
Collins, John J., 54, 83, 160, 196n13
commissive speech acts, 62, 68–69
common laws
    in *Miqsat Ma'aseh ha-Torah*, 31–34
    works and deeds from, 35–41
complaints, 143–47, 199nn6–9
confession, in new covenant initiation, 64
connecting links, breaking of, 76
constative utterances, 55
consubstantiality, 31–34
continuous peshers, 198n1
Cooper, Marilyn M., 3
corpse contact, impurity from, 112, 117–18, 121–23
covenant(s)
    defined, 110, 191n1
    purity and, 110–13, 129
    See also Mosaic covenant; new covenant

Coward, Rosalind, 106
Cross, Frank Moore, 187n1, 189–90n10, 193n10
curse, in new covenant initiation, 65, 69–70
Cyrus, 176
Czajkowski, Kimberley, 93

Damascus, and dissociative rhetoric in *Damascus Document*, 21, 95–98, 196n15
Damascus Document
    apparent and real Essenes and dissociation in, 21, 91–95
    apparent and real final remnants and dissociation in, 21, 88–91
    apparent and real humanity and dissociation in, 20, 82–85
    apparent and real Israel and old and new Israel and dissociation in, 21, 95–98
    apparent and real Israelites and dissociation in, 21, 85–88
    audience of, 9–10
    communal leadership of Essenes in, 181
    dating of, 193n1
    dissociation in, 20–21, 73–75, 80–82, 98–99
    fragments of, known to scholars, 74
    hortatory tone of, 194n7
    reference to Damascus in, 21, 95–98, 196n15
    rhetorical purpose of, 72, 73–74
    scholarship on, 193–94n2
    Teacher of Righteousness in, 180
    wealth in, 195n10
Daniel, 160, 161, 201n16
Dasenbrock, Reed Way, 193n8
David, 27, 45, 175
Davies, Philip R., 196n13
Day of Atonement, 126–28
Dead Sea Scrolls
    background of, 4–9
    dating of, 185n2
    discovery of, 1–2, 13–14
    documents comprising, 185–86n3
    hiding of, 13

importance of, 184
interest in biblical texts among, 2
lack of rhetorical criticism applied to, 17–18
rhetorical strategies in, 16–17
sale and publication of, 14–16
search for additional, 15
sectarian texts among, 2
and transition from biblical to talmudic rhetoric, 173–84
See also *Damascus Document*; *Habakkuk Pesher*; *Miqsat Ma'aśeh ha-Torah*; *Purification Rules*; *Rule of the Community*; *Temple Scroll*
decontextualization, 153
de Jong, Matthijs J., 201n14
demigod terms, 115, 124, 125
de Vaux, Roland, 15
devil terms, 194–95n8
dialectical materialism, 107
Dilthey, Wilhelm, 134
Dimant, Devorah, 161
discharges, impure, 116–17
Discoveries in the Judean Desert (DJD), 16
discursive embodiment / materialization
  of moral impurity, 124–25
  of ritual impurity in *Purification Rules*, 114–18, 119
dissociation and dissociative rhetoric, 9–10, 76–80
  apparent and real Essenes in *Damascus Document*, 91–95
  apparent and real final remnants in *Damascus Document*, 88–91
  apparent and real humanity in *Damascus Document*, 82–85
  apparent and real Israelites in *Damascus Document*, 85–88
  in *Damascus Document*, 20–21, 73–75, 80–82, 98–99
  of Judah from ideal Essene community, 196n18
  scholarship on, 194nn5–6
distinction, rhetoric of, in *Miqsat Ma'aśeh ha-Torah*, 34–41, 46, 48
double hermeneutic process, 132, 133
drunkenness, 152

dualism, as assumption grounding *Rule of the Community*, 52–53

Edbauer, Jenny, 3
Edelman, Samuel M., 17, 18, 173–74, 201n1
edh-Dhib, Muhammad, 13–14
editorial redaction, in book of Habakkuk, 153–54
Eemeren, Frans H. van, 193n8
Egypt, 145–46
eighth-century prophets, 200–201n13
Eliakim, 145
Elijah, 200–201n13
Ellis, John, 106
"end of days," 42–45, 54–55
Engels, Friedrich, 106–7
Enoch, 127
entitlement, 21, 109, 114–15, 118, 124–25, 130
Ephraim, and dissociative rhetoric in *Damascus Document*, 21, 95–98
eschatology
  as assumption grounding *Rule of the Community*, 54–55
  in *Habakkuk Pesher*, 166
  and rhetoric of persuasion in *Miqsat Ma'aśeh ha-Torah*, 42–45
Eshel, Hanan, 6, 12–13, 186n6, 187n3
Essenes
  apparent and real, and dissociation in *Damascus Document*, 91–95
  as audience of *Damascus Document*, 9–10
  challenges to boundary-creation practices of, 80–81
  commonalities between other Jews and, 31–32
  communal leadership of, 181, 186n5
  connection between Sadducees and, 189n8
  creation of, 100
  desire to return to Temple cult, 190n15, 191n17
  dissociation of Judah from, 196n18
  emergence community of, 189–90n10
  exile of, 2, 5, 8, 49
  introductory formulae used by, 26–27

224 | INDEX

Essenes *(continued)*
   as Israelites, 185n1
   legal rulings regarding religious observances among, 190n11
   observance of Torah law, 111
   as real final remnant, 21, 88–91
   and Roman occupation, 11–12
   self-identification of, 185n1, 191–92n2
   stops offering animal sacrifices, 183
   temptation and entrapment of, 81–82
   See also new covenant; Yahad
Evans, Craig, 54
Examiner, 82
exclusion, 94–95
exile, 2, 5, 8, 12, 39–40, 41, 49, 113
exodus, 149

felicitous speech acts, 57, 58–59, 60, 62–69
Fernández, Miguel Pérez, 187n3
Fernheimer, Janice W., 174, 201–2n1
festivals, 58–59, 168, 197–98n10
First Temple period, 4, 110, 132, 167, 185n1
Fitzmyer, Joseph A., 197–98n10
Floyd, Michael H., 162, 199n6
forgiveness, as result of atonement, 128
fornication, 97, 102–5, 170–71
Fragments of a Zadokite Work (Schechter), 74
fusion of horizons, 22, 138, 140–42
   in book of Habakkuk, 150–54
   in *Habakkuk Pesher*, 163–72

Gadamer, Hans-Georg, 22, 137–42, 199n4
Gentiles
   as apparent humanity, 20, 82–85
   impurity association with, 84–85
Gilders, William K., 127, 128
God
   acknowledgment of greatness of, in new covenant initiation, 63–64
   and assumptions structuring *Damascus Document*, 81
   and dissociation of apparent and real Israelites in *Damascus Document*, 85–88
god terms, 114–15, 194–95n8
Goldsmith, Galen L., 152
gonorrhea, 116, 117, 120–21, 122

Grabbe, Lester L., 178, 179, 181, 189n8
greed, 152, 169–70
Greene, Ronald Walter, 106
Greenspoon, Leonard J., 28–29
Gries, Laurie E., 107
Grootendorst, Rob, 193n8
Grossman, Maxine L., 79–80, 81, 196n14
Gruen, Erich S., 101–2
guiding concepts, and rhetorical dissociation, 74–75

Habakkuk, 12–13, 22, 199nn6–9, 201n15
   See also book of Habakkuk; *Habakkuk Pesher*
Habakkuk Pesher, 12–13, 21–22, 59, 131–33
   chapter of book of Habakkuk interpreted in, 198n2
   fusion of horizons in, 163–72
   hermeneutics/rhetoric in, 154–56
   Jerusalem Temple in, 177
   prejudices in, 156–59
   Teacher of Righteousness in, 180
   traditions in, 160–63
Habermas, Jürgen, 193n8
habitus, 110, 197n6
halakhah / halakhot, 187n1
Harding, Gerald Lankester, 15
Harkins, Angela Kim, 194n7
Harrington, Hannah K., 32, 40, 41, 105, 111, 117, 118, 119, 122–23, 129
Hasmonean high priests, 5–8, 11, 29–30, 48–49, 52–53, 101, 130, 168, 170
Hasmonean revolt (167 BCE), 4–5
Hasmonean rule, 100, 101–2
Heard, Chris, 200n11
Hebrew prophecy, 152
Hellenistic period and Hellenization, 4–5, 17–18, 70, 84, 101–2, 187n8
Hempel, Charlotte, 84, 194n7
hermeneutical rhetoric, 136
hermeneutic circle, 141–42
hermeneutics
   Gadamer on historical intersections of rhetoric and, 199n4
   Gadamer's philosophical, 137–42
   relationship between rhetorics and, 134–38
   rhetorical, 136–37

hermeneutics/rhetoric
  in book of Habakkuk, 132–33, 142–54, 199n5
  and fusion of horizons in *Habakkuk Pesher*, 163–72
  in *Habakkuk Pesher*, 21–22, 132–33, 154–56
  overview of, 133–42
  and prejudices in *Habakkuk Pesher*, 156–59
  and traditions in *Habakkuk Pesher*, 160–63
Herod the Great, 11, 186n6
Hezekiah, King, 144
Hidary, Richard, 174
high priests
  emergence of Essene community and succession of, 189–90n10
  rites and rituals carried out by, 179
  during Second Temple period, 178–79
  and transition from sacrifice to prayer, 181–82
  transition to rabbis from, 178–81
  See also Hasmonean high priests; Zadokite high priests
Høgenhaven, Jesper, 32, 33, 44
Horgan, Maurya P., 160, 161, 164
horizons, fusion of, 22, 138, 140–42
  in book of Habakkuk, 150–54
  in *Habakkuk Pesher*, 163–72
Hosea, 200–201n13
humanity, and dissociative rhetoric in *Damascus Document*, 20, 82–85
Hyde, Michael J., 135
Hyrcanus II, 11

identification, rhetoric of, in *Miqsat Ma'aśeh ha-Torah*, 31–34, 46, 48
illocution, 55, 56, 193n9
imitatio, 136
impurity
  associated with Gentiles, 84–85
  material, 109, 115
  moral, 10–11, 102–5, 110–12, 113, 123–30
  in *Purification Rules* and *Temple Scroll*, 108–9
  understanding, in context of larger discursive domains, 110–12

  and xenophobic exclusion, 94–95
  See also ritual impurity
incoherence, resolved by dissociation, 74–75
infelicitous speech acts, 56–61
  prevention of, in *Rule of the Community*, 69–71
initiation ceremony, in *Rule of the Community*, 20
interpretation
  atomistic pesher interpretation, 164–65, 167
  conveying structure and rhetoric of pesher, 165–66
  methods of pesher, 164–65
  practice of, 133–34
Isaiah, 200–201n13
isolation, as prescription for ritual impurity, 119–20
  See also exile
Israel
  conquered by Philistines, 175
  and dissociative rhetoric in *Damascus Document*, 21, 95–98
  during First Temple period, 185n1
  population growth of, 49
  Roman occupation of, 11–13
  during Second Temple period, 185n1
  shifts in rhetorical ecology of, 4–5
  State of Israel, 14
Israelite(s)
  change in meaning of term, 75
  and dissociative rhetoric in *Damascus Document*, 20–21, 85–88
  Essenes as, 185n1
  as real humanity, 20, 82–85
  redefinition of guiding concept of, 75
  of Second Temple period, 32
  shift social structure, 175
"it is written," 19, 31–34, 35, 190n12

Jameson, Fredric, 110, 197n6
Jassen, Alex P., 164
Jehoahaz, 145
Jehoiakim, 145–47, 167, 168, 199n8
Jeremiah, 146, 199n6
Jericho, 7, 103–4

Jerusalem
  borders of, 40–41
  destruction of, 23
  population growth of, 49
  prophecy on destruction of, 12–13
  Roman occupation of, 11–13, 179
Jerusalem Temple
  "book of the law" discovered during renovation of, 144–45
  construction of, 27, 175
  in Dead Sea Scrolls, 177–78
  defilement of, 29–30, 39, 82, 101, 145, 170–71, 183, 195n11
  destruction of, 23, 174, 175–76, 177, 179
  Essenes' effort to reestablish ties with, 190n15, 191n17
  Essenes' view on rhetoric of priests administering, 50
  infelicitous speech acts in, 57–61
  purification of, 30, 48
  reconstruction of, 176
  structure of, 123
Jewish revolt, 29–30
John Hyrcanus, 6–8, 49, 101, 102–3, 104, 105, 170
Jonathan, 4–5, 6, 30, 48, 101, 167–68, 189n8
Josephus, 17, 28, 105, 145, 156
Joshua, 28, 103–4
Josiah, 144–45
Judah
  dissociation of, from ideal Essene community, 196n18
  and dissociative rhetoric in *Damascus Document*, 21, 95–98
  during First Temple period, 185n1
  under Jehoiakim, 145–46
  as vassal to Assyria, 144–45, 175
Judea, 13, 29, 102, 130, 131, 143–46, 171
Judean oracles, 148
judgment, criteria of, in verdictive speech acts of renewal ceremony, 67–68

Kamm, Antony, 6, 11, 27–28, 104–5, 144, 145, 149, 188n6
"Kenneth Burke Meets the Teacher of Righteousness" (Newsom), 51
Kim, Jintae, 92

Klawans, Jonathan, 110, 112, 113, 195n12, 197n9
Koch, Klaus, 160
Konishi, Takuzo, 79

language
  entitlement and, 124
  Marx and Engels on, 106–7
  metaphorical, used by Old Testament prophets, 152
  tradition and, 141
late Second Temple period, 2, 17–18, 23, 41, 88, 132–33, 156, 161, 174
Leff, Michael, 134, 136
lepers, 59
Levine, Lee I., 102, 176, 179, 182
Lim, Timothy H., 165, 195n9
linguistic sign, 109, 114
links, breaking of connecting, 76
locution, 55, 56
lunar calendar, 168, 188n6
lying, 70–71

ma'aśeh ha-torah, 188n7
Machiela, Daniel A., 163
Mailloux, Steven, 136–37
Martínez, Florentino García, 35, 42–45, 188n7
Marx, Karl, 106–7, 197n3
Marxism, 106
Mason, Jeff, 193n9
maśśā', 148
material impurity, 109, 115
material rhetoric, 9, 105–9
  applicability of, in context of Dead Sea Scrolls, 197n5
  entitlement as form of, 115
  as methodology for exploring ritual and moral impurity, 130
  ritual erasure as form of, 118–23
McComiskey, Thomas Edward, 1–2, 184
McGee, Michael Calvin, 106, 107
Medala, Stanislaw, 42, 188n8, 189n8
Menasseh, King, 144, 145, 175
Menelaus, 5, 28–29, 58
me niddah, 121–23, 197n7
menstrual blood, as ritual impurity, 115–16, 120–21

Merkle, Benjamin L., 152, 201n14
metaphors, used by Old Testament prophets, 152, 158
Meyers, Eric M., 102
Micah, 200–201n13
Mica Pesher, communal leadership of Essenes in, 181
Milkowski, Chaim, 196n15
Miqsat Ma'aśeh ha-Torah (4QMMT), 19, 45–47
  audience of, 188–89nn5,8
  authorship of, 189n8
  called "Halakhic Letter," 187n1
  common laws and rhetoric of identification in, 31–34, 46, 48
  composite text of, 187n2
  connection between scripture and laws of, 190n12
  contents of, 25–26
  copies of, 24–25
  dating of, 187–88n3, 190n15
  eschatology and rhetoric of persuasion in, 42–45
  and Essenes' effort to reestablish ties with Temple, 191n17
  fragments of solar calendar in, 25, 188n6
  polemical, combative, or confrontational tone in, 190–91n16
  rhetorical ecology of, 5–6, 27–30
  rhetorical purpose of, 26, 48, 177
  works of law and rhetoric of distinction in, 34–41, 46, 48
miqva'ot, 120, 121
misfires, 56–57
moral impurity, 10–11, 102–5, 110–12, 113, 123–30
Mosaic covenant
  as assumption grounding *Rule of the Community*, 53–54
  blessings and curses associated with, 191n1, 200n11
  in book of Habakkuk, 149–50
  as broken, 62
  purpose of, 111
  transformed from unconditional promise to conditional agreement, 200–201n13
  and Yahad formation and covenant, 9
  See also covenant(s); new covenant
motivational rhetoric, 51
Mount Gerizim, Samaritan temple on, 7, 103
Mowinckel, Sigmund, 148, 154, 200n10, 201n15
Murphy, Catherine M., 81–82, 93, 97, 195n10
mysteries, interpretation of, *Habakkuk Pesher*, 12, 132-33, 156, 160–62, 180

Nebuchadnezzar II, 146–47, 175
Neco II, 145
new covenant
  as earned through obedience to Essene interpretation of law, 92
  felicitous speech acts and initiation into, in *Rule of the Community*, 62–66, 69–70, 72, 73
  felicitous speech acts and renewal of, in *Rule of the Community*, 66–69, 72, 73
  in *Habakkuk Pesher*, 162–63
  and interpretation of Torah, 196n13
  versus Mosaic covenant, 191n1
new Israel, and dissociative rhetoric in *Damascus Document*, 21, 95–98
Newsom, Carol A., 18, 50–51
Nichols, Ernest W., 200n13
Niehoff, Maren R., 165
Nissinen, Martti, 151, 159
nonbiblical texts, 2, 25, 188n4
nonremnants, and dissociative rhetoric in *Damascus Document*, 20–21, 85–88

oath of adjuration, 93–94
oaths, swearing, 92
obedience, as criteria of judgment in renewal ceremony, 68
O'Connell, Kevin G., 146, 149
Olbrechts-Tyteca, Lucie, 76, 77–78, 79
old Israel, and dissociative rhetoric in *Damascus Document*, 21, 95–98
Onias III, 27–28
oracles
  in book of Habakkuk, 147–49
  in complaint or lamentation liturgies, 201n15

oracles (continued)
    interpretation of, 142
    interpretation of, in book of Habakkuk, 150–54
    nature of, 147–48
    oral origin of, 200n10
    received during First Temple period, 132
Overholt, Thomas W., 157

pagan sacrifice, 85
Palestine Archaeological Museum, 15–16
Palmer, Richard E., 135
Pearce, W. Barnett, 3–4
Perelman, Chaim, 76, 77–78, 79, 194n5
performative utterances, 55–61, 62, 72
perlocution, 55, 56, 193n9
persuasion, rhetoric of, in *Miqsat Ma'aśeh ha-Torah*, 42–45
pesher method, 163–72
peshers, 12, 130, 198n1
    See also *Habakkuk Pesher*
Pharisees, 6, 17, 104–5, 182, 189n8, 196n15
Philistines, 175
Philo, 17
philosophical hermeneutics, 137–42
Pliny, 17
polygamy, 81, 195n9
Pompey, 11
pragma, 107, 197n4
prayer, transition from sacrifice to, 181–84
prejudices, 22, 138–39, 141–42, 143–47, 156–59
"princes of Judah," 96–97
prison-house, 197n6
promises, fulfilling, 124–25
prophecy, written, in *Habakkuk Pesher*, 156–59
prophetic interpretation, in book of Habakkuk, 151–53
Psammetichus, 145
public rhetorics, 3–4
punishment, 91–94
purification
    dissociation as act of, 79
    and material rhetoric in *Purification Rules* and *Temple Scroll*, 100–105
    ritual erasure through, 118–23, 125–29, 130
    See also purity
Purification Rules, 10, 21, 100–105
    creation and use of *me niddah* in, 197n7
    dating of, 197n2
    discursive embodiment, ritual impurity, and ritual erasure in, 114–23
    entitlement in, 109
    material rhetoric and explaining effects of inspiriting and erasure in, 108–9
    purity and covenant in, 110–13
purity
    covenant and, 110–13
    through ritual speech acts, 61
    understanding, in context of larger discursive domains, 110–12
    See also purification

Qimron, Elisha, 25, 188n7, 190n12
quasi-logical arguments, 76

rabbis
    transition from priests to, 178–81
    and transition from sacrifice to prayer, 182–83
Rast, Walter E., 148–49
rāz, 161
real, dynamic of appearance and, in dissociative argumentation, 77–79
real aspect, 74–75
real Essenes, and dissociative rhetoric in *Damascus Document*, 21, 91–95
real final remnants, and dissociative rhetoric in *Damascus Document*, 21, 88–91
real humanity, and dissociative rhetoric in *Damascus Document*, 20, 82–85
real Israel, and dissociative rhetoric in *Damascus Document*, 21, 95–98
real Israelites, and dissociative rhetoric in *Damascus Document*, 20–21, 85–88
reality
    arguments based on structure of, 76
    arguments establishing structure of, 76
rebuke, 91–94

redaction, editorial, in book of Habakkuk, 153–54
Regev, Eyal, 44, 129, 191n17
remnants, and dissociative rhetoric in *Damascus Document*, 20–21, 85–88
See also nonremnants; real final remnants
reproach, 91–94
rhetorical criticism, 18
"Rhetorical Criticism and the Dead Sea Scrolls" (Newsom), 51
rhetorical ecologies, 3–5
  of around 100 BCE, 100
  concepts relating to, 186n4
  of *Miqsat Ma'aśeh ha-Torah*, 27–30
  of *Rule of the Community* and *Damascus Document*, 73
  strategies for dealing with evolving, 46
rhetorical hermeneutics, 136–37
rhetoric(s)
  early effort to link speech act theory and, 193n8
  emergence of, 172
  Gadamer on historical intersections of hermeneutics and, 199n4
  hermeneutical, 136
  history of, 134
  motivational, 51
  periods of ancient Jewish, 17, 186–87n8
  public, 3–4
  relationship between hermeneutics and, 134–38
  study of Dead Sea Scrolls', 17–18
  transition from biblical, to talmudic, 173–84
  See also hermeneutics/rhetoric; material rhetoric
Ricoeur, Paul, 135
ritual erasure, 118–23, 125–29, 130
ritual illocutionary acts, 119
ritual impurity, 112–13, 129–30
  discursive embodiment of, in *Purification Rules*, 114–18
  and Essenes' interpretation of Torah law, 19, 59
  and material rhetoric, 108–9
  in *Purification Rules*, 10

sources of, 102, 115–18
understanding, in context of larger discursive domains, 110–12
ritual locutionary acts, 119
rituals, transition in, 181–84
Rivers, Nathaniel A., 4
Robertson, O. Palmer, 147, 150
Romans and Roman occupation, 11–13, 131, 172, 179
Roo, Jacqueline C. R. de, 127
Rule of the Community, 8–9, 19–20, 48–51, 71–72
  annual renewal ceremony in, 20, 66–69, 72, 73
  assumptions grounding, and its ceremonial procedures, 52–55
  communal leadership of Essenes in, 181, 186n5
  copies of, 186n5
  description of Sons of Darkness in, 193n7
  description of Sons of Light in, 192–93n6
  felicitous speech acts in, 62–69
  and infelicitous speech acts in Jerusalem Temple, 57–61
  Jerusalem Temple in, 177–78
  motivational rhetoric in, 51
  passages describing dualist nature of human spirit in, 192n5
  prayer as sacrifice in, 184
  prevention of infelicitous speech acts in, 69–71
  purpose of, 73
  rhetorical strategies in, 46
  scholarship on, 192n3
  speech acts as rhetorical strategies in, 55–57

Sabbath, 25, 58
sacrifice
  animal, 36–41, 58, 126, 181–84
  pagan, 85
  ritual erasure through, 125–28
  transition to prayer from, 181–84
Sadducees, 2, 6–7, 104, 189n8
Salahi, Faidi, 14

Salome Alexandra, 104
salvation, 60–61
Samaria, 7, 103
Samaritan temple on Mount Gerizim, 7, 103
Samuel, Mar, 14
Sanders, E. P., 31–32
Saul, 175
Schechter, Solomon S., 74
Schiffman, Lawrence H., 17–18, 183, 187n3, 189n8, 190n11
Schleiermacher, Friedrich D. E., 134, 135
Schrag, Calvin O., 135
Schwartz, Daniel R., 44, 187n3
Scoffer, 90, 196n15
Second Temple period, 23, 41, 88, 132–33, 156, 161, 174, 185n2
sectarianism, drive toward rhetorical dissociation as function of, 79–80
sectarian texts, 2, 25, 188n4
Seleucus IV, 27–28
Selzer, Jack, 106
seminal discharge, as ritual impurity, 116–17, 121
Septuagint, 17
sexual intercourse, ritual impurity through, 122
Shahin, Khalil Iskander (Kando), 14
Shanks, Hershel, 16
Sharp, Carolyn J., 25, 44
Shemesh, Aharon, 40–41
Sigal, Phillip, 181–82
Simon, 6, 30, 48, 101, 189n8
sin and sinfulness
   by association, 68
   and discursive materialization of moral impurity, 124–25
   intentional, 125
   moral impurity as acquired through, 113
   unintentional, 125–26
Six-Day War (1967), 15–16
slaughter, law concerning location of, 36–41, 58
Smith, Craig R., 135
solar calendar, 25, 168, 188n6
Solomon, 27, 58, 175
Sons of Darkness, 52, 55, 193n7
Sons of Light, 52, 55, 192–93n6
speech act theory, 21, 52, 55–57, 72, 109, 119, 130, 193n8
spirit
   dualist nature of human, 192n5
   dynamic character of, 67
State of Israel, 14
Stegemann, Hartmut, 194n4
Stökl, Jonathan, 157
Strugnell, John, 16, 25, 188n7, 190n12
swearing oaths, 92
Sweeney, Marvin A., 147, 151
synagogues, transition from temple to, 174–78

talmudic period, 17, 187n8
Teacher of Righteousness, 89–90, 163, 167, 169, 177, 180–81, 191n17, 201n16
Temple, transition from synagogues to, 174–78
   See also Jerusalem Temple
Temple Scroll, 10–11, 21, 100–105
   dating of, 197n2
   discursive entitlement, moral impurity, and ritual erasure in, 123–29
   entitlement in, 109
   material rhetoric and explaining effects of inspiriting and erasure in, 108–9
   purity and covenant in, 110–13
   subjects covered in, 196n1
   "tent of the meeting place," 39–41
thematic peshers, 198n1
Thompson, Michael E. W., 199n8
Titus, 13, 176
tohorah, 130
tôkaḥat, 143, 199n7
Torah law
   disagreements on application of, 19, 25–26
   and initiation into new covenant, 63
   interpretations of, 34–41, 49, 89–91, 111, 195–96n13
   punishment of violations of, 91–94
   relationship between covenant and, 110–11
Tov, Emanuel, 16

traditions, 22, 138, 139–40, 141, 147–50, 162–63
Truth and Method (Gadamer), 22

ultimate terms, categories of, 114–15, 194–95n8

VanderKam, James, 183, 196n15
Van Rees, M. A., 78, 79, 194n6
Vasholz, Robert I., 199–200n9
verdictive speech acts, 20, 66–69, 72
Vespasian, 13, 176
Volgger, David, 126–27
Vološinov, V. N., 106
vows, fulfilling, 124–25

Wacholder, Ben Zion, 95, 195n11
wealth, 81–82, 97, 102–5, 169–70, 195n10
Weaver, Richard M., 194–95n8
Weber, Ryan P., 4
Weddle, David L., 182–83
Weiler, Michael, 3–4
Weitzman, Steven, 185n1
Werman, Cana, 40–41
"we say" / "we think," 34–41
Whitehead, Philip, 153
Wicked Priest, 59, 167–70, 177, 191n17
Wilson, Robert R., 148, 201n15
Wolff, Hans Walter, 151

works and deeds, from common laws, 35–41
written prophecy, in *Habakkuk Pesher*, 156–59

xenophobia, 94–95

Yadin, Yigael, 14
Yahad, 8–9, 49–50
    establishment of, 177–78
    felicitous speech acts and initiation into, in *Rule of the Community*, 62–66, 69–70, 72, 73
    felicitous speech acts and renewal of membership in, in *Rule of the Community*, 20, 66–69, 72, 73
    and infelicitous speech acts in Jerusalem Temple, 57–61
    and new covenant, 52–54
    and prevention of infelicitous speech acts in *Rule of the Community*, 70
    See also Essenes; new covenant
Yom Kippur, 126–28

zab, 117
Zadok, 27
Zadokite high priests, 2, 4, 5, 6, 27–28, 30, 58, 96–98, 180
zera, 116
Zulick, Margaret D., 152, 153

www.ingramcontent.com/pod-product-compliance
Lightning Source LLC
Chambersburg PA
CBHW022051290426